AVIATION THERAPY

I0809149

AVIATION THERAPY

STORIES OF PERSEVERANCE AND PERSONAL GROWTH FROM THE COCKPIT

DAVID DALE

Stoney Creek Publishing

Stoney Creek Publishing
A Member of the Texas Book Consortium

Published by
Stoney Creek Publishing Group
StoneyCreekPublishing.com

ISBN: 978-1-965766-22-4
ISBN (ebook): 978-1-965766-23-1
Library of Congress Control Number: 2025910072

Cover design by Market Your Industry. Cover photo by Paul Bowen.

Printed in the United States

To my wife, Karin, who has made me a better person every day since April 1984.

To my children, Daniel and Shelby—we are so proud of the wonderful adults you are.

To my late mom, thank you for your boundless love and encouragement.

To my late dad, thank you for being a gracious provider to our whole family.

To my siblings, Jack, Lucy, and Hannah, you make me so happy whenever we are together.

To my late stepmom, Karen, I wish you were here to take a purple pen to my manuscript.

To my late stepdad, Ralph, for being the right man at the right time of my teenage life.

To Mr. Richard Lovell, for teaching me to fly.

CONTENTS

ACKNOWLEDGMENTS

I began writing this memoir using my paper logbooks for dates and details of various flights and missions. But a logbook contains just one line of brief information for each flight, and these flights took place many decades ago. One of the most fulfilling experiences of writing this book has been reconnecting with so many friends from high school, college, and every Air Force assignment. Karin and I had eleven assignments and sixteen addresses in twenty years, and I cannot thank her enough for her support then and now. She lived most of this memoir as well.

With so many moves and meeting so many people from 1978 to 2004, please forgive any inaccuracies found in this memoir. The mistakes are mine, and not intentional, but encompass recollections from many years ago. As a funny quote goes: "I only have two brain cells left —and I'm using one of those for breathing."

I sent various chapters out to friends far and wide for their review and comment, and I thank all who have helped shape this project. In particular, I'd like to thank Karin, my siblings Jack, Lucy, and Hannah, and also Carolyn McClelland for proofreading the early manuscript for clarity. This published edition of my memoir would not have happened without the encouragement of novelist Yi Shun Lai. I thank my editors, Christine Wolf and Bruce Hurd, for their probing questions that drew out more information. My publisher at Stoney Creek Publishing, Loren Steffy, and his editor, John Jarvis, helped shape this edition and have my immense gratitude. From my aviation past, I thank Larry Leonard, Michael Rafferty, Lee "Ice" Icenhour, and my friends and coworkers in the 62nd Bomb Squadron, 32nd Air Refueling Squadron, and 310th Airlift Squadron.

AUTHOR'S NOTE

Before every takeoff, pilots announce to the tower that they are "ready for takeoff." The systems have been checked, and the pilot is mentally prepared for whatever comes next. Psychologists know that some children benefit from equine therapy, interacting with horses to help them break out of their shell and gain self-confidence. I benefited from "aviation therapy." Aviation has influenced my life in so many positive ways. I grew up shy and lacking self-confidence, and it wasn't until I started taking flying lessons at age sixteen that I ventured out on my own to pursue my dream. Through aviation, I learned to make decisions, including some that could have life-or-death consequences. I scared myself a few times, but I also believe that I embody the slogan, "What doesn't kill you makes you stronger." The life lessons I learned through aviation made me ready to take off into adulthood and a successful military career.

Aviation Therapy recounts the extraordinary events of my ordinary Air Force career. I was not a combat pilot, so I didn't drop bombs on the Iraqi Republican Guard or dogfight over the Middle East. I did, however, fly during numerous historic world events. My career intersected many moments in history, and these stories represent the exploits that led to my personal growth through aviation, as well as my increasing self-confidence along the way.

This book is not meant to be an autobiography, nor a history of the Air Force, but an aviation memoir of my intersections with history. As I wrote this, my college friend and accomplished writer, Corey King, told me that if I'm going to write about myself, then I need to be willing to "walk through downtown naked." As a former swimmer, let's just say I'm willing to walk through downtown in a Speedo swimsuit. These are my often-told flying stories from 1978 to 2004, and the flight plan has been filed. You are ready for takeoff.

PROLOGUE: ASPIRATIONS

July 24, 1978: At age sixteen, I soloed at Weiser Airpark. I was hosed down and had my "tail feathers" cut by Mr. Andrews. (Larry Leonard)

Mr. Andrews, my first flight instructor, turned to me and asked, "So you think you're ready to solo in front of your friends?"

After my half-hour flight lesson of three takeoffs and landings, with my childhood friends Larry Leonard and Michael Rafferty watching from alongside the grassy airstrip, I was surprised by his question. At sixteen years old, I had no idea this might be "the day" I would solo at Weiser Airpark outside of Houston. It was all a blur. I don't remember what I answered; I think I just smiled and nodded. Up to that point, I had seven hours of flight instruction and had performed forty-two takeoffs and landings.

Mr. Andrews climbed out of the right seat of the Piper Cherokee, and I taxied to the end of the runway for my fifteen-minute solo flight, performing three touch-and-go landings with Michael and Larry snapping pictures with a yellow Kodak disposable camera.

When I looked left and then right, ensuring the path was clear before making a turn, there was nobody sitting to my right in the cockpit. I was alone. Nervous as I was, I was also very excited. This was where I wanted to be.

Like a lot of teenagers growing up, I enjoyed going to airshows. At one point in the 1970s, both the Air Force Thunderbirds and the Navy Blue Angels flew F-4 Phantoms as they put on airshows throughout the country. As they performed beautiful diamond-formation rolls and loops, trailing the ever-present tail of white smoke, or crossed the show's center flying cockpit to cockpit, I thought, *"That is one bad-ass airplane."*

Air Force flying was in my family. My uncle, Jack Sanders, was an Air Force fighter pilot, flying the F-100 Super Sabre during the Vietnam War. He then flew the A-7 Corsair II before finally transitioning to the new A-10 Thunderbolt II tank killer. He was an A-10 squadron commander, the pinnacle of a fighter pilot's career, before helping set up a new squadron of A-10s at Eielson Air Force Base in Alaska during the Cold War (no pun intended). He closed out his thirty-year career as a colonel and vice commander of 1st Air Force, in Tactical Air Command at Langley Air Force Base in Virginia, during Desert Storm in the 1990s.

In 1979, Uncle Jack was a lieutenant colonel A-10 squadron

commander at Davis-Monthan Air Force Base outside of Tucson, Arizona. That spring, I was seventeen years old and went to visit my Uncle Jack, Aunt Elaine, and two cousins, Christy and Tina. During that trip, I got to tour the base control tower, and from a bird's-eye view I watched the fighters take off and land. One of the highlights of my visit was when Uncle Jack arranged for me to fly the A-7 simulator. I pretended to be a real fighter pilot as I simulated low-level strafing attacks.

I came home from that trip determined to be a fighter pilot. I had already started flying lessons a year earlier in June of 1978 at the grass runway of Weiser Airpark. Using my restaurant busboy paycheck, I signed up for the Piper Flight School and gave the instructor $700, which he would draw from after each lesson.

Weiser Air Park had two WWII-era AT-6 Texan trainers on the grass field. Larry and Michael enjoyed airplanes as much as I did, so I invited them along for my seventh lesson. That's when I experienced the thrill of handling the Piper on my own, deciding when to extend the flaps and when to flare for a touchdown. Rumbling along the short grass strip, I reset the flaps to the takeoff position, added power, and pulled back on the yoke, climbing into the humid Houston summer air for another trip around the traffic pattern. Mr. Andrews wasn't there to offer advice or corrections; it was just me, a nervous teenage kid one year removed from driver's ed, now soloing a single-engine airplane. With each touch-and-go landing, I grew more excited at the realization I was doing this on my own. After landing for the third and final time, I climbed out of the Piper Archer and took part in the ritual of having my shirttail (my "tail feathers") cut off. The only problem was that I was wearing my older sister Lucy's favorite surfer T-shirt, a cool red shirt with an ocean wave on the front. *Oops.*

My name, the time and date of the flight—July 24, 1978—were written with a black marker on the cut-off portion of the red T-shirt and tacked to the wall of the flight school. I have no memory of what happened next; my brain was too focused on the momentous solo flight and getting everything right. Larry and Michael told me that Mr. Andrews then offered for them to join us on one more flight. The four of us, Mr. Andrews included, took off once again around the pattern, with me at the controls.

The rest of my private flying license lessons took place at LaPorte Municipal Airport in Pasadena, Texas, located near the oil refineries along the ship channel east of Houston. We called this area "Stinkadena" because of the foul smell of oil, referred to in Texas as "the smell of money." I worked as a busboy and cook at The Mason Jar Restaurant near my house on the west side of Houston to pay for my flying lessons. In addition, I joined the Aviation Explorer Post, a coed branch of Boy Scouts that focused on one main area. My neighbor, Libby Rafferty, was in High Adventure Scouting, going on campouts and rafting trips, and Larry was in computer science, using an IBM mainframe to learn about computing in the late 1970s.

My Aviation Explorer Post flight instructor was Richard Lovell. He was the owner of a beautiful 1973 Piper Cherokee, a white, 180-horsepower four-seater with a black-and-gray stripe down the side. He was in the Navy during the Korean War, but not as a pilot, and he didn't deploy overseas. He laughed about earning the National Defense Service Medal for never going anywhere. He was a short, tough old man—a Navy boxing champ with a permanently crooked nose to prove it. Day in and day out, he dipped Copenhagen tobacco ... and swallowed it. During flying lessons over the Texas Gulf Coast, as he gave me instructions, he'd periodically burp, filling the cockpit with the smell of Copenhagen. To this day, my Pavlovian response equates the smell of dipping tobacco with a Piper four-seater.

I owe Mr. Lovell a lot. He was demanding, telling me to "fight for centerline" when landing in a crosswind. As tough as he was, though, he also was very kind. He donated his instructor time for free, as a way of giving back to the Scouting program. My flight lessons from 1978 to 1980 started at $22 an hour and eventually rose to $25 an hour. This occurred at a time of high inflation, when a bank certificate of deposit earned thirteen percent—and I was making around $3 an hour at the restaurant.

Preflighting Mr. Lovell's plane

The hourlong lessons, flown near the Houston ship channel, consisted of airwork—flying circles with my wingtip pointed at a blue, lollipop-shaped water tower below while adjusting for the wind changes, or a series of S-turns flown over a railroad track. These exercises taught me to take the varying winds into account.

Stalling the airplane, which occurs when the plane is in a climbing attitude but no longer has the power to fly, is a pilot's nightmare, even in practice. To build my confidence, Mr. Lovell demonstrated his Piper's ability to handle a stall. By reducing the throttle to idle and pulling the yoke back to his chest, he proceeded to illustrate the magical gift of his aircraft. As I watched the airspeed bleed off, with the stall warning light and buzzer distracting my attention, I noticed his hands suddenly release the straining yoke of the shuddering airplane. My heart and stomach raced each other for my throat as the plane transferred from thirty degrees nose-high into a steep dive. "Shit!" I gasped as I looked down on the offshore drilling rig growing larger in front of the propeller. Without him touching the controls, the airspeed rose, and the trusty Cherokee slowly pitched up and down, finally settling at the original level-flight attitude. This breathtaking demonstration of aerodynamic stability allowed me to confidently rehearse stall recoveries on my own.

As my flight instructions continued, I also sought the advice of a neighbor, Pete Anderson, a captain for Delta Airlines who Air Force C-47s in the mid-1950s. When I told him over the phone that I wanted to be a pilot, he invited me over. I remember sitting on his living room sofa as he recounted his brief military career, and the flying he enjoyed with Delta Airlines. I set a goal at that time to have a military career, then become an airline pilot. Larry told me much later in life that he viewed me as unusual, because I knew from an early age what I wanted to be, but I never thought or realized that pursuing a dream was unusual.

Because of Mr. Lovell's instruction, encouragement, and generosity, I was ready for my private pilot's license checkride (flight evaluation) on August 20, 1980. I spent that afternoon with a renowned FAA-designated evaluator, Maybelle Fletcher, a fixture in the Houston aviation community. She and her husband operated Fletcher Aviation at Hobby Airport, located south of downtown Houston.

This nerve-wracking day began when I flew solo from quiet, tiny LaPorte Airport into the busy Houston Hobby Airport. As an eighteen-year-old in a small, single-engine propeller airplane, I had to fly into a big-city airport, sequenced between white Learjets, brightly colored Braniff Airline 727s, and Southwest 737s in their orange-and-red "corndog" paint scheme. My main motivation was, "*Don't embarrass yourself.*"

With that landing behind me, I then underwent a stressful oral ground evaluation, as Mrs. Fletcher quizzed me about aviation rules and navigation principles. Finally, we flew a one-hour flight to an outlying airport for three touch-and-go landings. I was "under the gun" for more than an hour, my every move and decision scrutinized by a lady about my mom's age sporting salt-and-pepper hair pulled high up on her head, but I successfully completed my first FAA checkride. I was now a licensed private pilot, just one week from starting college and the Air Force ROTC program at the University of Texas at Austin.

It had been an exciting day, but I still needed to fly back to LaPorte. It was 4 p.m. by the time I was debriefed and congratulated by Mrs. Fletcher. I sat in my small plane near the end of the Hobby runway, waiting for my turn to take off, but this was "rush hour," and streams of Learjets and colorful airliners continued to land.

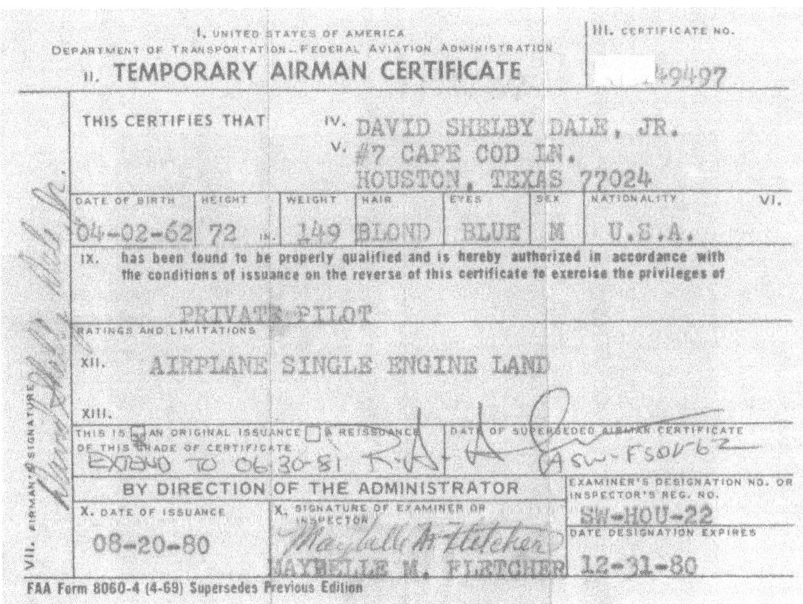
I. UNITED STATES OF AMERICA
DEPARTMENT OF TRANSPORTATION—FEDERAL AVIATION ADMINISTRATION
II. TEMPORARY AIRMAN CERTIFICATE
III. CERTIFICATE NO. 49497

THIS CERTIFIES THAT IV. DAVID SHELBY DALE, JR.
V. #7 CAPE COD LN.
HOUSTON, TEXAS 77024

DATE OF BIRTH	HEIGHT	WEIGHT	HAIR	EYES	SEX	NATIONALITY
04-02-62	72 IN.	149	BLOND	BLUE	M	U.S.A.

VI.

IX. has been found to be properly qualified and is hereby authorized in accordance with the conditions of issuance on the reverse of this certificate to exercise the privileges of

PRIVATE PILOT

RATINGS AND LIMITATIONS

XII. AIRPLANE SINGLE ENGINE LAND

XIII.

THIS IS AN ORIGINAL ISSUANCE ☒ A REISSUANCE ☐ OF THIS GRADE OF CERTIFICATE
DATE OF SUPERSEDED AIRMAN CERTIFICATE
EXTEND TO 06-30-81 R.A. ASW-FSDO-62

BY DIRECTION OF THE ADMINISTRATOR

EXAMINER'S DESIGNATION NO. OR INSPECTOR'S REG. NO. SW-HOU-22

X. DATE OF ISSUANCE 08-20-80

X. SIGNATURE OF EXAMINER OR INSPECTOR Maybelle M. Fletcher
MAYBELLE M. FLETCHER

DATE DESIGNATION EXPIRES 12-31-80

VII. AIRMAN'S SIGNATURE

FAA Form 8060-4 (4-69) Supersedes Previous Edition

Private pilot certificate, awarded August 20, 1980

Just before being cleared for takeoff, the Piper's engine began to sputter. The small plane had a left and right fuel tank, one in each wing, with a fuel selector by my left knee. Since most of my flying lessons lasted just one hour, switching fuel tanks was rarely required, but today the engine had already been running for almost three hours, and the left fuel tank was almost dry.

pointing at us from Cuba, ninety miles south of Florida. On that October 1962 evening, Mom and Dad feared for the safety of their young family, which now included six-year-old big brother "Jacky" (later known as Jack), cute little three-year-old Lucy, and me. Two years after that frightening missile showdown passed, Hannah Elizabeth arrived to complete our All-American family.

I was born April 2, 1962, in the Hunter's Creek area on the west side of the growing metropolis of Houston. We lived in a single-story, ranch-style house, the second one on the right side of Cape Cod Lane, a cul-de-sac with eight houses. It was one of many streets sprouting off Pifer Road, which was named for the family farm that been established there a century earlier. Every street in our neighborhood had a large yellow diamond-shaped sign announcing a dead end. We lived on a dead-end street off a dead-end street, but we were going places, and I didn't know or use the word "cul-de-sac" until I was in my twenties.

My parents met because of football. My dad, David Sr., was raised in a large two-story "almost mansion" in central Houston. His house was located just off River Oaks Boulevard, an eight-block street capped by the River Oaks Country Club at one end and Lamar High School at the other.

His father, Warren Dale Sr., was a successful lawyer with the renowned Vinson and Elkins law firm. Dad was a "happy surprise," arriving in 1933, thirteen years after his brother and sister. He was sent to a boarding school in Connecticut, but ran away as a young teenager and took a train back to Texas, after which his parents enrolled him at The Kincaid School, the local private preparatory school. Dad excelled at track and football there, but there was one problem: Kincaid played seven-man football, and Dad wanted to play "real" football.

Football was life for my father, and in the late 1940s he attended nearby Lamar public high school and kicked his football on their field. One Sunday afternoon, another young man, albeit six years older, also was there practicing his kicking. The twenty-two-year-old man's name was George Blanda. Dad spent that Sunday afternoon shagging footballs for the future Houston Oilers quarterback, kicker, and Hall of Fame NFL player.

By 1950, at age seventeen, Dad convinced his parents to let him attend Lamar High School and join the real football team as their tailback. That's where he met Judy Sanders, my beautiful mom.

Mom was the daughter of Jack Sanders Sr., a proud railroad man who was born in the tiny Arkansas town of Crossett, in the state's southeastern pocket. Her mom, Joecile Garrison Sanders, was a grade-school teacher and talented piano player, born in Abilene, Texas. My grandmother's birth name was Lucile, named after her mom, and her dad was Joe Garrison; as time went by, she began going by Joecile, a combination of both of their first names. She eventually changed her name legally to Joecile, which is what my grandfather lovingly called her.

In 1922, at the age of fourteen, Jack Sanders began working for the Missouri Pacific (MoPac) Railroad. Standing by the railroad tracks far from the terminal, he handed out the lane assignments to the incoming freight train operators using a large hoop made of bamboo.

My grandparents married during the Great Depression and started their family, and Papa moved his family all throughout the Midwest, never saying no to a MoPac job. Despite not having a college degree, he progressed up the office hierarchy, eventually retiring as vice president of MoPac freight. By the late 1940s, the Sanders family, which included Mom's little brother, Jack Jr., moved to Houston. Mom enrolled at Lamar High School, where she fell in love with a slim, six-foot-tall tailback with thick, wavy, rust-colored hair, and sparkling blue eyes.

Dad was athletic, playful, and apparently very smart, too. In the early 1950s, he became a third-generation Texas Longhorn, following his maternal grandfather, Ebenezer Dohoney (UT Class of 1896) and both of his parents (Class of 1918) at the University of Texas at Austin. Within three years he completed his bachelor's degree in an accelerated program, and in another three years, Dad—like his father —earned his law degree from the prestigious University of Texas law school. He married Mom while still in law school, and their first son (another Jack!) arrived two years later.

I spent the 1960s in a loving, happy family, free to roam around our suburban neighborhood. My best bud, Larry Leonard, was born six months after me, and he lived just around the circle at the end of our street. We spent afternoons learning to ride our bikes without training wheels as our moms gave us a push while chatting by our mailbox.

Our idyllic life was rocked when mental illness took hold of my dad by 1969. Dad was diagnosed as manic-depressive (bipolar II disorder) in the late 1960s and sought treatment in Topeka, Kansas. A person with this disorder experiences major depressive episodes, rather than shorter cycles. I was too young to understand what was going on, but I soon learned that we'd be moving to Topeka in 1970, after I completed second grade. In July of that year, we rented out the Cape Cod Lane house, packed up our maroon Ford station wagon, and I sadly said goodbye to my neighborhood buds, Larry and Michael.

Uncle Jack helped Mom drive us thirteen hours north to Topeka, where our life resumed, and Dad received the treatment he needed. We joined the Westminster Presbyterian Church, just across the street from Boswell Junior High, and Dad began teaching oil and gas law classes at Washburn University, not far from our two-story "Little White House" on High Avenue.

Life was very different in Topeka, but not in a bad way. We had been born and raised in a very white area of Houston, where almost every suburban housewife had a maid who rode in weekly on a bus from Houston's East Side. I now attended Kansas public schools that had more Black children than I had ever seen before.

The good thing about being an eight-year-old was that I didn't care about skin tone. I had many great friends throughout grade school, junior high, and in Scouting who were Black, and I thought nothing of it. In seventh grade, I had a crush on Shelley Douglas, a beautiful girl with straight, black, shoulder-length hair, and a huge smile. She often wore pretty, embroidered denim shirts. We flirted but never kissed.

Like many families in the 1970s, our family fell victim to divorce. I don't remember my parents arguing; instead, I believe they simply fell out of love from the strain of Dad's condition while trying to raise four children, with the third one (me) being hyperactive. I was always fidgeting and had difficulty concentrating in class.

I remember when I was in sixth grade (eleven years old), sitting on our red living room sofa, when my parents told me they were separating. At that moment I didn't think it was a big deal, so I wasn't upset. Dad was just moving five blocks down the street into an apartment, and I thought this was a temporary arrangement.

While still in grade school that year (junior high in Kansas was seventh to ninth grade), I talked to a classmate named Kirk Porteous, the only child I knew with divorced parents.

"What's it like having your parents divorced?" I asked as we walked home from school.

"Sometimes it sucks when my dad can't be around," he answered.

Some days he went to his mom's place, he said, and on other days he went to his dad's house. I let that soak in.

By 1974, my brother, Jack, graduated from Topeka High School and moved into a nearby apartment, working full time as an auto mechanic. Mom continued to raise Lucy, me, and Hannah on High Avenue. To me, Lucy was the extrovert of the family—beautiful, athletic, and self-assured. From junior high through high school, she and her best friend, Diane Deeter, were on the cheerleading squad. Hannah and I enjoyed hours of playing outdoors with neighborhood youths on both sides of our house.

Around that time, Dad and I bought matching running shoes. I would run to his apartment, and we then would jog around the Washburn college campus.

At the time, Dad was battling midlife sedentary weight issues, and I was trying to outgrow my skinny, asthmatic body. When I was fifteen, Dad told me something that prompted my life fitness goal. I weighed just over 120 pounds, while Dad, with his basketball-sized belly, weighed more than 200. One day he said, "Just remember, Davy, when I was your age I looked just like you, too."

I vowed that day to never have a pot belly. I'm sure my dad taught me some other life lessons growing up, but that's the only one I remember to this day. He didn't dispense advice, but instead told stories of what happened in his younger days.

Later that same year, Mom gathered Lucy, Hannah, and me in the living room and told us that she and Dad would not be getting back together, and this time I sobbed on my mom's shoulder as the news sank in. Dad and I were buds, playing tennis, throwing a football or baseball, and jogging. As sad as this was, it helped knowing that Dad was still just a few blocks away in his apartment.

Back then, I suffered from low self-esteem and a lack of confidence, because I was never impressed with my looks or abilities. Our family was fairly active, and we all tried to stay physically fit. From YMCA activities through junior high teams, I tried but didn't succeed at the popular sports of basketball, football, and wrestling, the last of which my parents suggested as a way to toughen me up.

There was no doubt I was a "momma's boy," either. With little guidance from Dad, my loving mom set her expectations. We siblings had to learn piano before picking another instrument (the trombone for Jack and me). In high school, we had to take a year of Latin before choosing a language. I chose poorly; I later rebelled against the local Hispanic community surrounding me at work and chose French. My siblings all chose Spanish, which turned out to be a much more useful language later in life, as I now fly throughout the Caribbean and Central America. Mom gave me a classical upbringing (music, theater, and even choir and band camp), and I freely admit that, because of her, I enjoy singing, and I love watching plays or musicals.

As for wrestling, the practices were good, but it was hard to toughen up when my matches only lasted about thirty seconds. I never had a killer instinct, but I did learn some cool moves.

My neighbors on High Avenue were three boys: Aaron, Bret, and Craig Zlatnik. Their mom thought that out: A, B, and C, to Z. All of them wrestled in school and rough-housed with each other at home, which I often joined. I mainly hung out with Craig, who was Hannah's age (two years younger than me), probably because he was less of a threat since I was older.

Bret was one year older than me and became an inspiration, though I never told him so. He was a back-to-back state champion wrestler with muscular arms. Bret earned almost all straight-As, and he was the first-chair trumpet player in the junior and high school band. He also could kick your ass if you made fun of him for being in the band. I never attained his greatness, but he showed me what was possible.

Tennis was our family sport, and by ninth grade I earned the top spot on our Boswell Junior High tennis team, thanks to private lessons, my double-handed Bjorn Borg backhand, and my "Tasmanian devil" serve. I had a very powerful serve for a fourteen-year-old, but I didn't always know where it was going. In later years, fellow aviators would call this "all thrust, no vector." My matches usually consisted of a mix of double-faults and aces, and I lived and died by my serve. I was quick and agile on a tennis court over the short distances, but I was never fast enough for basketball and football.

I also took up swimming while in junior high. Hannah and I swam both in a summer league and at the Topeka YMCA throughout the school year. This was great for my growing body, and for overcoming my childhood asthma. My best event was the hundred-yard backstroke, but my performance was lackluster.

Throughout our seven years in Kansas, we visited Houston almost every year. I'd get to spend a week with my two good friends, Larry Leonard and Michael Rafferty. Michael lived next door to Larry and diagonally across from me. Like Craig, he also was two years younger, while his older sister, Libby, was my age. I knew from these Texas visits that most of my friends swam on the Dad's Club YMCA team, and that Larry was quite good.

Academically, I was a solid B student who hated to read. Unless it was mandatory reading, I rarely read anything for fun. After ninth grade, though, my budding interest in aviation led me to read a biography about Charles Lindbergh. I was captivated by how he taught himself to fly an old Jenny biplane years before making his famous solo flight over the Atlantic Ocean. Watching Jimmy Stewart portray Lindbergh in *The Spirit of Saint Louis* inspired me to become a pilot, and Dad even told me that his mom was at the 1927 New York ticker-tape parade honoring Lindbergh after he returned from Paris.

I enjoyed creative writing at school and was pretty good at math, but I specifically remember the day in eighth-grade algebra when the lightbulb came on. Suddenly the equations made sense, and my hand shot up excitedly time and time again in Miss Andrews' class. I can still picture her smiling face, and I'm sure it made her feel good to see one of her students "get it."

By 1977, Lucy had graduated from Topeka High, and I graduated from Boswell Junior High. Mom married a very nice family man named Ralph Slavens, whom she met at our Presbyterian church. Although my dad was a kind provider, he was non-confrontational and would never broach a touchy subject (relationships, finances, you name it.).

I never heard "the talk" from Dad, or how to interact with girls. As a result, I think I learned how I wanted to parent by what was missing in my life. To this day, I enjoy bear hugs with both of my grown children. When our son, Daniel, was in grade school and junior high, I spoke with him about how to treat others, and how to talk to them.

"Ask questions, and let a girl tell you about herself rather than you talking about yourself," I told him.

Ralph filled that fatherly void and was the "dad" that took me hunting once on a Kansas prairie. We were hunting doves and pheasants, but I shot a rabbit with my .410 shotgun as it ran through the

Kansas woods, which my mom graciously cooked. Ralph was a barrel-chested man with a hearty baritone laugh. He was an accountant for hospitals by day, but turned into a pool shark in local taverns in the evening. With a big laugh, along with a wink, he admitted, "I had a misspent youth." Ralph knew how to have fun.

Hannah, Ralph, and Mom at Lucy's wedding

We shot a lot of pool, and I became pretty good at it. Ralph smoked cigarettes, as well as a pipe of whiskey-flavored tobacco. I never took up smoking (the first and only cigarette I tried burned my throat), but I never minded the smell, either.

Ralph suffered from heart disease throughout his life. After his brief marriage to my mom ended, he married a wonderful lady named Betty and eventually retired to Tonganoxie, Kansas, just west of Kansas City. Ralph died of a sudden heart attack in 2019 in his back yard, and when his oldest son, Sean, called to give me the news, I cried hard later that night for the man that got me through my teenage years. In his eulogy, Sean quoted what I had once said: "Ralph was the right man at the right time of my teenage life."

With Lucy graduated from high school, Mom decided it was the right time to move Hannah (now thirteen) and me with her back to Houston. At age fifteen, I was thrilled to be moving back to my "hometown" to start high school. Lucy enrolled in Abilene Christian University, where she continued her cheerleading and studied to be a teacher.

Meanwhile, our brother, Jack, had a full-time job in Topeka, and a serious girlfriend named Carol Wolf. Academically, he personified perseverance, even though he didn't head to college after high school. In his late thirties he earned his bachelor's degree at night school—and, once the study bug kicked in, he applied for and was accepted into Washburn Law School, where our dad had taught two decades earlier. In a bit of serendipity, some of my brother's professors were Dad's students. Jack earned his law degree in his early 40s, never giving up on his dreams.

Dad, Hannah, me, Lucy, Jack, and Carol in 1979

After seven years of renting out our Houston home, Mom, Hannah, and I moved back to Cape Cod Lane, and I prepared to enter tenth grade at Memorial High School. I knew I'd play trombone in the concert band, but it was time to decide on a sport. I chose swimming over my promising tennis abilities because of my friendship with Larry, who was on the swim team. Looking back, I think this speaks volumes about me, as I had a great fear of rejection and wanted to belong. I didn't want to launch out on my own and join a tennis team where I didn't know anybody. To this day, my high school friends have no idea how good I was at tennis. Neither swimming nor tennis were "cool" sports, but who wants to be alone playing an uncool sport?

Instead, I attached myself to Larry's hip and continued my teenage years as a mediocre swimmer. I succeeded in qualifying for the Texas State Regionals swim meet in my hundred-yard backstroke event before calling it quits. It's obvious to me now that I chose to live in Larry's shadow.

Like Bret Zlatnik in Kansas, Larry was smart, excelling in the equivalent of advanced placement courses today, and learning computer programming through his Explorer Scout post. He was a strong swimmer, and his freestyle relay team won the state title during our 1978 junior year. In my mind, Larry was everything I wasn't: cool and confident—and he had a girlfriend. I couldn't even talk to girls for fear of rejection. I was fortunate to go to two proms because friends made it clear that both girls would say yes if I asked them.

By 1978, Dad had also returned to Houston, teaching law at the University of Houston (known locally as U of H), where he met my stepmom, Karen Lewis, who also was a UT graduate. She was an English professor at U of H—and a force of nature, too. She smoked constantly, with a husky voice, large-framed glasses, and an ego as big as her home state of Texas. In her mind, she was never wrong. She was opinionated, but I loved her, especially for loving my dad.

Karen encouraged my writing, and that was one thing we could talk about. I wrote a paper about aviation safety, detailing all the steps a pilot goes through in preparing to fly a small airplane. She entered my paper in a Houston-area writing contest, and although I really don't remember the results of the contest, I liked that she was impressed with my writing.

Dad and Karen in 1997

Karen had a very bright young daughter, Alison, who was a dozen years younger than me. Eventually, my dad adopted Alison, and his face lit up whenever they were together. I truly did not resent that at all; in fact, I was happy to finally see him act like a dad, so perhaps he just hadn't known how to relate to his sons. As a testament to my loving family, my mom and dad remained close throughout their life, and we often got together for the holidays. I particularly remember a 1978 Thanksgiving gathering where my mom held Karen's four-year-old daughter on her lap. In 2007, as a pilot for Southwest Airlines, I wrote an article for our local paper, titled "*Thanks, Mom AND Dad*" (referenced in Appendix 1) that illustrated the relationships within our loving but unusual family.

Karen passed away unexpectedly in mid-January 2020, at the outset of the COVID-19 pandemic. She was hospitalized just days after a family Christmas party, and the doctors were perplexed at her fatigue and low oxygen levels. They thought she either had the flu or a mild heart attack, but she had given up smoking many years earlier. Like my father, she did not want an autopsy or a funeral, so we will never know the cause of her death, but it saddens me greatly that she wasn't here to tear up this manuscript with her vicious purple pen.

My dad, even with his mental illness, was never violent or threatening. He would have a lot of "great ideas" during a manic episode—but when the depression took over, he'd become very withdrawn for months. Fortunately, he was stable and enjoyed his life at the end, watching sports in his assisted-living facility and attending family gatherings.

Dad passed away suddenly in his bed on a cold afternoon in February 2014. I was in our Florida kitchen with my wife and daughter when Lucy called, her voice shaking, to say that Dad had unexpectedly died. She had stopped by his retirement home with a few requested items (probably ice cream) and found him in bed, unresponsive. I started trembling and paced around the kitchen island, letting the news sink in: Whatever took him happened so fast that he didn't press his Medical Alert emergency button that he wore on a lanyard.

My mom continued to thrive in Denver. She embodied the motto "live, laugh, love" by always demonstrating a love of life, enjoying socializing with everyone, and playing her favorite games of canasta and Scrabble. She was an interactive grandmother for her growing family, and was a brave example of being a survivor by persevering through life after breast cancer, and by facing Parkinson's disease head-on until succumbing in August 2024. She was a loving example for all her children, grandchildren, and great-grandchildren.

There is a saying that goes, "We can't choose our circumstances, but we can choose our response," and Judy chose happiness.

She didn't want for her husband—our father—who she loved so much, for all her life, to go through his bipolar episodes. She didn't want to be a divorced mother of four. She certainly didn't want to endure radiation and chemotherapy treatment as she overcame breast cancer, and she would never wish upon anybody the ravages of Parkinson's disease. But, through it all, she chose to be cheerful, and strove to brighten everyone's day to the best of her ability.

Like me, my little sister also struggled with low self-confidence. Hannah is the kindest, most caring member of our family, is non-competitive to a fault, and has a heart of gold. And what does every girl want? A horse. So our dad bought fourteen-year-old Hannah an Appaloosa horse named Poco. The horse should've been named BOGO—the acronym for "buy one, get one"—because Dad unknowingly bought a pregnant horse. By the following Mother's Day, Poco delivered Bonnie, a beautiful brown filly.

Hannah's horses were stabled in Katy, Texas, a half-hour west of us. She had the responsibility of feeding, cleaning, and caring for them, and her self-confidence soared. I watched my shy little sister take control of her full-grown mare and train a cute filly. This was equine therapy at its finest, and I needed something like that.

My therapy ended up coming from airplanes. At age sixteen I joined the Aviation Explorers post, attending meetings at Ellington Air Force Base on the southwest side of Houston, where I rose through the ranks to become the leader of the post by my senior year. I began my flying lessons at Weiser Airpark in northwest Houston and learned to solo a small plane. Flying helped me "cut the cord" and come out from behind Larry's shadow so I could become my own man.

2

SWING AND A MISS

Cadet Dale, University of Texas Air Force ROTC

I REMEMBER the sensation of my first military haircut as a college freshman beginning my ROTC training. I hadn't felt the wind on my ears since grade school. I kept rubbing the exposed tops of my ears and the back of my clean-shaven neck as I walked back to The Castilian dormitory from the barber shop on Austin's Guadalupe Street. Between joining the 50,000 students at the University of Texas and beginning my Air Force training, very little was the same as my life in Houston. My new haircut made me look and feel different as I transitioned from scruffy teenager to sharp cadet.

There are three avenues to becoming a military officer. One of them is to attend a military academy, such as the Air Force Academy in Colorado Springs. Another is to graduate from college and then attend three months of Officer Training School, where the graduates are known as "Ninety-Day Wonders." The third avenue, and the way the majority of officers are trained, is through university ROTC programs, where cadets attend classes twice a week and march or "drill" one day each week. I had hoped to attend the Air Force Academy, but I didn't think my 990 SAT score was high enough. The decision ended up being made for me at age seventeen, when I dug the application out of a box in my room and discovered I had missed the deadline by two weeks. So I became a fourth-generation Texas Longhorn, following my great-grandfather, both of my dad's parents, and my dad.

Seventy-five Air Force cadets started as freshmen at UT in August 1980, but not everyone wanted to fly. Many cadets looked forward to non-flying career fields, such as engineering, missile operations, security forces, nursing, or the new Space Command, as the space shuttle program was preparing for its first launch in April 1981. I had high aspirations of becoming either an Air Force fighter pilot and member of the Thunderbird Flight Demonstration Team, or a NASA astronaut, so I enrolled in aerospace engineering to improve my chances of becoming a test pilot.

Those of us hoping for a pilot slot went to Bergstrom Air Force Base on the southeast side of Austin for our first military flight physical. This was a few years after the post-Vietnam military drawdown, and in the last few months of the Carter administration. Because of severe defense budget cuts, there were not many pilot slots available.

My eye-test results were disappointing; I had 20/20 vision in my right eye, but 20/25 in my left eye. There were far more pilot candidates than pilot slots, so no waivers were granted for poor vision.

Swing and a miss.

Although I was disappointed, I never considered dropping out of ROTC to pursue a civilian aviation career. This news was a setback to my aviation plan, but after my first semester the ROTC staff offered me a navigator candidate slot with a full scholarship, which I accepted. Although the scholarship certainly helped and was considered an honor, it felt to me like a consolation prize.

I was mostly a B student, and I couldn't envision busting my butt for five years to earn an engineering degree just so I could be a navigator in the back of some aircraft. After my first semester, I changed majors to computer science for a year, then switched to business management. That way, I figured, I could graduate in four years and get on with my Air Force career. The Air Force didn't care what my degree was in, so I hoped to graduate from college as quickly as possible.

Thanks to my sophomore college roommate, I improved my eye-test score during college. Doug Griffith, whose dad was an Army ophthalmologist, told me that I only needed to correctly identify five of the eight characters on the vision test to receive credit for that line. If I could distinguish (or guess correctly) between Cs and Os, or Xs, Ks, and Rs on the eye test, I would be able to demonstrate 20/20 vision after all. By squinting into the eye-test viewer like a wanderer lost in the desert, I guessed correctly and demonstrated 20/20 vision during my sophomore annual physical.

Luckily, this took place just before attending summer ROTC field training at McConnell Air Force Base outside of Wichita, Kansas. With fingers crossed, I headed off to the Land of Oz, hoping for a pilot slot.

There was great incentive to do well during this intense four-week "officer boot camp" training program. Field training was the centerpiece of the entire four-year program, and the top graduate in each flight of twenty cadets could either receive a coveted pilot slot or a full scholarship for the final two years of college. I already was on scholarship as a navigator candidate, but the ROTC program would not combine a pilot slot with a scholarship. If I was the top graduate in my flight, I would happily trade in my navigator scholarship for a pilot slot.

A few days before the end of field training, our section of cadets took an orientation flight on a KC-135 (similar to a Boeing 707) air refueling tanker. During the noisy flight, I chatted with a fellow cadet and friend named Ivan. As a Michigan State University gymnast, Ivan had been an alternate on the 1980 Olympic gymnastics team. Those Olympic Games in the Soviet Union were boycotted by the United States after the Soviets invaded Afghanistan in 1979. Now, Ivan needed a scholarship to continue his college degree. As we talked in the rumbling cabin of the gray tanker, our flight commander, an active-duty Air Force captain, joined the two of us.

"It's good to see you two talking, but it doesn't make my job any easier," he said.

"Why is that, sir?" I asked.

"I have you two neck-and-neck for my nomination for top cadet," he replied.

That was a problem. I could earn the pilot slot I dreamed of, or Ivan could win a badly needed scholarship. My dad already had assured me that my college education would continue with or without my scholarship, but I had mixed feelings about this situation. I wanted the best for Ivan, but I also really wanted that pilot slot. This is not the part where I graciously backed down and allowed Ivan to win—but, in the end, he won the award fair and square, and on his own merit.

Swing and a miss.

One year later, during the flight physical of my junior year, I again demonstrated 20/20 vision in both eyes. The Reagan-era military buildup was beginning, but not quickly enough for me. In the spring of 1983, I presented my new pilot-qualified physical to the Air Force ROTC detachment technical sergeant in charge of the administration section. Unfortunately, I was disappointed again.

"That's great, but all of the pilot slots for your fiscal year have been awarded," he said.

Swing and a miss.

I was feeling deflated, but I still had to make the best of this situation for the time being. The Air Force allowed fifty active-duty navigators to attend pilot training each year. I'd have to postpone the goal of my ambition until I was on active duty.

3
HANGING OUT IN AUSTIN

Hang gliding with Texas vultures in an accidental double-exposure shot. (Michael Rafferty)

BY THE SUMMER OF 1983, I had finished my junior year of ROTC, and our old neighborhood gang was reunited again. Larry Leonard and I roomed together our college freshman year at The Castilian dorm, which was where I eventually met my wife-to-be,

Karin. Before starting our senior year in 1983, Larry and I moved into the same Austin apartment complex, each in a one-room efficiency, and Michael Rafferty was in his sophomore year at UT.

After driving through the West Austin hill country one late summer day, Michael and I spied a hang glider for sale in a front yard. We both were aviation enthusiasts who wanted to take up hang gliding after watching the opening scene of the James Bond movie *Live and Let Die*. Although we didn't buy that particular glider, the owner did put us in touch with the Austin hang glider club on the north side of the city. The club was run by Steve Burns and Steve Stackable, a 1975 U.S. motocross national champion. "Stack" was the ultimate cool dude. This wavy-haired motorcycle standout had raced in the Houston Astrodome in the 1970s and was married to a Playboy playmate.

Michael and I entered Austin Air Sports' small wooden shop and asked about hang gliding lessons—and through Steve Burns' connections, we found a great deal on a hang glider. Michael and I split the $800 cost of a 1980 Spirit Electra Flyer, which featured an innovative crossbar, making the large, 200-square-foot glider nimble and maneuverable. It had multicolored earth-tone panels with brown in the center, then orange, tan, yellow, and red panels extending out to the purple wingtips. The entire disassembled glider was fairly easy to transport, fitting into an eighteen-foot-long blue canvas bag about two feet in diameter.

Launching a hang glider required a hill to run down, though, and that meant we needed a four-wheel-drive vehicle, so I bought my brother's green 1978 Subaru Brat. It was a tiny, two-seat pickup with a four-speed manual transmission, and its four-foot truck bed was covered by a white plastic camper shell. Once loaded, our "glider-in-a-bag" extended two feet past the front and back of the little fourteen-foot truck, but we were in business.

Much like learning to fly any airplane, learning to fly a hang glider requires a mastery of taking off and landing. For that, we only needed a small hill, so Austin Air Sports used the football field that was sunken in a shallow bowl at Murchison Middle School. Our beginner's lessons reminded me of Charlie Brown skiing down his pitcher's mound, and the flights lasted only a few seconds, but they suited our needs.

Our glider came with training wheels mounted on the control bar, so to fly it I stepped into the blue harness that stretched from shoulders to crotch like an old-fashioned men's swimming suit. The knee-hanger harness had two thick six-foot ropes shrouded in material that was stitched into the harness at my shoulder blades and attached by wide Velcro straps just below my knees. This simple harness style kept my legs and feet free as I ran down the launch ramp. The two thick ropes, held together with a large coupling (a carabiner), hooked to the glider frame above and behind my shoulders.

Once safely buckled in, and with my white half-shell motorcycle helmet in place, I hoisted the triangular control frame assembly onto my shoulders. My arms were draped around the tubes of the triangle, and both my wingtips extended out seventeen feet. I ran a few steps down the small hill, and the large wing became airborne within seconds.

For the initial training, my only goal was to fly straight ahead into the football field and belly land. This allowed the wheels to touch, after which I coasted to a stop. After a flight shorter than the twelve seconds of Orville Wright's, I stood up and unhooked the carabiner. Holding onto the pointed nose of the kite, I then pushed it up the hill for another go.

Larry joined Michael and me, and we each practiced numerous takeoffs before learning the art of flaring the large kite for a normal landing. To land it, I would push gently forward on the control bar to raise the glider's nose, but not enough to climb back into the air. This allowed for a feet-first landing, like a duck landing on water. I found that if I pushed too aggressively on the control bar, I risked climbing ten feet in the air, stalling, then crashing to the ground. Hang-glider pilots have broken their legs from these kinds of botched landings.

After a few weeks of practice, we were ready for a real flight. The nearest location for that was a 400-foot hill on Packsaddle Mountain, ninety minutes west of Austin between the smaller Texas communities of Marble Falls and Llano. Michael and I strapped our bagged glider to the top of the Brat and set off for the Hill Country behind our instructors, Stack and Steve.

Michael Rafferty preparing for his first launch from Packsaddle Mountain, with Steve "Stack" Stackable and Larry Leonard.

We bounced our way along a two-mile dirt county road off Highway 71, finally turning off at the base of an outcropping of an oblong hill. Two hills merged at that point, raised at both ends and with the right side higher than the left, giving it the appearance of a horse's packsaddle. Our launch point was the southern, higher hill, and the Brat ascended the rutty dirt trail up to the 400-foot summit.

With the kite fully assembled, and with my harness and motorcycle helmet donned, I carried the kite on my shoulders to the wooden launch platform, which was painted like a gigantic Texas flag in red, white, and blue. Stack said the first few rides would just be "sled rides," meaning a simple flight with mild S-turns from the launch platform to the cow pasture directly below. Given the increased speed of this flight versus the small football stadium hill, I was instructed to just make a belly landing on the training wheels until I gained more experience.

Balancing the kite on my shoulders, I jogged down the ten-foot ramp and was airborne after just three steps. The wind whistled in my ears as the craggy hillside fell away below. Ahead lay a vast pasture used for grazing cattle, which made for an easy landing zone. My inaugural flight lasted perhaps a minute, and I glided toward the dry, brown, summer grass for a soft landing.

After that came the tedious part. During my short flight, Michael drove the Brat down the bumpy road and into the pasture, and together we partially disassembled the kite, folding the wings together along the central spar and taking apart the aluminum triangle. We then hoisted our glider back onto our trusty little pack mule and drove back up the hill for another flight.

Early on, Michael and I decided we would each take three short flights in a row, then turn the kite over to the other person. It became a very long day for just a bit of flying, but the experience was exhilarating.

After a few more sled rides, I began to get a feel for handling our glider from takeoff to landing. I started to add gentle turns to the flights, cruising back and forth along the hillside in what is called "ridge lift," created from the southerly wind flowing toward Packsaddle Mountain. As long as the breeze blew and I stayed in a thermal, or ridge lift, the glider could stay airborne indefinitely. There were just two things limiting our flight time: One was that Michael was waiting for his turn, and the other was that, while gliding, I was in a front-leaning-rest push-up position, which became very tiresome.

Our flights usually lasted about twenty minutes, which was

plenty of time to take in the rustic sights of the Texas Hill Country. Like a hawk scanning the land below, I could see the Colorado River to the north and east, divided by dams to form Lake Buchanan, Lake LBJ and Lake Travis. To the south, I saw Highway 71 snaking its way west toward Llano, and miles and miles of cedar and scrub oak-covered hills. Gliding was very peaceful, with only the soft hiss of the wind in my ears accompanying the creaking and clinking of the aluminum glider frame.

Our desire to fly like a bird occasionally was enhanced when we were shadowed by a pair of turkey vultures that launched from the surrounding trees to follow our kite. As the pilot, I was rarely aware that I was leading a formation of birds, because they would follow the glider just aft of my wingtips. I couldn't see them, but they made for some excellent photographs.

Communing with nature occurred not only during flight, but during the evening landings, too. Our landing zone was the preferred dining spot of a roaming herd of cattle, and as the sun began to set and we were getting our last flights in, about thirty black cows began grazing right in our landing zone. Just as aircraft pilots have been known to buzz sheep or cattle, I also took part in that ritual. After cruising in the hillside ridge lift for half an hour, I flew away from the hill and out of the lifting wind currents to begin a shallow descent to the brown, grassy field below. I gained enough speed to allow for a "go-around" if things didn't look right before landing, then whistled over the uninterested bovines just five feet above their backs. It was pure fun in the Texas sun.

Once clear of the munching moos, I pushed forward on the control bar, raising the nose slightly, then circled back to a clear grassy spot for a flare, where I touched my feet to the ground and shouldered the kite. I loved the calm, thrilling experience of hang gliding.

Unfortunately, my flights didn't always go as planned. One incident occurred on an evening when the winds started to pick up as our day came to an end. I suited up for a last run and ran down the launch, becoming airborne just as a gust of wind hit my left wing. It blew me immediately toward the radio tower guy wires about fifty yards to the right of our launch ramp, so I immediately shifted my position to the left corner of the control bar, throwing it up and to my right in an effort to counter the gust with a hard left turn. Fortunately, my right wingtip missed the guy wires by a few feet, and I cruised away from the tower and into the hillside updraft.

Another incident involved a revolutionary way to launch hang gliders by towing them behind a powered ultralight. Just as airplanes tow sailplanes in soaring, a French company pioneered a tether system for their power gliders to tow us up from a pasture. Part of their three-ring release assembly included a weak link designed to snap if too many g-forces were pulled by the trailing glider. This way the powered leader would not drag a flailing kite, which would pull them both back to the ground. Michael took the first flight, running with the kite for a few feet until the power glider gained speed and towed him safely to altitude for a smooth flight.

I suited up in the harness and helmet and gave the towing tricycle glider a thumbs-up, indicating that I was ready. As he increased the thrust of his small propeller, I walked, then jogged, as he gained speed. Just like launching from our hillside ramp, I was airborne quickly, but the cool sensation this time was that I was just a few feet above the grass. I enjoyed the low-altitude cruise at grass-top level as the power glider gained speed and altitude. We flew up to 200 feet, and he began a gentle turn to the left. I must have been looking down or off to my right at the Hill Country scenery, because I didn't notice his turn and started mine too late. I didn't aggressively get back into position behind him, and within a few seconds my kite was straining the tow rope—and the weak link then snapped as designed.

I now needed to make a quick landing back at the cleared field behind me. It's a situation I had been trained for in flying small planes, just like an engine failure after takeoff, so I calmly continued my wide left-hand turn. I saw trees and a power line between me and the pasture. With no ability to add power, I could only hope to steer clear of the obstacles as the trees and powerline loomed closer. Luckily, my feet cleared the powerline, and I successfully landed in the field. I was pretty shaken up by that episode, knowing that I had caused it by getting out of position. While Michael would go on to enjoy years of hang gliding and soaring in a sailplane, I decided I would stick to powered flight. Give me an engine any day.

4

THE HAPPY PESSIMIST

David Briscoe, Stacey Samuels Bie, and me, the "Happy Pessimist."

SOME MILITARY AVIATION emergencies involve parachutes, so why not go skydiving? That's what my college friend Stacey Samuels

Bie and I did in October 1983, the fall of my senior year. On a beautiful Halloween weekend, we set out for Skydive Austin, located east of the city near the town of Manor. Instead of the really cool-looking, steerable rectangular airfoils used by skydivers today, our parachutes were military surplus dome chutes used by Army airborne units.

Stacey and I, along with her friend David Briscoe, sat through a short ground school, where the instructors showed us how to strap into our parachute harnesses. They then hung us in our harnesses from a metal frame, simulating the motions of the parachute descent and landing. We practiced turns by pulling on two sets of risers above our shoulders, which allowed us to turn or spin to the left and right so we could land into the wind.

We also practiced the proper way to land, which the instructor called the "banana" technique of touching down with both feet together, then immediately rolling onto our right or left calf, thigh, hip, and butt to absorb the impact. David said he didn't want to mess up the banana landing shape and land flat, with his innards exploding from his "banana skin."

Ours wasn't a tandem jump like beginning skydivers experience nowadays, where jumpers are tethered to an instructor. We were doing a static-line, solo jump, with a ripcord attached by a twenty-five-foot-long lead to the airplane to deploy our chute. As we each fell away from the aircraft, the static line released our parachute once we were a safe distance from the airplane. The Army refers to this jump method as "dope on a rope."

With our ground school successfully completed, the three of us headed out to the flight line with our heavy parachutes on our backs, waiting for our turn to board the high-wing Cessna. In an amazing small-world coincidence, my future girlfriend and wife, Karin, sat on the curb waiting to watch her then-boyfriend skydive. I recognized Karin from our days in the dormitory and around campus.

"Hello," I said.

"Hi there," she replied as I prepared to board the plane with Stacey and David.

The white Cessna took off with we three rookie skydivers onboard, accompanied by one instructor. We climbed into the blue October sky, gaining altitude as we circled up over the intended landing zone. One of the landmarks pointed out to us was a white clapboard house used as the "house of ill repute" in the Burt Reynolds and Dolly Parton movie *The Best Little Whorehouse in Texas*. It was filmed during my sophomore year—and, in an ironic twist, University of Texas students around campus were employed as extras. They portrayed the Texas A&M Aggie cadets in khaki uniforms and knee-high brown leather boots who frequented the infamous Chicken Ranch near LaGrange, Texas.

Our pilot finally gave the indication that we were over the zone, meaning it was time to "Skydive Austin." I eased my way to where the side door of the Cessna had been removed, reached out with both hands, and grabbed the wing strut, a smooth piece of metal running at a forty-five-degree angle from the fuselage to the lower skin of the airplane. I then stretched my right foot out to touch the footrest alongside the right main landing gear. My right foot now held my weight on the small six-by-twelve-inch metal plate, while my left leg dangled in the 120-miles-per-hour wind. I was now standing outside of an airplane! Like a "wing walker" in the barnstorming shows of the 1920s, I was now riding along outside a small plane similar to those I had been piloting since 1978.

Not being the least bit scared, I took in the Texas countryside and a small, white-colored wooden house below. I wish I could have remained a barnstormer longer, but the instructor must have wondered if I had frozen up, because he yelled, "Go! Go! Go!" He was rightfully concerned that I would drift out of the landing zone. There really wasn't much to this type of skydiving: I just had to let go of the wing strut and let gravity do the rest. I fell away from the airplane, arching my back and looking up as the plane grew smaller.

As expected, the static line stretched to its limit and released my main parachute. Had this not gone as planned, though, we had been trained to pull the cord on the smaller back-up chute on our chest, pound the side of it hard enough to get the pouch to open, then throw the auxiliary parachute out and away from us to inflate.

Fortunately, there was no need for any such dramatics this time, and within a few seconds I was dangling beneath a green silk parachute. Many people never attempt to skydive because they're afraid their parachute might fail to open, but because I had trained for that circumstance, I wasn't concerned at all.

Now, though, with my full weight under the chute, I had a different uncomfortable thought: "*What if the leg strap buckles at my crotch fail?*"

If that happened, I knew I would fall out from the bottom of the parachute, and that would suck. It would be all over but the shouting.

Aviators are trained to always think about the next thing that can go wrong, which can lead us to have a rather pessimistic view of things, but it also keeps us ready to react with the correct procedure. Over time, I've come to realize that I am a "happy pessimist." While I have a positive view on life—and I deeply appreciate, and love, my family and friends—I think quite a lot about things that can go wrong.

Perhaps this hasn't served me well for investment opportunities or entrepreneurial prospects, but I've always kept my guard up. I once delayed a laminated flooring project at home because I knew that just one degree of error would compound into a botched job. My exasperated wife finally yelled, "Just start it!" We did, and it turned out fine. Regardless of those "what can go wrong next" thoughts, I'm not full of dread and gloom. Instead, day in and day out I'm a happy, smiling person.

As I continued drifting peacefully toward the field below me, I pulled the left riser to get a view to my left, then pulled the right riser to scan the opposite brown, flat Texas horizon. My entire parachute experience lasted perhaps three or four minutes and was quite different from the free-fall experience I enjoyed as a fifty-year-old from 14,000 feet with my children and their friend. This jump took place from 5,000 feet instead, and near the end of the descent I turned to land into the wind as instructed. With the ground rushing up, I assumed the landing position, eyes on the horizon (although I might have cheated and looked down), with my feet together and knees slightly bent. My touchdown felt fine as I rolled along my right leg and onto my back before watching the green silk drift softly to the ground.

I immediately released the parachute harness buckles at my shoulders to avoid being dragged by the chute in case a gust of wind kicked up, then stood up, uninjured, from my satisfactory banana-technique landing. I gathered the military surplus parachute in my arms and walked over to join Stacey and David in a celebratory high-five, all of us smiling from ear to ear. With the huge orange sun setting in the west, there was no chance to skydive again that day, so I'm glad we jumped at the opportunity when we did.

5
HELO OR NAV?

IN APRIL 1984, one month before commissioning, my ROTC detachment commander at the University of Texas, Col. Larry Smulczenski, called me into his office.

"Dave, we've just received word that there are helicopter pilot slots available if you want one," he said.

"Oh, wow," I thought. I certainly hadn't expected this news so close to graduation.

I definitely had mixed feelings about the opportunity. After four years of trying, here was my chance to get my Air Force pilot wings—but in a helicopter. I wasn't excited enough to accept it on the spot, but I also wasn't going to turn it down right then and there.

Colonel Smulczenski said he could give me a few days to think about it.

At that time, the only Air Force pilot on the ROTC staff was Capt. Gary Smith, who recently had piloted the KC-135 tanker in the Strategic Air Command (SAC). I asked for his thoughts on the advantages and disadvantages of this new opportunity. He said that, to him, the primary purpose of Huey helicopter pilots—the only Air Force helicopter operations he was familiar with—was to ferry SAC nuclear missile crews out to the underground silos scattered across the central United States.

As the Air Force's primary helicopter, the UH-1 Huey flew at miles per hour, and I was already doing that in a rented Cessna 172 at the Bergstrom Aero Club. Also, one conventional military saying at the time was, *"Once a helicopter pilot, always a helicopter pilot."* There might be an opportunity for a crossflow tour to a fixed-wing airplane unit, but that wasn't guaranteed—and even if I was selected for one, I was told I eventually would have to return to a helicopter unit. At no point was I told about, nor did I think about, special operations forces helicopter units and their exciting, secret missions. I just knew I wanted to follow in my Uncle Jack's footsteps and fly a combat aircraft, not a support aircraft, such as an airlift transport or an air refueling tanker.

I was in a real quandary. For four years I had fought to get a pilot slot, and now one was offered—but it was for helicopter training, which I had never even considered. In my mind, the Air Force flew jets and C-130 propeller-driven transports, and I fully expected to fly something much faster than a rented Cessna. Did I want pilot wings so badly that I was willing to fly a "whop-whop" whirlybird for the next twenty years? Or did I want to be a jet navigator and then hope to be selected for pilot training?

At the time I was a pretty gung-ho, physically fit cadet. During my final spring semester of college, I was the cadet corps commander, overseeing the detachment of 150 Air Force cadets. I often exercised with my sophomore college roommate, Doug Griffith, who attended the Marine Corps' Officer Candidates School (OCS) in the summers at Camp LeJeune, North Carolina. We encouraged each other through sixty sit-ups, thirty pull-ups, and a three-mile run along Austin's Town Lake, and I scored high enough on the Marine Corps' personal fitness test to be asked by a clipboard-toting Marine recruiter if I wanted to switch services. But I was content to pursue an Air Force career, fully intending to fly in a combat fighter unit.

Another factor I had not considered, nor was I told about by

Captain Smith, was that pilots typically had stronger career opportunities in the Air Force than navigators. He probably was aware of this fact but didn't want to portray navigators as second-class citizens. Leadership positions in flying units almost always went to pilots, while a navigator wanting to lead usually had to cross-train to become the commander of a non-flying unit, such as a maintenance or security forces squadron. I witnessed this as my career progressed, but at the time it didn't enter my decision-making process. As a twenty-two-year-old, soon-to-be second lieutenant, I couldn't imagine what life would be like as a forty-year-old lieutenant colonel.

I also found out later that helicopter pilots could indeed become fixed-wing airplane pilots and could remain so for the rest of their careers. I eventually crossed paths with numerous Air Force and airline pilots who began their careers flying helicopters.

In the end, I told Colonel Smulczenski I would rather be a combat aircraft navigator than a low-and-slow helicopter pilot. I wasn't thrilled at the prospects of attending helicopter pilot training, but I also wasn't enthusiastic about navigator training, either. Either route would just be biding my time until undergraduate pilot training became available. One of my ROTC classmates took the helicopter pilot slot—and, sure enough, ended up ferrying missile crews in his UH-1 Huey out to the nuclear missile silos around Wichita, Kansas.

On May 19, 1984, I was commissioned a second lieutenant and prepared to head out to Mather Air Force Base, near Sacramento, California, to become a navigator.

My commissioning ceremony as an Air Force officer

6

KARIN SMITH

Karin Smith Gamma Phi Beta sorority photo, University of Texas at Austin

AIR FORCE UNDERGRADUATE navigator training (UNT) was a nine-month course consisting of academics and flights in both the T-37 "Tweet" (a side-by-side jet trainer carrying an instructor pilot and a student navigator) and the T-43 (a Boeing 737, carrying twelve student navigators and three instructors). To successfully complete the program, we needed to master multiple methods of navigation. The first method was dead reckoning, which involved tracking our position on a map by using a stopwatch and compass headings to find landmarks and turn points. We also learned radar navigation by interpreting the terrain from the images we saw on ground-mapping radar. We became proficient in celestial navigation, too, using a sextant and the same trigonometry methods the ancient mariners did to "shoot the stars" as we plotted our plane's location.

Each block of training included a written test, and I was satisfied to receive a on my first Air Force exam, but my fiancée, Karin, always the smarter of the two of us, asked why I didn't make a 100.

"You're only studying one subject, after all," she said.

Her gentle nudge reminded me of a well-known story of a wealthy businessman and his wife as they were pulling into a gas station. The lady recognized the greasy auto mechanic as a former high school boyfriend and pointed him out to her husband.

"Just think," her cocky husband said. "If you had married him, you would be an auto mechanic's wife."

"No, honey," she replied. "If I married him, HE would be a wealthy businessman."

I'd say that story fits my marriage.

I was lucky enough to begin dating Karin in what I refer to as "just-in-time dating"—four weeks before our college graduation. We originally met our freshman year while living in the coed dorm The Castilian across the street from the college campus. Karin, like myself, is six feet tall, so she is hard to miss and easy to look at. I worked in the dormitory cafeteria and served her as she passed through the food line, so we now tell people, "We lived together our freshman year."

Some couples have cute pet names for each other. Mine, apparently, was "There." Karin was a "little sister" to the Navy ROTC unit in a service organization called Anchorettes. The Air Force had a similar organization called Angel Flight, and many ROTC classmates met their future spouses this way. When I spotted her walking through the ROTC building, I would say, "Hi, Karin." Not knowing my name, she would reply, "Hi there." None of my Air Force friends ever caught on to this joke between us; otherwise, "There" might have become my Air Force call sign. Can you imagine: Maverick, Goose, Iceman, and ... "There"?

We officially met at the Silver Dollar Dance Hall on the north side of Austin, where two long tables were occupied by twenty ROTC cadets, Anchorettes, and Angels. Karin was sitting at the far end with a married Marine Corps friend of hers, who told her she should dance with me.

When she came over and asked me to dance, I answered, "No, not to this song."

I wasn't playing hard to get, though. I wasn't a strong country dancer and didn't know the song the band was playing, so the last thing I wanted to do was step on the toes of the woman I'd been falling for since our freshman year. From grade school through college, I was terribly shy around girls, and I didn't have the self-esteem to put myself out there and risk being turned down. Instead, I just admired Karin whenever she walked by, never imagining that I'd be talking to her that night.

After being told no, Karin sat down and asked what I was drinking, and I became sheepish. This was the final nickel beer night before the Silver Dollar closed for good on Saturday. They served nickel beers and fifty-cent pitchers of Budweiser on Thursdays ... and I was drinking water. "*How NOT to make a good impression!*" was all I could think. But I had a good reason: I hadn't planned to be there that night.

I'd been going to the Silver Dollar for four years (not every Thursday, but close), and on the previous Saturday I had completed a college triathlon, which consisted of a thousand-yard swim, a thirty-mile bike ride, and a six-mile run. I was in the best shape of my life, but when my friend Wade called to say everyone was heading out to the Silver Dollar one last time, I said I was burned out on the place. Wade didn't relent, though. He told me that our mutual friend Alex Bays was not planning to drink that night, so I could "just come along and not drink with Alex." Alex and I had downed numerous pitchers of water by the time I finally met Karin.

She and I did dance that night, and it was the first time I ever looked directly into the eyes of a dance partner. I was entranced, and I will never forget that first dance. Luckily for me, Karin needed a date for her final sorority spring dance in April 1984, and she picked me. Our whirlwind romance continued through college graduation four weeks later, and on into the summer.

My original report date for navigator training was October 1984, so I worked a construction job after graduation. I helped build an apartment complex on the south side of Austin and roomed with my ROTC classmate, newly commissioned 2nd Lt. Jim Thomas. Meanwhile, Karin moved into a South Austin apartment and began using her finance degree as a bookkeeper for Pok-e-Jo's, a local Austin barbecue eatery.

Jim and I were scheduled to attend nav school together in the fall, and we planned to share an apartment in Sacramento, California, but in July I received an unexpected phone call from the Air Force Personnel Center in San Antonio. A slot had opened up in the August navigator training class, and I was asked if I wanted to report for training two months early. I didn't hesitate for a second.

"You bet!" I replied, without even consulting Karin. I knew I wanted to marry her, but now my timeline was accelerated, and I hadn't even met her parents yet.

I soon found out that she came from a family of very tall people. In late July we headed down to her hometown of Corpus Christi, where I met her six-foot-six-inch father, Jerry; six-foot-seven-inch brother, Clark; and five-foot-ten-inch mother, Barbara. At six feet tall, at least I wouldn't be the shortest in this family.

Later that afternoon, Jerry and I sipped Miller Lites in their pool while Karin and Barbara went shopping. Jerry had enlisted in the Air Force during the Korean War because, as he said with a laugh, "I would've been the tallest person in Korea, and the Army didn't make foxholes deep enough for me!"

Instead, Jerry attended the Defense Language Institute, located near Monterey, California, and served as a Russian linguist in northern Japan, eavesdropping on the submarine pens in Vladivostok. After his enlistment, Jerry became a store manager of various Woolco locations, moving his family around the country. He served as an assistant store manager in California, Arizona, and Ohio, before being promoted to general manager of his own Woolco on the north side of Houston. This imposing gentle giant then had the task of turning around a poorly performing Woolco in Corpus Christi. The family settled there in 1974, where Karin graduated from high school in 1980.

Lounging in the pool, he asked me what a second lieutenant made in the Air Force these days.

"About $17,000 a year," I told him.

"Oh, that's pretty good," he said, smiling.

My $700 paycheck every two weeks far exceeded the $400 per month he made as an enlisted man thirty years earlier.

Once I worked up my courage (thank you, Miller Lite), I told Jerry that, after completing navigator training next summer, I would like to marry his daughter. I was totally going off-script at this point; Karin and I knew we wanted to get married, but during the drive down to Corpus from Austin I had wondered if I really should ask her dad for his permission on this first meeting. But here I was, full of beer, sunshine, and courage, doing just that.

Leaning up against the side of his pool, my future father-in-law said, "It's OK with me, but you'd better ask her."

A few minutes later, Karin and her mom, whom I had hardly met, walked in the gate by the pool.

"Barbara, you better go get dressed," he told his wife. "We're going out to dinner."

"Why?" she asked.

"David wants to marry our daughter," he said.

I am certain Barbara was floored. She must have been thinking, "*Who is this twenty-two-year-old kid sitting in my swimming pool? I don't know the slightest thing about him.*"

Karin also was stunned, caught off-guard that I would ask Jerry after telling her I wouldn't bring it up on this first visit. It was a bit out of character for me, but I just decided to go for it.

A few days later, on a triple-digit July day, I drove Karin up to Mount Bonnell in her 1979 Monte Carlo. I had recently bought a brand-new 1984 Monte Carlo Super Sport, but it was delivered without freon, so the air conditioner wasn't working on that blisteringly hot day. As we overlooked Lake Austin, I officially proposed, and Karin said, "Yes."

"Good," I replied, sweat dripping down my face. "Let's get back to the car!"

We drove to the Austin Hyatt Regency for a rooftop dinner celebration.

The day after Karin agreed to marry me, I stood in my Austin living room and told her, "Now that you said yes, I need to talk you out of it."

"Why?" she asked.

"Because our life in the military might be hard, and I don't want to get a divorce," I said.

Being a child of divorced parents, I really didn't want to start a family and then have the marriage break up.

"I promise I won't divorce you," Karin replied.

Our first vows had just been spoken.

I certainly didn't know what the future held for us, since I had never been in the military, but I knew from watching my uncle, aunt, and two cousins move around a lot that married life might get challenging for both of us. We weren't going to live close to our families, and we'd be on our own for major parts of our married life. I wanted Karin to know what she was signing up for, and I hoped that we could weather the challenges together. Establishing those parameters kept us from throwing in the towel when times were tough.

Karin interviewed with major oil companies after graduating from UT with her finance degree. She had also been accepted to Saint Mary's University School of Law in San Antonio. Fortunately for me, Karin gave all that up to follow me across the country.

Life in the 1980s (and earlier) was not easy on working military spouses. Employers would ask the now-illegal question, "Is your husband in the military?" The true meaning behind that question was, "Will you be leaving us soon?" Answering that question either meant not getting hired, or being hired for a low-level job with few chances of advancement. Karin never earned what her degree and brainpower were worth, selflessly serving instead as a military spouse, as thousands before and after her have done with unwavering strength and grace.

I left for Sacramento a week later, then flew home during my Christmas break from training on December 22. One week later, on December 29, we were married in Corpus Christi. We had only dated for four months before my departure for Air Force training, and have been married ever since.

Karin's family on our wedding day

7

"WHAT'S SIXTEEN MINUS SIXTEEN?"

Second Lieutenant Dale, student navigator at a T-43 navigator station

"WHY DIDN'T YOU MAKE 100?" Karin asked. "You're only studying one subject."

I had just scored a ninety-three on my first test in navigator training, and Karin had a point. I wasn't trying to balance four or five college courses on various topics. Thanks to her push, I made 100 on the remaining academic tests in navigator training and later in pilot training.

The first navigation evaluation is visual low-level navigation in the T-37 "Tweet," a twin-engine jet trainer known for producing more noise than thrust. The instructor pilot sat in the left seat, with a full panel of aviation instruments. The student navigator sat in the right seat and had a control stick, but with fewer instruments to observe and no expectation to fly the jet. Students flew several training rides to learn how to navigate visually, using "timing and heading" to navigate to a target. This meant the student told the pilot to fly a heading for a prescribed number of minutes, identify a landmark, then turn to a new heading to complete a low-level route across the Sierra Nevada mountains east of Sacramento.

For my low-level evaluation, the target was a radio tower atop a Sierra Nevada mountain. This might sound like it would be easy, but flying at 500 to 1000 feet above the ground limits forward visibility, so all that can be seen are easily identifiable landmarks: lakes, roads, or railroad tracks in the immediate vicinity. The low-level route was plotted on a colored map, with a black line zig-zagging across the mountains toward the target. Flying a zig-zag pattern could help avoid detection in a real combat sortie over enemy territory.

I knew one important landmark was the second of two small mountain lakes. My stopwatch was running as we clipped along at four miles per minute, just 500 feet above the treetops. At the prescribed time, I looked out of the cockpit and saw a lake.

"OK, where is the second lake?" I thought. *"Or was THAT the second lake?"*

Hmm.

I glanced at the map and looked back outside a few more times. The pilot then calmly asked me the all-important question: "What do you want me to do?"

I was nervous, bewildered, and unable to hit a pause button. I decided I had to trust my timing and told him to turn to the new heading. He threw the little jet into a hard right turn, rolled out, then turned his dark-visored helmet toward me. His oxygen mask concealed what must have been a smile as he keyed the interphone and said, "They drained that other lake years ago."

A few minutes later, after several more turns, we rolled out on the final leg to the target. Peering ahead, I saw the red-and-white radio tower poking above the horizon on the wooded hilltop ahead of us.

"Nice job," he said.

The radar navigation portion of training consisted of interpreting the green-and-black round radarscope to pick out terrain features and use them as turn points en route to a destination or target. Radar emissions bounce off anything solid, whether it's the buildings of a city or the rain in a thunderstorm, so the radarscope would display the distance and rough shape of an object, including how solid it was.

The scopes we used were not the modern-day, multicolored weather radar depictions. Ours just showed various shades of green and black. A favorite trick of the instructors during the simulator training sessions was to place a thunderstorm near a large city to see which one the student would avoid, as we had to keep clear of thunderstorms by twenty nautical miles to avoid potential hail damage. During one simulator session in a room full of twenty students facing their scopes, the instructor slapped the student next to me on the shoulder and sarcastically said, "Congratulations. You just successfully deviated around St. Louis."

I successfully completed the radar navigation portion of training and moved on to the hardest phase, which was celestial navigation. After each navigation phase, those who did not pass the evaluation were "washed back" to the training class behind us. Students needed to pass each phase of the course, and if they failed a portion after their second attempt, they washed out of training completely. After that, it was up to the Air Force to either retrain the officer in another career field or dismiss them from the service. "The needs of the Air Force" was a common mantra that we heard, and it never was a certainty that a student would pass a test or evaluation and move on to the next phase.

A navigator training class started every two weeks at Mather Air Force Base, so it was easy to wash back for many reasons. Catch a cold and miss three training flights? Wash back. Sprain your ankle playing volleyball? Wash back. Fail a checkride? Wash back. I knew if I stayed on track, I would graduate in April—but, as I told Karin, "I have no idea when I'll graduate. I've seen guys wash back at the drop of a hat."

For this reason, our original spring or summer wedding in 1985 was moved up to the Christmas break of 1984. I learned that only one thing is certain in Air Training Command: The school shuts down between Christmas and New Year's Day. By the time we started celestial navigation, we had lost a third of our original classmates. Many of them would go on to graduate, but not with their original class.

I had enjoyed mathematics ever since junior high algebra, and I took trigonometry in high school, but I also was the smart-aleck student who asked, "Mrs. Benedict, when am I EVER going to use this?"

Well, I found out that the terms tangent, sine, and cosine are all used in celestial navigation. A line of position (LOP) from three different celestial objects (stars, planets, or the moon) will plot a small triangle, identifying a location over the Earth. Or, in daylight, a LOP from the sun or moon can be crossed with a radio signal from a known beacon, and the geographic position is at that intersection. It was all math, and I really enjoyed it. During a later visit to Houston, I stopped by Mrs. Benedict's math class to tell her, "I found out where you use trig!"

After many weeks of theory, each student was loaned a sextant to take home for practice. Many of us second lieutenants lived in apartments in the Rancho Cordova area, and I was now newly married, so I thought, "*What better way to entertain my new bride than to bring home a sextant to look at the moon and stars?*" From the monkey bars of the playground equipment in our apartment complex, Karin and I hung the ten-pound metal sextant and looked skyward. It may all sound very nerdy and geeky, but my wife will always remember our evenings "shooting the stars."

The airborne training consisted of three flights in a T-43, a 1970s-era Boeing 737 with the skinny engines. It was the same model that Southwest Airlines was famous for flying in the days of flight attendants in hot pants and go-go boots. The T-43 cabin had three sections (A, B, and C), each containing four navigation stations, one sextant porthole in the ceiling, and one instructor navigator to monitor his four students. In total, there were twelve student navigators and three instructors, plus the two pilots up front.

During a training flight, each student was responsible for navigating one segment of the flight. Even when it was not my leg, I had to keep up with the airplane's position so I would be ready to give the pilots a heading to fly when my turn came. Things quickly turned interesting if a weak student navigator was in charge. If the student made a math or position error, he or she would believe the plane was way off course and direct a large heading change to the pilot ("Pilot, come right thirty degrees!"). Now we all had to continue to plot this errant course, so that when our turn came we could direct the pilot back on course.

To prepare to take a celestial shot of a star, navigators completed a pre-computation (called a precomp) worksheet so that we knew what area of the sky to look for our intended star. One navigator from sections A, B, and C stood on a stool, looking out the sextant port in the ceiling above their section. During the initial training flights, all three were supposed to shoot the same star. The best rule of thumb was to hope that we all faced the same direction once we stood on a stool. Math errors could easily lead to some students facing exactly backward from the intended stars, and sometimes "one of these navs didn't look like the others," to paraphrase the old *Sesame Street* song.

I cruised through both daytime and nighttime celestial navigation with perfect scores on all the training rides and was third in my class of thirty. Being in the top 10 percent virtually assured me of my first choice of aircraft on assignment night, two weeks away, when we found out what airplane—and to which Air Force base—we would be assigned. An officer's entire life changed that night, making it a thrilling and nerve-wracking event.

I eagerly submitted my "dream sheet" of what I hoped to fly. At the top of my sheet were the F-111, FB-111, F-4, and RF-4, in that order. Behind them all, in a distant fifth, was the B-52 Stratofortress bomber. I knew I wanted a combat aircraft, and those five choices fit the bill. The F-111 and F-4 fighter aircraft all had two sets of flight controls, so even the navigator had a "stick." But in the F-111 and FB-111, the navigator sat beside the pilot, not behind him like in the F-4 and RF-4. I knew all I had to do was ace my daytime and nighttime celestial navigation evaluations, and a fighter assignment would be mine.

The daytime celestial checkride (flight evaluation) consisted of three position fixes taken throughout the four-hour midday flight. Each position fix had to be within five miles of our actual position. Up to this point, all of my previous fixes on the training rides had been spot-on. I ran my precomputations, completed the fixes and plotted the aircraft position on the navigation chart. To me, everything seemed to be going just great. At the end of the flight, each student rolled up his navigation chart and handed it to one of the three evaluators monitoring the flight. The charts would be graded overnight, and the results debriefed in the next class. I slept well that night.

The next morning, we took our seats in the classroom—and because I sat on the back row, the evaluators entered the room behind me. As they came into class, I was suddenly whacked upside the right side of my head by a rolled-up navigation chart. It was my instructor, who looked at me and asked, "What's sixteen minus sixteen?"

"Zero," I answered. *What a weird question for him to ask*, I thought.

"Well, yesterday you thought it was ten," he said, shaking his head.

Instantly, I knew that was not good. A critical math error meant my position fix was ten miles off and out of tolerance. But I also knew that one of the three fixes could be out of tolerance and I would still pass the checkride—but with a rating of good instead of excellent.

I soon found out there was another problem. My checkride came at an unfortunate time. My second position fix was a LOP from the sun, crossed with a radial from a VOR (VHF omnidirectional range) beacon in Wyoming. VOR stations are navigational beacons that give aircraft directional guidance. For one reason or another, I discovered that my second fix also fell outside of the five-mile tolerance.

The next day, that particular VOR was posted as temporarily out of service. I can only assume that the radial reading I took during my checkride that day was not an accurate bearing. With two of my three fixes out of tolerance, I failed the checkride with only two weeks before assignment night. Because of my near-perfect performance before that, and my successful completion of the nighttime celestial checkride, I was still projected to graduate on time. My class standing, however, fell from top ten percent to top third of the class. Not simply checking my math proved to be a pivotal moment in my life. That was my first episode of "Don't get cocky, Lieutenant Dale."

I was still hopeful I could get a fighter. After all, F-111s and F-4s don't have sextants or use celestial navigation, and I did well on the low-level and radar navigation evaluations. My flight commander, Captain Dahlgren, agreed. In the days leading up to assignment night, students in my class met with our flight commander, where we were given an assessment of our training performance and his thoughts on what aircraft we would receive. According to Captain Dahlgren and the other instructors, they thought I would receive an F-111, which made me very relieved and excited.

On the other hand, the last flight in the T-43 was a low-level excursion near the Grand Canyon, bouncing along in the stubby-wing aircraft at a thousand feet above the canyon rim. Nine of the twelve student navigators threw up on that turbulent flight. I was one of the three that did not. It looked like I could handle low-level flying in a large aircraft.

"Uh-oh," I thought.

Although the aircraft assignments were made by the Air Force Personnel Center in San Antonio, and not by the local Mather training staff, I didn't like the way this was shaping up.

On assignment night, as I drove through the Mather main gate, I told Karin, "I think I'm going to get a B-52. I have it too high up on my list." The dream sheet had room for thirty choices, and many students put the old bomber at number thirty—and would have listed it even lower if they could have.

When my turn came, I was called up on stage and turned to face the crowd of classmates, spouses, and the navigator training staff. Captain Dahlgren said a few kind words about my performance and then announced, "Congratulations. You've been assigned to the 62nd Bomb Squadron at Barksdale Air Force Base, Shreveport, Louisiana."

At that moment, a picture of a B-52 flashed on the screen behind me.

I turned to face Captain Dahlgren and shook his outstretched hand. As we locked eyes, I thought, *"That sure doesn't sound like the F-111 you thought I was going to get."* I'm certain he felt bad about getting my hopes up. Although I was prepared to receive a B-52 assignment, I was disappointed when it came true. All that I could think in this moment of confusion was, *"Where is Shreveport, Louisiana?"*

8
RUNNING AROUND IN THE BUFF

B-52G taking off

I CALLED my grandfather to tell him the news of my B-52 assignment, telling him over the phone: "Papa, I'm going to Barksdale Air Force Base. That's in Shreveport, Louisiana."

"I know where Barksdale is," he answered with a chuckle. "I helped build that base."

My grandfather, born in 1908, was a single twenty-three-year-old in 1931 when he rented a small room at the Shreveport YMCA while he coordinated the MoPac train shipments of material used to build the air base outside of Bossier City. This two-year project near the Red River was the job that saw him through the Great Depression, and I was surprised to hear Papa's story. Now I had a family connection to Barksdale, and that put a positive spin on my less-than-ideal assignment.

Flying on a B-52 crew had its highlights. Although the Stratofortress may not have been a popular assignment, the camaraderie of working with the same six-man team and enjoying each other's company, as well as getting to know their families, helped me enjoy my job. This was the beginning of my very gratifying Air Force career.

B-52 training for navigators consisted of a seven-month course at Castle Air Force Base outside of Merced, in California's Central Valley. Navigators received an all-expenses-paid move there to learn about the new offensive avionics system, or OAS. B-52 copilots arrived a month later to begin learning the aircraft's hydraulic, electronic, pneumatic, and fuel systems.

The B-52G models were built between 1958 and 1961, and in the 1980s they were just coming out of a major bombing system upgrade. Gone was the old punched-card computer; in its place was a new bombing computer that received its data via metal cartridges. The updates also included a new radar and inertial navigation system (INS) to guide the plane and its crew to a target.

The 1964 dark comedy *Dr. Strangelove* depicted the inside of a B-52 fairly well. The famous actor James Earl Jones portrayed a B-52 radar navigator, whose equivalent job during World War II was called bombardier. He sat downstairs in the bomber, to the left of the navigator, which is where I sat. In the bomber crew hierarchy, all navigators started in the right navigator seat. After two years, we typically upgraded to the left seat to become the radar navigator, just like a copilot starts in the right seat and upgrades to aircraft commander in the left seat.

Strangely enough, I remembered watching *Dr. Strangelove* in my high school civics class during my senior year in 1980. Now, five years later, I was training to be a B-52 crew member.

Leading up to our first training mission, we watched several training films of B-52 incidents or accidents. Although their purpose was to instill a safety mindset, or to demonstrate the importance of teamwork in overcoming a bad situation, these definitely were not confidence boosters. One accident, caught on grainy, black-and-white film, captured a B-52 crash-landing before breaking apart as it slid off the runway and into the grass. The cockpit portion snapped off to the side of the runway, and the entire crew scrambled out before the bomber burst into flames. In the love/hate relationship we all had with our B-52s, we referred to the old bomber as the BUFF, which stood for "big, ugly, fat fellow"—except the last word wasn't "fellow."

At that time, the B-52 had a six-man crew. Two pilots comprised the pilot team, with the aircraft commander (AC) in the left seat and the copilot (CP) in the right. There also was an electronic warfare officer (EWO), and an enlisted gunner who sat facing aft, behind the pilots. The radar navigator and navigator sat on a lower level, under the pilots but facing forward. In 1992, following the collapse of the Soviet Union, the gunner position was removed from the crew—and by the mid-1990s, women were allowed to join the combat crew force.

Training missions typically lasted seven to nine hours, so that crews were ready for the rigors of long-range bombing missions. The missions consisted of a rendezvous with a KC-135 or KC-10 tanker for mid-air refueling, followed by simulated high-altitude bomb drops and air-launched cruise missile (ALCM) releases. The intense portion came next, as the bomber descended into a low-level route over the Midwest, flying at about 400 to 1,000 feet above the ground, depending upon cloud cover and weather conditions.

When the time came for my first takeoff in the BUFF, I was pretty anxious. Before departing for an eight-hour training mission, I stood for several minutes in the bathroom of base operations—not throwing up, but nervously trying to pee instead. Once onboard, there would only be a standpipe to use as a urinal, and that often proved to be difficult on a bumpy flight.

The training videos of mishaps lodged in my head as our plane lumbered toward the runway, and I wondered if it was the exception or the rule that our flight would end successfully. Once off the ground, though, I was too busy doing my job to think about anything bad happening.

We spent the next several hours flying around the western United States, refueling behind a KC-135 tanker over Arizona, then descending for a low-level route over southern Colorado and New Mexico. We spent the next hour flying at the height of a modern-day cellular tower before the mission concluded with forty-five minutes of practice landings (called touch-and-go landings) for both pilots sitting directly above us.

My radar navigator during this training was a middle-aged major just returning to the B-52 following his air staff tour. As we taxied back into our parking spot at the end of that first flight, he couldn't contain himself any longer and finally threw up in his ever-present barf bag. Throughout my years of flying, getting airsick was one fate I never experienced.

The navigator ensures the aircraft stays on course and on time, and also is responsible for overall crew pacing, from preflight through arrival back home. Performing that job instilled a sense of timing that has stuck with me for the rest of my life. I hate running late, and I have difficulty being around folks with poor time-management skills. I tend to fidget irritably in a group setting when a person rambles along with a story, even if a meeting has five more minutes to go. That lack of timing awareness grates on my nerves.

Time's up! Move along!

My family knows I get antsy when things don't run on time.

Our low-level routes were flown over the farmlands of Kansas, Nebraska, the Dakotas, Colorado, and the deserts of Nevada and New Mexico. Each route had three bombing targets separated by about twenty minutes' flying time along the twisting, turning route, over rolling pastures and around small towns. In an era before GPS was available, navigators used two-prong compass dividers to plot the aircraft's coordinates on paper charts. My job was to keep the plane within four miles of the route's centerline.

At cruise altitude, we still wore our flight helmets but allowed our oxygen masks to hang off to one side. It was more comfortable that way, and it usually wasn't important for us to talk instantly to the rest of the crew. If we needed to communicate, we'd raise the mask to our face and speak into the embedded microphone. At low altitudes, however, each crew member cinched the oxygen mask containing the microphone tightly to our faces, so we could continuously talk while working with both hands. If anything went wrong while flying close the ground, we were immediately ready to eject.

Important safety note: The downstairs navigator ejection seats ejected *downward,* and the minimum altitude for ejection was listed as 150 feet in our operating manual to allow for our ejection seats to blast out of the bottom of the aircraft. The navigators would then be propelled from their seats, with the parachute opening just seconds before impact. We called that "one swing in the chute." At that low altitude, we navigators knew we probably would still be traveling close to 100 miles per hour when we hit the ground.

The dangers we faced with low-level flying weren't just theoretical, either. I know of two bomber crews that crashed during low-level training missions. One of those involved a B-1 bomber that hit the rugged mountains at night in South Texas near the Mexico border. The radar navigator, Capt. Scott Genal, had been a B-52 navigator friend of mine at Barksdale before transferring to the brand-new B-1. All of the crew members died on impact. It was sobering to realize the training flights we enjoyed flying as a crew could have a deadly outcome.

The second crash involved a B-52 from a northern base that clipped the top of a thin, tall, tower-like peak in Arizona while descending into a low-level training route. The damage from the glancing blow was bad enough that the pilot knew the plane was unrecoverable. He pulled up quickly after striking the peak and began to roll the big bomber, commanding, "Bail out! Bail out! Bail out!" Everyone with an ejection seat immediately grabbed the yellow ejection handle between their legs and punched out. Because the aircraft was rolling sideways, all six crew members had an equal opportunity to escape as both the upstairs and downstairs ejection seats blasted out of the now-sideways bomber.

Later on, the navigator was assigned to my squadron, and he briefed us during a quarterly safety meeting on his harrowing ejection. He was a living testament for the Nomex flame-retardant flight suits worn by military crews as he recounted descending in his parachute as the bomber exploded, drifting through the aircraft's fireball. Miraculously, his only burn marks were on his wrists and the back of his neck— the only exposed areas on his body. He provided a great reminder to keep our sleeves down and collars up during a B-52 mission. Although six people survived the crash he was in, there were two other instructors on board—one pilot and one navigator—who did not. Instructors were not afforded an ejection seat and instead occupied a metal box seat. Neither instructor was able to escape through the holes left from the now-departed ejection seats, probably because of the centrifugal force of the rolling airplane.

The B-52 low-level missions were exhilarating, requiring intense concentration from all six crew members for almost an hour and a half. Each of the three bombing runs started by arriving at the initial point (IP) on time. The IP was the last navigation point before we reached the target and the beginning of the bombing run. From there, the radar navigator provided steering data to the pilot's display upstairs. As long as the pilot kept the two lines centered and flew at the requested speeds, the bomber arrived at the release point on time. The pre-release checklist was succinctly choreographed, with each step called out by me and replied to over interphone by the appropriate crew member.

Although the B-52 (with its 185-foot wingspan) flew low to evade simulated enemy radar, the bomb release altitude was a bit higher. Seconds before the release, the pilots began a short, abrupt climb to allow the bombs to be "pitched" or "lobbed" toward the target. Finally, the radar navigator would announce, "Bombs away," indicating the weapon had been released. During training missions, the only thing released was an electronic signal for scoring. On a real-world combat mission, a drag chute would be deployed on the bombs, which would drift slowly down to the ground as the bomber flew away.

The pilots then quickly changed course to the next target and pitched down to 400 feet again, creating negative g-forces and a floating sensation in the cockpit. Any unsecured objects (such as ink pens, or my sharp, pointed dividers) floated around the cockpit if we weren't careful. About twenty minutes later, the roller coaster ride repeated itself until the final simulated bomb release. After the last "Bombs away!" call-out, instead of pitching over, the pilots brought the eight-engine bomber out of the low-level route and back up to high altitude for the flight back to our base. During these climbs I would drop my mask, lean back from my tabletop, and take a long swig of water from a nearby bottle. I could finally relax a bit for the flight home.

B-52 missions required detailed planning from all six crew members because the training route covered so much territory, with mission progressing from air refueling, to high-altitude bomb and missile releases, to low-level routes, and then back to base. Planning a mission took an entire day before the flight. My final B-52 checkride from Castle Air Force Base was scheduled for January 29, 1986, which meant the mission-planning day was January 28. As we all huddled around the charts that morning, a major walked in to the room around 8:45 a.m. telling us that the space shuttle Challenger had just exploded. It was a somber moment as we let the news sink in.

We were told that if we did not feel up to taking our checkride the next day, it would be understandable. Although it was a terrible tragedy, we completed the planning, then headed home to watch the news updates about the shuttle explosion and the repeated scenes of the horrific mishap. Our crew knew we were well-prepared for our final evaluation, and all of us showed up early the next morning to fly our seven-hour checkride. By the end of January, I was a qualified BUFF navigator, and Karin and I packed up our Monte Carlo Super Sport for the move to Louisiana.

In a bit of good luck, Karin, following in her dad's footsteps, worked as a retail manager for Miller's Outpost, a California-based clothing store. Fortunately for us, Miller's Outpost was expanding east and had just opened a store in Shreveport. A job as store manager was waiting for her when we arrived.

9

BARKSDALE B-52 HIJINKS

The 62nd Bomb Squadron at Barksdale in 1986

MY AIRCRAFT COMMANDER during initial qualification training in California was Maj. Glenn Lunsford. We both were assigned to the 62nd Bomb Squadron (62 BMS) at Barksdale Air Force Base, arriving in February 1986. New crew members usually were combined with experienced crew members to form bomber crews, and Major Lunsford and I were paired together as part of a permanent crew. His copilot was 1st Lt. Dan McMillan; later, 1st Lt. Stan Buelt joined our crew as well. Capt. Joe Wolf, six years older than me, was the radar navigator. The electronic warfare officer (EWO for short, or simply "E-Dub") was 1st Lt. Alan McGreer, and our gunner was Airman 1st Class Mike Barker.

Major Lunsford—or Glenn, as only Karin and the other spouses could call him—was a chain-smoking, soon-to-be-divorced Californian with thinning blond hair. He reluctantly returned to the B-52 after a Pentagon staff tour where he worked in the targeting office, planning strikes against the Soviet Union. Even at just thirty-five years old, he was the old man and adult supervisor of our crew.

Captain Wolf, who was the same age as my brother, Jack, hailed from Baltimore and joined the Air Force after obtaining his biology degree from the University of Tampa, which my daughter attended years later.

"You know what you do with a biology degree?" he once asked me. "You join the Air Force and become a navigator."

Captain Wolf was a lean, athletic triathlete, excelling in swimming, biking, and running. He had a narrow face with a sharp, pointed nose, and he tackled every challenge with maximum effort. When he took up tennis, he bought the latest high-tech, big-face racket, and the tennis apparel to look the part. Once he became interested in golf, he immediately started making his own clubs—and made my first set, too.

On a rare B-52 trip away from Barksdale, our crew flew a bomber to Tinker Air Force Base, near Oklahoma City. Joe, Al, and I took advantage of this rare off-base trip by packing our golf clubs in the huge storage compartment behind the bomb bay. Once we changed out of our flight suits, we headed to the base golf course, as all Air Force officers should.

We were true golf novices, but I knew enough not to tee off from the women's red tee box markers, or the blue markers for the pros, so

Al and I walked up to the men's white tee box. Mr. Athlete, Joe Wolf, stood back at the blue markers and yelled, "Get back here, you wussies!"

Alan and I grabbed our tees and balls and sauntered back toward Joe, at the blue professional tee box. We then proceeded to spray our tee shots in quite a military fashion; our three golf balls flew left, right, and left from the intended fairway. At that moment, a voice from the pro shop's loudspeaker announced the following, for all to hear: "Will the party on the first tee please move up to the white tees?" Thanks, Joe. Golf is a stupid game.

Alan, the EWO, was responsible for providing our self-defense on missions by electronically jamming enemy radar, and by dispensing chaff (long strips of metal) and flares to confuse incoming missiles. Mike, the gunner, sat in the cockpit alongside the aft-facing EWO, controlling the tail-mounted .50-caliber machine guns. He had a tiny four-inch scope to hopefully track any attacking fighters behind us, and his job was to shoot at any enemy fighter that got close enough for a gun kill.

We used to tease Mike, asking if he brought a roll of quarters for his video game, since that's what his gunner's station looked like. His system was so low-tech that even he knew his job was to "spray and pray," i.e. shoot enough bullets to hopefully hit something. The gunner was a carryover from the days before accurate air-to-air missiles were widely used. Technological advancements meant modern enemy fighters no longer needed to get within machine-gun range, and the gunner's position was eventually removed.

The majority of our training missions took off and landed from our home base. It was always known that Strategic Air Command (SAC) provided a stable family life, because we were rarely away overnight. Barksdale had two squadrons of twelve B-52s (twenty-four bombers on the base), and each crew spent one week out of every four to six weeks on nuclear alert. "Sitting alert," as it was called, was akin to being a fireman on duty at a firehouse, only our rotation was 24/7 for a full week. At other, smaller SAC bases, the rotation schedule was once every three weeks, which could be a real morale killer. Once our crew gained experience, flying the same training missions and always returning to Louisiana started to become routine. Fortunately, though, our crew got a break from the routine when we were selected to head to England in fall 1986 for a month of flying.

Each fall, four U.S. crews and two bombers deployed to Royal Air Force (RAF) Fairford, a base near Swindon in southwestern England. From there, we flew live bombing missions over Texel Island off the coast of the Netherlands. Other missions flew over France and West Germany to a low-level route along the East German border, or we practiced anti-shipping operations over the Mediterranean Sea. This specialized off-station training was far better than flying the same nine-hour flights over a Midwestern prairie. The annual Busy Brewer exercise, as it was officially named, was considered a "good deal tour," which is any trip that makes others envious. This was at the height of the Cold War, and our trip also occurred several months after our Air Force's F-111 raid on Col. Muammar Gaddafi's bases in Libya. Pictures of our B-52s were splashed across the front pages of the British newspapers as the press speculated that we were there to conduct a follow-up raid.

TIO PEPE SPAIN'S SHERRY GONZALEZ BYASS

SUNDAY TELEGRA

No. 1319 August 31, 1986 Price 40p

Frenzied mob hails Gaddafi a! tension rises in Tri

US prepares B-52 bombers for Libya

By CON COUGHLIN in Tripoli and NORMAN KIRKHAM in London

An American B-52 bomber at RAF Fairford, near Bristol, after its arrival

British newspaper headline the day we arrived in England for Busy Brewer

Al and I roomed together in a small hotel room. He was a year older than me, and his wife's name was Davilynn. She hailed from Sacramento, and they met while he was at nav school. One night our room phone rang in the dead of night—at 2:30 a.m.—startling both of us. Davilynn didn't realize the time zone difference between us, and she couldn't wait to share her news with Al. Since he was away, she had bought a cute little Shih Tzu puppy for $400. This was at the time when lieutenants made $800 every two weeks.

"A what?" he asked. "I don't even know what that is!"

After hanging up, Al looked at me and said, "She bought a $400 dog! Do you even know what a Shih Tzu is?"

"It's a little white dog about the size of a football," I told him. "You should call it Wilson."

From that day forward, he referred to Davilynn's precious puppy as Wilson.

Meanwhile, I had two navigator friends flying F-111 fighter-bombers from RAF Lakenheath and RAF Upper Heyford. One was Jim Thomas, my college and nav-school roommate, and the other was a nav-school classmate named Jon. One of them asked me if we would take the B-52 down Loch Ness in Scotland at low level, the way they did. Apparently it was allowed, and even condoned, since the Brits loved military aviation.

One afternoon, our planned B-52 mission over central Europe was scrubbed because of bad weather. On this particular flight, our wing commander, Col. Eugene Habiger, an experienced B-52 pilot himself, joined us. As a backup plan, I took my F-111 friend's advice and came up with a route to fly counterclockwise around the eastern coast of England, up to the northern coast of Scotland, then down the Loch Ness at 500 to 1000 feet above the water before returning to RAF Fairford.

Besides working in a compartment with a downward ejection seat, the navigator station also lacks windows. To give us a view of the outside world, the B-52 has two cameras under the nose. These are the two "bulges," or "blisters," seen below the cockpit in B-52 photographs. One of the cameras is forward-looking infrared (FLIR), and the other is a low-light television (LLTV). These cameras provided night vision on television screens at both the downstairs navigator stations and on the pilots' display panels. As navigator, I had a trackball that I could use to swivel the cameras up, down, left, and right.

Our B-52 dropped down over Loch Ness on its mission and cruised over the water, slightly higher than the cliffs on both sides. I swiveled the cameras left and right, viewing the old stone buildings along the loch. It was a quick trip, but as we climbed out of our low-level flight, Colonel Habiger said over our plane's interphone: "That was nice, but it's a bit like our Grand Canyon, so I don't think anyone else should do that."

Good thing I got to see it when I did.

Our month of European flying also included showcasing the B-52 to local dignitaries, including the U.S. ambassador to England, Charles Price. Our training sortie for the day was a simulated mine-laying mission over the Mediterranean Sea, south of Sicily. Instead of Major Lunsford commanding the flight, our B-52 demonstration flight was piloted by Lieutenant Colonel Northington, the new commander of our sister squadron, the 596 BS, also located at Barksdale. Our crew hardly knew him and had never flown with him before, but we all knew he was an up-and-coming commander with stars in his future.

We departed RAF Fairford and, like our WWII forefathers in their B-17s, pointed south over the English Channel toward France—where, by previous agreement, four French Mirage F1 fighters intercepted our Stratofortress. Our flight continued over the Alps and down the Adriatic Sea, along the eastern coast of Italy. With the ambassador seated on the instructor pilot jump seat behind Lieutenant Colonel Northington, we descended through a dense layer of clouds to 400 feet above the ocean, and I navigated our bomber westward to the initial point for Joe's mine-laying run, just south of Sicily.

For this particular flight, our B-52 carried a metal training weapon, but it lacked a warhead or the means to disperse active sea mines. On Joe's command, the inert sea mine splashed into the sea, and the deployment was scored by Navy observers from a nearby ship as we banked left in a wide, 270-degree turn, heading back toward the eastern side of Italy.

As the B-52 climbed back into the clouds to 1,000 feet (the low-level training altitude for poor weather conditions), Lieutenant Colonel Northington began chatting with the ambassador over the plane's interphone, blocking our ability to chime in. From our green-and-black radar screen, Joe and I could see the mountainous coastline looming ahead as the pilots flew westward in a thick overcast. As a young second lieutenant, I should have been more emphatic, but I wasn't being assertive enough with the high-ranking officer sitting above. Al and Mike became nervous as they heard Joe trying repeatedly to break into the VIP conversation. Unable to stand it any longer, Joe finally yelled, "Pilot! If you don't climb now, we're all going to die!" Al and Mike reached for their ejection seat handles until we were sure we had cleared the "cumulus granite" directly ahead. I kicked myself for not speaking up and doing my job, even as *just* a second lieutenant.

Our Stratofortress climbed back up to 30,000 feet for the return flight to England, and the ambassador was invited to sit in Dan's copilot seat, to the right of Lieutenant Colonel Northington. Hours later, in the dead of night, it was time to descend over the English Channel and enter the traffic pattern of RAF Fairford. Ever the diplomat, our aircraft commander said to the ambassador: "OK, sir, I think it's time for Dan to get back into his seat."

"What's the matter?" the ambassador replied. "Don't you trust me?"

Silence, then a question: "Well, sir, do you have any flight experience?"

"I have my private license in a Cessna 172," our VIP told him.

That apparently was a good enough answer for Lieutenant

Colonel Northington, as he prepared to demonstrate a touch-and-go landing of our eight-engine bomber to our distinguished visitor. The opinion of the three lieutenants and one captain onboard wasn't sought, and Joe and I looked at each other, a bit wide-eyed with concern.

After any touch-and-go landing, the tower controller will send a query—"State your intentions"—asking the aircrew what approach and landing they will request to fly next. Upon hearing the query, Joe dropped his mask and shouted to me (not over the interphone): "Live! We want to live!"

Soon afterward, the ambassador relinquished his seat to our "Lieutenant Dan," and we safely completed our training mission. To show his gratitude, the ambassador treated our crew to traditional post-mission beers—but, in the land of English ales, Scottish ales, and Irish Guinness, he opted to serve us Budweisers.

During our off-duty hours, we shopped and toured London. The dollar was so strong that year that many of us bought cashmere sweaters, Waterford and Stuart crystal, and Wedgwood fine china. Joe, still single at this point, chose a blue-and-silver Wedgwood Amherst pattern of china (it was Air Force colors, after all). He purchased the entire sixty-four-piece set, telling me, "I don't know who I'm going to marry, but I hope she likes my china."

The B-52 had a huge storage compartment aft of the bomb bay, just forward of the tail, so we packed our goods there before returning to the States. Upon arrival, we parked our three B-52s on the Barksdale flight line, and each crewman downloaded his collection of British goods. Major Lunsford's E-61 crew had the largest pile stacked beside their bomber, prompting Colonel Habiger to remark as he strolled by: "Looks like you guys win the 'Support the English Economy Award.'"

After a month in England, we resumed our rotation of sitting nuclear alert. We ate three meals each day in the alert facility's chow hall, and Joe and I shared a dormitory-style room with two twin beds. The alert facility housed aircraft maintenance personnel, along with the eight six-man B-52 crews and eight four-person KC-135 crews. It was like a firehouse packed with up to eighty men, plus a few women from the KC-135 crews, for the next seven days. (Women joined the B-52 crew force ten years later.)

Outside of the alert facility, rows of blue Chevrolet pick-up trucks were parked, one for each crew, so we could reach our aircraft quickly if the klaxon went off. That blaring horn signified that we needed to get to our aircraft, start the engines, and decode an encrypted message. The message, from SAC headquarters, would instruct us whether or not to taxi to the runway, and also whether this was a training event or the beginning of World War III.

The wartime scenario we trained for assumed that Russian submarines had launched missiles at our military bases, and that we had only a few minutes to return fire over the Soviet Union with the cruise missiles mounted on our wings and ordnance in the bomb bay.

While sitting on alert, just a week after returning from England, our crew was told to report to the base clinic for a tuberculosis test because we had been out of the country for a month. Of the entire crew, our gunner, Mike, was the only one not married or in a serious relationship, and while in England he met a lovely young British lady named Sally, who eventually became his wife. They had enjoyed a few weeks of togetherness during a whirlwind romance before we returned home, and as he and I strolled down the hallway toward our transport vehicle, Mike asked, "Why do we have to go to the clinic?"

Without any forethought, I jokingly said, "Probably to see if we brought back any sexually transmitted diseases."

"No," Mike said. "Really?"

I smiled and left it at that.

We dutifully walked into the immunization clinic and had our forearms pricked, knowing we would return three days later to have the results examined. Once back in the truck, Joe and I sat in the bed of the pickup truck while Mike and the others all took seats in the cab, and I told Joe about my STD comment to Mike.

"Oh, that's good," he said, laughing. "We can do something with that."

The day before returning to get our tests read, Joe called the immunization clinic and told the young technical sergeant about our upcoming prank on Mike, and the sergeant readily agreed to go along. The next day, our crew returned to the clinic and, one by one, showed the sergeant our forearms. Everyone was in the clear until Mike put out his arm.

"Oh, wow," the technician said. "This might be a problem."

"What?" Mike replied. "Mine looks the same as theirs!"

The med tech did a great job at that point, getting out a micrometer and measuring the spot several times, making Mike's arm redder with each press.

"Who's in charge of your crew?" the med tech asked.

"I am," said Major Lunsford, going along with the joke.

Looking very serious, the tech said: "Sir, we need to make some calls and see about getting this guy off alert."

"Whoa!" Mike exclaimed upon hearing that. "We're not calling ANYBODY!"

I was biting my lip to keep from laughing, so I stepped out into the hallway, where I encountered a young mother who was waiting with her grade-school-aged daughter for school immunizations. She asked me what was going on, and I told her about the STD joke we were playing on Mike.

"Oh, y'all are bad," she said, smiling all the while.

The scam continued inside the clinic, as Major Lunsford pretended to make a phone call to the alert facility to remove Mike from alert status. Moments later the whole crew came out of the clinic, with Mike still thinking he had tested positive for an embarrassing disease.

While I did not instigate what happened next, I couldn't have planned it better. As Mike walked past the young mom, she reached out and patted his shoulder—and, with great sympathy, she said to him, "Everything will be all right."

Mike looked around at all of us and yelled, "Does EVERYBODY know?"

At that point, we couldn't contain ourselves any longer. We all burst out laughing, and he knew he had been had. In the end, having a young enlisted man on our crew provided some pretty fun moments.

Capt. Alan McGreer (EWO), me with headphones, Senior Airman Mike Barker (gunner), and Capt. Gordy Neff (evaluator navigator), standing by our Barksdale B-52G while visiting Hill Air Force Base, Utah.

10
A CRAPPY FLIGHT

I WORKED with many memorable Air Force leaders throughout my career, and I learned a lot from several of them. Many of them provided positive lessons on effective leadership, while others taught me lessons on what not to do. Most of my leaders served as positive role models, but occasionally there were those I didn't want to emulate.

One night we had to fly a B-52 training mission with our operations officer, Lieutenant Colonel Bright, tagging along as the instructor pilot. He wasn't very well thought of within the squadron, so to us his call sign was "NotSo." The mission concluded with a one-hour, low-level route over La Junta, Colorado, and New Mexico. After the low-level portion was completed, we climbed to 31,000 feet for the two-hour flight across Texas back to Barksdale Air Force Base.

Once we leveled off, NotSo came on the interphone and said, "Guys, I'm really not feeling well. I need to clear off and use the 'honey bucket.' " Our 1959-model B-52 was built to accommodate a six-man combat crew, but there was no flush toilet. Instead, there was a standpipe to pee in, and a metal box with a plastic-lined hole—the aforementioned "honey bucket"—to poop in. The mantra among B-52 crews was, "You don't poop where you work." Taking a dump was strictly *verboten*—unless you're the operations officer with diarrhea, that is. Then you get to foul up the cockpit for everyone within the twenty-foot radius of the honey bucket. That man made our eyes water, even after he tied off the plastic bag.

We still had more than an hour to cruise before returning to Barksdale for the mandatory thirty minutes of approaches, which allowed the pilots to practice their touch-and-go landings at 10 p.m. for all of Bossier City to enjoy. But NotSo had an idea: "Guys, let's drop down to 10,000 feet, depressurize, and I'll put the bag in the forward wheel well."

As described earlier, the B-52 had two levels, with both pilots, the electronic warfare officer, and the gunner sitting on the upper level, and the two navigators sitting below the pilots. Behind the navigator seats in the lower level was a small door that led to the wheel well, and the bomb bay beyond. After live-weapons drops, it was the navigator's job to crawl through the door, over the massive tires of the forward wheels, and along the catwalk to peer into the bomb bay to ensure there weren't any live bombs hanging either from the bomb racks or on the bomb-bay doors. It's not neighborly to accidentally drop live weapons on our fellow countrymen.

NotSo's idea was to open the small door and place his stinking bag of poop on the wheels, so that when the gear doors opened over northwestern Louisiana, the offending bag would drop harmlessly from the bomber as we completed our training mission.

With the bag now resting on the landing gear, we repressurized the cabin, climbed back up to altitude and completed our trip to Barksdale. The gear doors opened, and both pilots completed their obligatory touch-and-go landings. After the final full-stop landing, we taxied to our assigned parking spot and waited as the crew chief plugged in his headset. As the eight engines wound down to a stop, we could hear the sergeant yell, "Oh, my God! What the hell?"

It seems the offending bag of poop had other ideas than to drop to the ground below. In a confounding display of fluid dynamics, the air swirled in the wheel well like a tornado once the landing gear doors opened, and our sorry sack of shit managed to smear itself all over the gear well, becoming the smelliest graffiti ever. As we started to download all of the crew gear, I heard the crew chief tell NotSo, "I am NOT cleaning this up!"

We clambered aboard the crew van and went to the maintenance debrief, never knowing how that crappy night ended.

11

BLUE RIBBON CREW

OUR B-52 CREW continued to work together for a year and a half, rising through the crew ranks from R (ready) crew, to E (experienced) crew to S (select) crew. Select crews normally were assigned to the standardization and evaluation (Stan/Eval) division, but Major Lunsford's S-61 crew held the distinction of progressing rapidly up the chain to become one of the few non-evaluator select crews.

I found the saying "timing is everything" to be quite true, in both bad ways and good. My career got off to a slow start because there weren't enough pilot slots to go around, but now, thanks to the Reagan administration's military buildup in the late 1980s, the Air Force had a great need for pilots. The annual quota of navigators accepted for pilot training doubled to 100, but the competition was pretty stiff, considering there were hundreds of navigators vying for those 100 slots. Additionally, navigators had to serve two years in their assignment before applying for undergraduate pilot training (UPT), and they had to be in training by age twenty-seven.

In the spring of 1986, I was twenty-four, one year into my B-52 navigator assignment, and the 2nd Bomb Wing at Barksdale was preparing for its operational readiness inspection, or ORI. This was a make-or-break event in SAC, dating back to its founder, Gen. Curtis

LeMay. Jimmy Stewart's 1955 movie *Strategic Air Command* offered a great depiction of how important passing an ORI is to a bomber unit and the crew members who took part.

The ORI tested the base's ability to carry out its nuclear mission, and failing it would result in the firing of the wing commander. The crews had to pass a written evaluation, and selected crews were chosen to fly an in-flight evaluation.

At the very least, we wanted to pass. At most, we hoped to be recognized as a SAC Blue Ribbon crew, meaning that we excelled at both the written test and in-flight evaluation. The test portion concluded with a scenario-based question—and, depending upon timing calculations, the crew had to decide whether to drop a nuclear bomb on a target. We could elect to withhold the release of our nuke, but if the correct answer was to drop, then points would be deducted for a wrong answer. If we elected to release the bomb when the correct answer was to withhold, though, then our crew would fail, we would immediately become unqualified aircrew members, and it also was likely that our entire wing would fail.

Nothing like a little bit of pressure!

As we went through the scenario, we ran the calculations again and again, and each time we came up with the answer to release our nuke over the target. Joe was insistent that it was the right answer, but we all had to agree on "release" being the right answer. We opted to release, then nervously awaited the results. What a relief it was to find out we were correct!

The following day, we boarded our B-52 for an eight-hour training flight that included ninety minutes on a low-level route through both South Dakota and North Dakota. After striking the three simulated low-level targets on time, we returned home to a late-night landing. As we climbed down the short crew-entry ladder, the two ranking colonels of the base leadership met us, smiling broadly. The wing director of operations (Wing/DO) shook each of our hands, telling us how proud he was of our timing and bombing results.

Days later, the crew members of S-61 learned that we had earned the elite status of B-52 Blue Ribbon crew during the Reagan-era Cold War. Our performance contributed to the 62nd Bomb Squadron and 2nd Bomb Wing winning both the Sweeney Trophy and the Kenney Trophy for the highest bombing-effectiveness results of the 1986 Strategic Air Command's operational readiness inspection. As an instructor and Blue Ribbon crew navigator, my application for pilot training grew stronger.

S-61 Bluo Ribbon crew. From left. Senior Airman Mike Barker (gunner); 1st Lt. Van Heckman (EWO); me; 1st Lt. Stan Buelt (copilot); Maj. Glenn Lunsford (aircraft commander); Lt. Col. Randy Wooten (62nd Bomb Squadron commander); Capt. Joe Wolf (radar navigator) is not pictured.

At this point in my progression, I could have opted for a quick upgrade to radar navigator or become an evaluator navigator in the Stan/Eval office. Knowing that I wanted to get to pilot training as quickly as possible, though, I decided that spending the next year as an evaluator probably looked better on my résumé than becoming a radar nav on a newly formed ready crew.

Some of the best advice given to military personnel is this: *Do the best at the job you're given.* It ties in well with another saying, which is: *You can't pick your circumstance, but you can choose your response.* I didn't choose to be a navigator—especially not a B-52 navigator—but I rose to instructor and evaluator on a SAC Blue Ribbon crew.

I built a pilot training application package that included an endorsement signed by the 7th Air Division's two-star general, bolstered by my status as a Blue Ribbon crew member. I submitted my pilot training candidate package in the summer of 1987 at age twenty-five.

I told Karin that the Air Force would probably try to get more time out of me as a navigator, so all I could do was hope for the best.

In November 1987 I was called to the squadron commander's office, where Lt. Col. Randy Wooten, a six-foot-four-inch-tall East Texan, stood waiting. With a big grin on his face, he handed me a letter, signed by our 2nd Bomb Wing commander, Col. Brett Dula. I stared at the official Air Force letterhead and read the words I longed for: "Congratulations on the selection of Lieutenant Dale as a primary selection to attend undergraduate pilot training."

I'm not one to whoop or holler, so with a huge smile instead I thanked my squadron commander while shaking his hand. I was on my way to Vance Air Force Base, a pilot training base in Enid, Oklahoma.

Finally!

12
WILD BLUE YONDER

TO BECOME AN AIR FORCE PILOT, trainees attend a rigorous twelve-month course, preferably somewhere that has very few distractions, like Enid, Oklahoma. Karin and I packed up our two cars and two dogs—a cocker spaniel and a beagle—on Super Bowl weekend in February 1988. We moved into a 1,400-square-foot, $400-per-month rental house on the outskirts of Enid, a farming and oil town in western Oklahoma.

Book cover of my pilot training yearbook.

Undergraduate pilot training, or UPT, began with four months of aviation academics and specialized training, such as experiencing the high-altitude environment in an altitude chamber, and undergoing basic parachute training. We students had to adjust to wearing an oxygen mask in the altitude chamber, which could induce claustrophobia, but the suffocating feeling of breathing into a rubber mask went away after a few weeks.

Meanwhile, the parachute training was like a Caribbean vacation on the prairie: parasailing behind a blue Air Force pickup, then landing in a flat Oklahoma field.

After completing academics, our class went parasailing in the flatlands of Oklahoma. The ejection-seat sequence only takes a few seconds, but pilots have to learn how to hit the ground to minimize injuries. Just like the "banana" landing technique I was taught while skydiving in Austin during college, the proper sequence of touchdown was feet, side of one leg, then roll to our backs, letting our body gracefully absorb the impact. This three-step method was the textbook parachute landing fall, or PLF. Its counterpart is the PFL, or "poor fucking landing," which consists of feet, knees, and face-plant. The objective of our Oklahoma parasailing excursion was to learn the PLF and not the PFL.

Once we successfully completed that training, we headed to the flight line. Students received eighty flying hours in the T-37, an underpowered, twin-engine jet, learning acrobatics and instrument flying. We then transitioned to the supersonic T-38 jet trainer for 120 flight hours of acrobatics, formation flying, and instrument flying. The biggest difference between the two was that the T-38 was a faster, more responsive jet, once used by the Air Force Thunderbirds in the 1980s.

Our class began, like most others, with thirty students, most of them second lieutenants right out of college. As a first lieutenant, though, I was one of three senior officers in my class. I was joined by Skip Shoenheit, another first lieutenant B-52 navigator from Minot Air Force Base in North Dakota, and Lori, a female captain maintenance officer from McConnell Air Force Base near Wichita, Kansas. Lori was the highest-ranking officer, so she was the senior ranking officer, or SRO, of our pilot training class. Skip was second in line, with a date of rank higher than mine, and that was fine with me because I could concentrate on learning to fly—and graduating.

Pilot training got off to a good start for me, probably because of my experience as a navigator, and also because I already had 125 hours of private flying. I was familiar with Air Training Command written tests, and I already had gone through several altitude chambers to get a sense of hypoxia (oxygen deprivation during a pressurization malfunction) and the benefit of our oxygen masks. Although I had not piloted an Air Force plane, I had begun to develop situational awareness, and I no longer felt claustrophobic wearing an oxygen mask. I could also talk on the radio without getting tongue-tied and nervous. Some of my classmates, on the other hand, had hardly ever flown before.

The T-37 is now a museum piece (Dan Smallwood)

On the first day of T-37 training, I met my instructor pilot, 1st Lt. Brian "Vic" Morrow. Vic was his call sign because his last name was the same as the popular 1970s actor Victor "Vic" Morrow. At this point it was time for everyone to receive their first Air Force call sign, and many were a play on their real names. Lieutenant Lee enjoyed a quick promotion (in call sign only) to "General." Lieutenant Kling became "Static," while Lieutenant Schweinberg became "Pig Mountain," then just "Pig" for short.

Some call signs were geographical, so a pilot from Oklahoma became "Okie," while another from the Tennessee Smoky Mountains announced "Smokey" for his call sign before another classmate, Lieutenant Robinson, could grab it. Lt. Brian Robinson, the only African-American in our class, went by "Velcro," which I know would not be allowed now. After graduating from pilot training, Brian later changed from "Velcro" to "Smokey" as he progressed up the ranks to become a three-star general.

I successfully avoided the call sign of "There" that Karin had given me when we first met. During my previous two years in B-52s, SAC decided to include first names as well as last names on our flight suit name tags. Our radar navigator, Joe Wolf, thought it would be funny for our whole crew to order an additional set of nametags with the last name of Yossarian, the last name of fictional character Capt. John Yossarian in Joseph Heller's 1961 novel *Catch-22*. The six of us "Yossarians" walked through the Barksdale Base Exchange (BX) making the cashiers think we were all brothers. With that precedent, I became "Yossarian," then "Yos" for short—kind of lame, I'll admit, but at least it wasn't embarrassing. After UPT, I never went by "Yos" again. Most of my Air Force friends have called me "Double-D" or "D2." I should have gone with one of those.

Within the first few minutes of meeting my instructor, Lieutenant Morrow, we both realized we were 1984 college graduates, and I learned that he had attended the University of Colorado at Boulder. When I told him that my dad still lived in Parker, south of Denver, he happily announced, "T-37 cross-country to Colorado!"

That was a great idea! The only problem was that I had to pass three checkrides and numerous ground evaluations before the "good deal" cross-country trip could be scheduled. It certainly made for a nice incentive, though.

Flying the nimble Tweet began with basic aerobatics, including the gasp-producing spin recovery. Before soloing the T-37, we had to prove we could recover from a spin should one occur while we were flying solo. To recover from a spin, a pilot first had to intentionally stall the small jet and throw it into a spin, so I pulled the nose up to what felt like near vertical, bleeding off the airspeed as the Tweet struggled to climb. At the last moment I kicked the rudder, throwing the plane into a nose-down, dizzying spin, the ground spinning like a turntable around the nose of my blue-and-white Air Force trainer.

Now was the time to perform the spin recovery procedure. Here's the abbreviated version: idle, neutral, aft, needle left, spinning left, right rudder, count to three, then push, pull, recover.

That simplified version was much easier to remember in the heat of battle than the forty-three-word memorization procedure we had to recite verbatim before a flight:

- Throttles—idle
- Rudders and ailerons—neutral
- Stick—abruptly full aft and hold
- Rudder—abruptly apply full rudder opposite spin direction (opposite turn needle) and hold
- Stick—abruptly full forward one turn after applying rudder
- Controls—neutral after spinning stops and recover from dive

Nothing to it.

The abbreviated procedure above is how a spin recovery actually worked.

The first checkride in pilot training is called the mid-phase contact checkride. Its purpose is to prove that student pilots could handle the aircraft by accomplishing specific acrobatics and performing a dizzying spin recovery. I was the first one in my class to take the mid-phase checkride, undergoing a one-hour ground evaluation, answering my evaluator's questions, which was followed by a one-hour, twenty-minute flight. Like all evaluations, I was nervous, mainly because my every move and decision were being watched by the guy sitting next to me, which could lead to a lot of second-guessing on my part. Thankfully, I passed with an excellent (on a scale of outstanding, excellent, and good), so I was off to a strong start.

Each morning of training began with a morning briefing, which let us know what was taking place that day. The briefing ended with a "situation of the day," a stressful scenario designed to make trainees think about, and state, how they would correctly handle a specific emergency. An instructor pilot (IP) would describe a flying scenario, including such details as weather conditions and what the jet's instruments were reading. The IP would then give a clue about the impending malfunction, and we all listened intently, not knowing who would be called upon to answer. After running through the scenario, the instructor would pause and look around the room before continuing in a manner such as this:

"Lieutenant Morgan! You have the aircraft."

Lieutenant Morgan would then stand and ask questions to verify the situation, then apply the correct checklist steps verbatim from memory. If Lieutenant Morgan said the wrong thing at any point, the IP would shout, "Sit down!" and the disheartened student would not fly that day. A dreaded "pink sheet" would be added to the student's training folder, indicating a deficiency, and the IP would move on to his next victim.

"Lieutenant Smith! You have the aircraft."

Lieutenant Smith would then proceed to enumerate the correct procedures until the T-37 was safely back on the ground.

Having already completed undergraduate navigator training, I can attest that pilot training was intentionally—and definitely—more stressful. Navigator training focused on academics and was mainly a mental exercise, and we certainly were nervous before each test or navigation checkride, but there was a different element in UPT. Pilot training was not only physical, as we controlled the airplane as it danced around the sky, but it also was purposefully stressful to ensure we could react correctly under pressure. Those who could not were weeded out.

There is a saying that goes, "Given enough time, even a monkey can learn to fly," but the military did not have an infinite amount of time or money to spend on trainees, so we had to keep up with the fast pace of this program.

In our class of one woman and twenty-nine men, we had a country boy, Nick Coleman, from Lubbock, Texas, who already owned his own Piper J-3 Cub taildragger aircraft. He was cool! I already had my private pilot license, but Nick already had his own airplane—and he spoke with a slow West Texas drawl.

One morning, the IP described the following scenario: A T-37 is coming in for landing, and as the wing flaps are extended an unexpected rolling motion begins. This is a description of a condition called "asymmetric flaps," where the flaps on both wings are not extending equally. The correct first step is "flaps retract" to stop the rolling motion—and that first step must be stated verbatim.

The IP barked, "Lieutenant Coleman, you have the aircraft!"

Nick slowly rose to his feet and, in his best Slim Pickens country drawl, said, "Well, I'd get my flaps a-comin' up."

"SIT DOWN!" the IP barked. Poor Nick did not fly that day.

T-37 training continued through the instrument phase, with students learning to fly in poor weather by using the cockpit instruments.

As the training came to a close, I was surprised to find out that I was the only student to not have a bust on my record. Everyone had either hooked (failed) an in-flight checkride or had failed a stand-up scenario, all of which resulted in receiving a pink sheet. I survived the T-37 evaluations unscathed, and even pinned on the rank of captain in early July. Almost every officer pins on their captain bars four years after commissioning, so it wasn't a huge event, but I certainly found it easier to answer a military phone call with "Captain Dale" rather than "Lieutenant Dale."

At this point, our SRO, Lori, had failed a checkride and was not progressing on schedule, so she was washed back to the class four weeks behind us to re-accomplish some of her training. Washing back happened quite frequently in all classes, just as it had in navigator training. The only issue for us became who was going to move up to

SRO of the class. Skip outranked me, but he was struggling and didn't want the added responsibility, so I assumed the role of SRO.

Even as a newly pinned captain, I was still expected to salute Lieutenant Morrow, my instructor pilot, and call him "Sir," but I wasn't so hung up on rank to believe there was anything wrong with this temporary arrangement. In military etiquette, the junior officer always salutes first, then the senior officer returns this salute. Some military officers are especially rank-conscious and would never render the first salute to a junior ranking officer. In my mind, though, that instructor pilot had the wings I wanted, so I easily played the role of cooperative student. Each morning, I gladly offered Lieutenant Morrow the first salute.

With my three checkrides completed, Lieutenant "Vic" and I finally planned our T-37 cross-country flight, and two other crews joined us for our weekend trip to Colorado. The three T-37s departed Vance Air Force Base on a Friday morning, June 18, and headed to Amarillo to fly practice approaches before proceeding up to Peterson Air Force Base near Colorado Springs.

While the planes were being refueled, Vic grabbed the paper low-level terrain charts of the nearby area and started to circle each of the well-known ski resorts west of Colorado Springs and Denver. After tracing circles around the turn points of Aspen, Vail, Copper Mountain, Breckenridge, and others, Vic drew a line connecting them all. The route headed west from Colorado Springs and eventually turned east to come over the Rockies just south of Denver, where my dad lived in Parker.

The other pilots copied Vic's route onto their own charts and, knowing that the mountains extended up to more than 14,000 feet, we decided to fly the route at 16,000 feet to avoid the terrain. With me piloting from the left seat, Vic and I took off first from Peterson and climbed westward toward the Rocky Mountains.

The summer sun gleamed off snow-covered peaks as we made our way up to 16,000 feet and searched for the first ski resort turn point of Breckenridge. After forty-five minutes of weaving above the mountains and overflying famous ski resorts, we headed east toward Interstate 25, which pointed us north toward our destination of Buckley Field on the east side of Denver. In the vicinity of Castle Rock, I descended to 1,500 feet above the flat plains to stay below the Denver airport arrival corridor, then circled to allow the other two T-37s to catch up with us. Once the third T-37 was in sight, Vic announced over the radio, "OK, Dave has navigation."

We headed north at 1,500 feet in search of my dad's house, on the outskirts of Parker. Dad lived on five acres of land in a two-story, rough-cedar house, and most of the houses looked just like his. I located the golf course and tennis court "bubble" I knew he used, so I was close.

Then our family's hobby paid big dividends. Ever since the 1970s, my family has enjoyed visiting the western U.S. national parks of Zion, Arches, and Bryce Canyon, and we camped at many of those parks in a pop-up camper. Now, in the late 1980s, my dad, stepmom, Karen, and stepsister, Alison, still enjoyed camping in a new pop-up camper. As I scanned back and forth for Dad's house, a flash suddenly appeared to my left. Looking down, I saw the bright sun glistening off the top of Dad's camper in his driveway.

"There it is!" I shouted to Vic, and we gave Dad a quick, low-altitude fly-by.

Dad told me later that he was in his walk-out basement when he heard our jet whistle by. The Tweet was known for its shrill-sounding engines, and he made it outside just in time to see the second and third Tweets cruise overhead on our way north to Buckley Air Force Base. There, Vic and I rented a car and headed south to Dad's country house for dinner. It had taken four months to pull off, but Vic and I completed the cross-country flight to Colorado that he had promised on my first day of flying the Tweet.

13
MISSING THE MARK

T-38 Talon, supersonic jet trainer (Military.com)

TRANSITIONING to the T-38 got off to an exciting start. I was now class leader, as well as the only student in my class with an unblemished record. My instructor for the flight was our flight commander, Capt. Mo Beale, a former A-10 pilot and soon-to-be Air Force Thunderbird, flying "opposing solo" (one of the two jets that cross at show center) for the Air Force demonstration team.

I will never forget that first T-38 flight on a hot August afternoon. After years of flying with an instructor sitting beside me in an airplane, I was now in the front seat of a tandem-seat fighter-trainer, sitting in the pointy end.

The Air Force Thunderbirds have flown the F-16 since the early 1980s, but before that they flew the same model of T-38 I was now flying. Now it was my turn to push up the throttles and sink back in the seat as the twin-engine jet sped down the runway. The sensation I most remember was going into that first turn; I felt like I was in a kayak that was tipping over. The edge of the bubble canopy was at shoulder level, so I could see the sides of the plane as I banked left or right. And the power! It felt so nice to be in a powerful jet that didn't lag as I pushed on the throttles.

All I had to do to get my pilot wings was pass three more checkrides: contact (basic aircraft handling and aerobatics), formation, and instruments. What could possibly go wrong?

The training flights in the first phase went well. I loved flying the "Cuban eight" maneuver, where I pulled the T-38 into three-quarters of a loop, with my view shifting from blue sky to brown ground while flying forty-five degrees upside down. I then quickly pushed forward on the stick and rolled the wings 180 degrees so that I was now upright, but the airplane's nose never wavered from the spot it was pointing at on the ground. At this forty-five-degree dive angle, I felt like I was on a bombing run in a fighter-bomber, keeping my target in sight while rolling from upside down to right side up. The maneuver was repeated as I traced sideways figure-eights in the Oklahoma sky.

After performing the aerobatics, I returned to the landing pattern to perform landings in an abnormal configuration, including a landing without wing flaps extended, so I would know what to do should a no-flap landing occur while I was flying solo. As a bit of foreshadowing, any plane landing without extending its flaps has to come in at a higher airspeed to make up for the lack of lift normally created by extending the flaps, which requires a longer final approach.

On September 12, the day of my contact checkride, I breezed through the required aerobatic maneuvers before heading back to Vance for several approaches. The Oklahoma winds had shifted, and I now was faced with something I had not encountered before: a no-flap landing with a significant tailwind. Under normal conditions, pilots prefer to land into a headwind, because the wind over the wing helps generate lift. At this point, though, the air force base had not "turned the airport around," i.e. switching to landing in the opposite direction and into the wind. The rule of thumb when taking a checkride is to not do anything dumb, dangerous, or different during that evaluation—and, for me, a no-flap landing with a strong tailwind was very different.

I knew that I needed a long final approach from my overhead pattern; how much, I couldn't imagine. The overhead pattern consists of flying straight down the landing runway at 1,500 feet above ground level (AGL) with the landing gear and flaps up, known as a "clean" configuration. Halfway down the runway, pilots go into "the break," throwing the plane into an aggressive U-turn to the left at nearly ninety degrees of bank to bleed off speed. At the end of our downwind turn we are flying parallel to the runway and offset about two miles to the side.

As our speed decreases, we extend the landing gear and flaps (in a normal configuration landing), and when the runway is forty-five degrees behind our left shoulder we begin a descending left turn to the runway. In a no-flap condition, our downwind leg is extended well beyond the forty-five-degree angle to the runway. This allows the faster-flying aircraft to make the turn and still land within the allowable touchdown zone, which is the first 3,000 feet of the runway. This zone is delineated by white stripes painted at 500-foot increments. Landing beyond the last set of stripes is considered outside of the touchdown zone. Add a tailwind into the mix, and I knew I needed a really long final approach to complete the landing.

At this point in my training I had not been "issued enough judgment," or gained enough experience, to understand how long of a final approach I needed to land safely. I badly overshot the runway on my first attempt, so I aborted the landing, pushed up the throttles, raised the landing gear, and went around to try again. Feeling unsure and nervous, I extended my final turn on the second attempt, but it still wasn't enough, so I went around again.

The runway supervisor officer (RSO) monitoring landings that day was Captain Beale, my first T-38 instructor. He emphatically broadcast the winds over the radio, indicating that there was a ten-knot tailwind, which is the legally allowed tailwind limit for landing. On the third attempt, I extended my final turn even further and rolled out on final approach, and the T-38 glided at a high speed down to the runway. Unfortunately, the last set of white stripes sailed by, and I touched down beyond the allowable touchdown zone.

Welcome to the T-38, Captain Dale, you've just hooked your first checkride.

As I taxied toward the parking ramp, the tower announced over the radio that they were now using the opposing runways, which pointed into the headwind. I felt as deflated as an eighteen-wheeler's shredded tire lying on the freeway. I quietly sat through the evaluator's checkride debrief, disappointed in myself for screwing up.

14

WHERE'D HE GO?

Vance Air Force Base T-38s flying in formation (Military.com)

THE FOLLOWING week I successfully passed my T-38 contact recheck, demonstrating that I could safely perform a no-flap landing, so I then moved on to the formation phase. Now for the fun! If you've ever seen the Thunderbirds or the Navy's Blue Angels at an air show, then you may have heard the announcer tell the audience that all military pilots are trained in the maneuvers the team is performing. The demonstration teams just do them with a lot more aircraft—and for a longer period of time—while simultaneously looking very cool.

Now it was my turn to learn how to do a formation takeoff, joining on the wing of the flight leader with three feet separating our wingtips as I followed him through the skies. *"Where you lead, I will follow."* A little later, the second plane slides into a position called "close trail," flying just beneath the tail of the lead aircraft, and resumes the game of follow the leader.

Halfway through the flight, the lead aircraft switches to being the second plane, and the new leader practices leading his flight of two T-38s before returning to the airfield for a formation landing. During both the formation takeoff and landing, the leader flies normally, as if flying solo, while the other pilot focuses solely on the lead aircraft, becoming airborne and touching down only when the leader does—and without referencing any other visual cues.

I rotated between two different instructors during formation, and their instruction—and my subsequent performances—were like night and day. My first instructor, another Captain Dave, was a burned-out first assignment instructor pilot (FAIP) who had been at Vance for four years. This was his initial assignment as a second lieutenant after graduating from pilot training. Most FAIPs serve three years before moving on to another Air Force aircraft, but this Captain Dave had been at Vance four years and also had been a high-level evaluator on the base. He was now "just an instructor," as he put it, grudgingly flying with new students again and wanting badly to move on to his next C-141 cargo airlifter assignment.

Captain Dave had spent the past year giving checkrides, focusing on evaluating students rather than instructing them. He often was in a foul mood and was very nervous about flying with new students. I became tense while flying with him, and my performance showed it. Flying in formation required small inputs on the controls, using a light touch, but me being tense led to a heavy grip and erratic flying. I flew poorly with him and began doubting my abilities, wondering if I had "the touch" to smoothly fly three feet from the other aircraft.

After a particularly bad training flight, Captain Dave berated me for what I did wrong.

"What are you doing?" he yelled.

Being a fellow captain and about his same age, I finally told him, "You're telling me what I'm doing wrong, but you're not teaching me how to do it right."

I told Captain Beale, my flight commander, that I thought I needed an instructor change, and he agreed. Along came 2nd Lt. Larry "Judas" Deist. His call sign rhymed with Judas Priest, the popular heavy metal band at the time.

Judas was a very fun-loving T-38 IP, and he always was in a good mood. Everything about him made me laugh, and I vividly remember my first formation flight with him instructing from the backseat. I was piloting the second aircraft, taking off and climbing out three feet to the left of the leader's wing. Judas yelled, "Oh, yeah! We are Thunderbirds today!" before adding a little later: "You're on him like flies on shit!"

I grinned from ear to ear—and, because of his encouragement, I really enjoyed formation flying. Attitude is everything, and after a few more training rides it was time for my formation checkride.

The plan for my November 17 evaluation called for me to lead the formation of two and switch to the second position halfway through the flight. We taxied our T-38s to the Vance runway, each with an evaluator in the back seats. As we approached the runway for takeoff, the tower instructed us to hold short of the runway for an incoming emergency landing. We sat ... and we sat ... and we sat, burning crucial gas as a malfunctioning T-38 flew a long, fifteen-mile straight-in final approach, then proceeded down the runway with fire trucks in fast pursuit. Once the airplane and trucks cleared the runway, we finally rolled down the runway side by side, but with a lot less fuel than originally planned. I led our flight of two through the required maneuvers, which included a loop, pulling the required minimum of three g-forces, while the second plane stayed tucked in below and behind me in the close trail position.

Once my portion was complete, we performed a lead change, and I followed the leader around the skies of western Oklahoma. At the appointed time, I slipped into the close trail position behind the lead pilot. He began his loop, but he wasn't pulling the required minimum of three g-forces. When he noticed this, he aggressively yanked on his control stick—and once he did that, he quickly pulled away from me, causing me to lose my formation position. Our flight of two had now broken up, and I needed to rejoin the formation. All of this was taking more fuel than we could afford to burn and still return to Vance with our required minimum amount. The end result was that we returned to the airfield without completing all the required formation maneuvers. It was the second bust for class leader Captain Dale.

That checkride bust had major implications. By this point, I wanted to be a "Strike Eagle" fighter-bomber pilot in the brand-new, twin-engine, two-seat F-15E. This plane seemed a bit more survivable than the single-engine F-16. It also had a weapon system operator (WSO) navigator in the back seat and dropped bombs, like I had done in the B-52. Like any fighter assignment, it required that I be "fighter, attack, and reconnaissance qualified" (FAR'd). Two failed checkrides, one of them being formation, took me out of consideration for being FAR'd. My hopes of flying fighters crashed like the Hindenburg zeppelin over New Jersey.

For my recheck a few days later, my evaluator was the lieutenant colonel director of operations (DO) for the training squadron, the second in the chain of command. He was an experienced Air Force fighter pilot but did his best to put me at ease about the upcoming re-evaluation. Now I was really under the gun, because UPT had a "three strikes and you're out" policy. I was two-thirds of the way toward elimination, and now I was flying with an "old" (probably forty-year-old) fighter jock for my recheck. I had to get my nerves under control to demonstrate I could fly smoothly in formation for the next hour.

With the sortie briefed, our formation took off again, this time with me in the trailing position, since that was the part of the checkride I needed to re-accomplish. The clouds that day were high and thick. I stayed on the wing of the lead aircraft as its pilot climbed to 14,000 feet. We finally popped out into the Oklahoma blue sky and continued with formation evaluation. In the words of Judas, I stuck on the lead plane like a fly on shit, my mood improving with each maneuver. After several minutes of following my leader around the blue Oklahoma skies, the lieutenant colonel evaluator said, "There's nothing wrong with your formation flying. Take me back home."

Recheck complete.

Even with a thirty-pound parachute still on my back, I felt the heavy burden lift from my shoulders as we walked across the flight line. His positive debrief of my flight performance was reassuring, and it bolstered my confidence.

"I can do this," I thought. *"Time to get back in the game."*

15
A MONUMENTAL EVENT

THROUGHOUT ANY FLYING TRAINING PROGRAM, simulators are used to practice emergency procedures—and also save the cost of fuel—by perfecting skills such as instrument flying. Once a simulated emergency is successfully handled, the instructor resets the simulator for the next scenario. A well-known expression was, "OK. New day, new jet," meaning everything experienced was now in the past, and we were proceeding with a clean slate. At this point I had failed the first two T-38 checkrides and was heading into the final phase: instrument flying.

OK. New day, new jet.

During instrument training, the assumption is we're flying in clouds and unable to see the horizon ahead, or the ground and runway below. This phase took place about two months before graduation, consisting of both simulator training and flights from the back seat of the T-38, relying solely on the airplane's instruments. I progressed through the training flights, and in mid-January 1989 I was four weeks—and one flight—away from my final UPT checkride.

Throughout the year, physical fitness was emphasized for us to stay in good shape to be able to sustain the g-forces encountered in the jet trainers. Plus, we were, after all, in the military. There were numerous physical training sessions throughout the week, and we also played intramural sports. Volleyball and softball were my favorites, but my downfall was pretending that I could play basketball.

One night I attended my one and only intramural basketball game, showing my support as the class leader. Other than shooting around for fun, I hadn't played in a real basketball game since junior high. I dressed out for the game and sat on the bench, waiting for my chance. During the free-throw attempts after a foul, I subbed in and assumed my place on the side of the lane. The ball went up, bounced off the rim and came in my direction, and I leapt off the court for the rebound. I caught the ball, then immediately came down on my opponent's foot, rolling my left foot to the side. I felt a pop and collapsed to the floor, then hobbled to the bleachers where my wife was waiting, shaking her head. Neither of us could believe that I was injured in just three seconds of playing time.

I iced my ankle at home and got ready for bed. The next morning I noticed my ankle was a bit swollen, with an ominous blue streak running down the outside of my left foot toward the little toe. It was painful to touch, and I couldn't put any weight on it without feeling a shooting pain.

I headed to the base flight surgeon and had it X-rayed. The young flight surgeon wasn't much older than I was, and he lacked any bedside manner or sympathy.

"You broke your foot," he said. "Looks like we'll need to wash you back a class."

I couldn't believe it. I was the class leader of twenty-eight guys that I had trained with for the previous eleven months. Now I was supposed to wash back to the class behind me just before graduation? I asked if there were any other options. Vance is a small air force base, without a main hospital and only a health clinic, so the young flight doc referred me downtown to the hospital, where I met a kindly old doctor.

The gray-haired doctor looked at my X-ray and pointed to the hairline crack just below my little toe as we talked about my broken foot. I told him I was scheduled to graduate in four weeks and had two required flights left in the program, one being a training ride and the other an instrument checkride. I explained that I was the class leader, and I desperately wanted to graduate with the guys I had come to know so well over the previous year.

The doctor knew all about Air Force pilot training and took pity on me. He explained that, normally, the crack would heal wearing only a hard shoe or boot. He then graciously offered a solution that made us both happy.

"How about we cast it for two weeks and you stay off it completely, then we'll take another look at it," he said. "That'll give you two weeks to fly those last two flights."

During those ensuing two weeks, our class held its assignment night. This was very similar to what I had experienced on assignment night in navigator training, except without any ill-conceived guesses as to what I might receive.

Our class wore flight suits that night along with our standard-issue black flying boots. I pulled a large black sock over my plaster cast, and our class waited in the back of the room for our introduction. The master of ceremonies introduced "Class 89-05"—and, with rock music blaring, I led the class in a limping jog down the center aisle. In the video of the event, I look as though I'm strutting to the song. It wasn't until many days later that I saw the video and realized my whole class took up my "strut" and limped/jogged up to the front of the room, coming to attention in front of the base leadership. Since we all had the same gait, many attendees never realized my foot was broken and in a cast. Had I known the class was doing this, perhaps our introductory song should have been Aerosmith's *Walk This Way*.

The momentous evening proceeded with each member of the class being called up individually to stand in front of a dual screen featuring a "hero shot" of the pilot trainee holding a helmet and standing on the ladder next to the sleek T-38 cockpit. The emcee enjoyed roasting the trainees with embarrassing tales before finally announcing the assignments.

Top graduates were thrilled to receive an F-16, as others received A-10s, or larger cargo and refueling aircraft. One necessary but dreaded assignment was to be retained as a first assignment instructor pilot (FAIP), meaning an extended stay in Enid, Oklahoma. Those pilots would remain at Vance, flying the T-37 or T-38, training new students for three more years before receiving a follow-on assignment to a fighter, bomber, tanker, or cargo aircraft.

This was not happy news for one young couple. As the young second lieutenant stood on the stage, the emcee said these fateful words: "Tactical Air Command is going to have to wait three more years to put you in a fighter. You're staying here at Vance to fly the T-37."

Staying in Oklahoma and becoming a T-37 instructor pilot was not what he expected or wanted at all—and his young bride didn't want it, either. Sitting one row behind the wing commander and squadron commanders, she stood up and drunkenly cried out, "What the hell?" before the other wives sitting nearby quickly pulled her back into her seat.

My top choice was the newly built B-1 bomber. It was the latest and greatest bomber, could fly at supersonic speeds, and was known to handle like a big T-38. Behind that, I wanted a B-52 to Loring Air Force Base in northern Maine, or Andersen Air Force Base on the Pacific island of Guam. Those two bases focused on sea-mining operations and conventional bombing, and the crews did not have to sit nuclear alert. After two years at Barksdale, I now embraced the bomber mission and thought my career would go further if I eventually flew the future B-2 stealth bomber. The Air Force initially planned to use former navigators as pilots in this long-range, two-pilot aircraft.

My third choice was the newest plane in the inventory, the KC-10 Extender. This was a modified McDonnell Douglas DC-10 used by the military for air refueling and cargo transport.

Unlike assignment night in navigator training, I was not resigned to receiving a B-52, but I truly hoped a B-1 would be my next plane. Hopefully one B-1 training slot would be allocated to our class, but that was not a given. As my name was called, I awaited my fate. Playing in the background was the Rolling Stones song *You Can't Always Get What You Want,* with these foreshadowing lyrics: "*But if you try sometimes—well, you just might find you get what you need.*"

"Captain Dale, even though you placed two bombers as your top two choices, you will be returning to Barksdale Air Force Base, Louisiana, to fly the KC-10."

That was certainly a stunning surprise. It was unheard of to list an unpopular B-52 above a KC-10 and receive the new plane over the older. But it happened. I was shocked but not disheartened. I just never imagined this would be the result.

Now I just needed to pass my final instrument checkride. Over the previous two weeks I had been unable to fly with my foot in a cast, but I was given daily use of the T-38 full-motion simulator to practice my instrument approaches. That was a godsend.

The day came to return to the in-town doctor for re-examination. He removed my cast and sent me back to X-ray, and we met in his office a few minutes later. With the two X-rays side by side, I could still see the hairline crack on my left foot.

He asked, "How does it feel?"

I answered, "It hurts a little, but otherwise it's fine."

"So you think you can fly with it in your flight boot?" he asked.

"Yeah, I can do that," I said.

He reached for the paperwork to put me back on flying status, and in a slow drawl he said, "OK, just don't get me in trouble," as he handed me the signed medical clearance form. I headed back to Vance ready to schedule my remaining T-38 flights, with graduation just two weeks away. I was given one practice instrument flight to warm up and then scheduled for my final pilot training checkride.

On February 10, fifty-one weeks after moving to Enid, I met my evaluator, and we briefed the flight. The location was up to me, weather permitting, so I planned to perform my final checkride at Barksdale Air Force Base, my old B-52 home and future KC-10 base. Once there, I would fly a series of instrument approaches from the back of the T-38, with a cloth curtain pulled over the windscreen to block my view of any outside visual references.

As we headed toward the crew van, I noticed the evaluator also limped as he walked. In his case, though, he was favoring his right foot. We boarded the van with several other pilots, all waiting to be dropped off at our respective jets. A fellow IP on the van knew both of us and said to my evaluator, "Didn't you sprain your ankle at the basketball game last night?"

"Yes," he replied. "But it's only minor."

This was news to me. Turning to me, the IP said, "And didn't you break your foot in a game?"

"Yeah, I just got the cast off a few days ago," I replied.

"How are y'all going to fly and hold the brakes on the T-38?" he asked.

Since my left foot was cracked and his right ankle was sprained, I said, "Well, I'm going to hold the right brake, and he's going to hold the left brake." I was kidding, but we hobbled off the bus and wobbled down the flight line toward our T-38.

I flew back to my old Louisiana stomping grounds, completed my three instrument approaches, then landed to refuel. We parked very close to my future 32nd Air Refueling Squadron (32 ARS), so I asked my evaluator if I could stop in for a visit.

"Sure," he said.

Still wearing my G-suit and carrying my helmet bag, I walked into the 32 ARS and told the first pilot I saw that I would be coming to this squadron in a month. He said, "Well, let's go upstairs and meet your future boss!"

We headed upstairs to the squadron commander's office, where I was introduced to Lt. Col. Wally Dill. He shook my hand, and in a friendly voice said, "Look at you with your 'fast pants' on," referring to the G-suit. It was a quick visit, but I felt it was a great way to close out pilot training and start my future assignment in the KC-10.

Days after my last checkride, on a bitterly cold February day, my parents and brother arrived in Enid for the graduation activities. It was exactly one year after Karin and I arrived. I gave my family a tour of the base, and Jack enjoyed flying the T-38 simulator. The ceremony culminated with me standing proudly as Karin, four months pregnant with our first child, pinned silver pilot wings on my uniform where my navigator wings used to reside.

Once back at our house after the ceremony, my dad and I headed outside to walk our cocker spaniel and beagle around the block. Dad was a fairly quiet man, very stoic toward me and my brother, rarely showing affection. We received handshakes instead of bear hugs, and when I said, "Love ya, Dad," he would smile and say, "Right," but never uttered the word "love." I'm sure it was generational, because many of my friends have said the same thing about their dads.

Dad loved to tell lots of funny stories, and he was very kind, but he also was mostly ambivalent toward my aviation career. My dad didn't discourage me from flying, but he wasn't curious or enthusiastic about it, either. On this brisk, blue-sky day as we walked the dogs, I finally realized my dream of becoming an Air Force pilot. I didn't follow in my dad's footsteps of being a lawyer, but rather my uncle's. As we walked side by side, something monumental happened. My father quietly said, "You know, Davy, I'm proud of you."

It was the one and only time my dad ever said those words.

T-38 "hero shot": UPT graduation photo, February 16, 1989

16

BECOMING A GUCCI BOY

Barksdale KC-10, 1989

MY KC-10 initial qualification simulator instructor was a Korean War F-86 fighter pilot veteran named Jim, who was kind of full of himself. After having served as a MiG-killing fighter pilot over Korea, Jim was not happy about being reassigned in the late 1960s to the fairly new KC-135. Instead of flying fighter sorties against the enemy, Jim flew KC-135 tanker missions during the Vietnam War.

After several weeks of academic training, I started to notice that Jim only had two responses when I asked a question. It was either, "Well, what does the book say?" or, "Well, it's obvious that ... "

While on a break one day, feeling frustrated, I told my training partner, Randy, that if everything was either obvious or in the book, then why did we need Jim as our instructor? Randy sympathized with me, saying, "Dave, I gave up asking him questions a week ago."

I completed my KC-10 training in the summer of 1989 at Barksdale. The fleet of fifty-nine KC-10s was divided among three bases: Seymour Johnson Air Force Base in North Carolina, March Air Force Base in southern California, and Barksdale. Each of the three bases had its own simulator and staff of instructors, so all training was done in-house. This was unlike other Air Force aircraft, where new crew members went to a training base that specialized in a particular aircraft and mission.

I was paired with Capt. Randy Fopiano, an upstanding guy who became a good friend of mine. Randy was the first in his family to attend college, and he played tennis as a cadet at the Air Force Academy. After pilot training at Columbus Air Force Base in Mississippi, Randy flew T-37s as a FAIP (first assignment instructor pilot) for three years before coming to Barksdale to fly the KC-10.

The KC-10 is a modified McDonnell Douglas DC-10, the long-range version of the commercial DC-10 jumbo jet airliner. The Air Force modifications added extra fuel tanks underneath the main cabin floor, plus the air refueling equipment and plumbing required to perform midair refueling mission.

Many people step into the cockpit of a large aircraft and wonder, "What do all of those buttons and knobs do?" I spent the next three months finding out. My impression of KC-10 training was that I had to learn how to fly the huge airplane twice. First, it is a massive, 590,000-pound aircraft with three powerful General Electric engines. Randy and I came to this plane from very responsive T-37 and T-38 trainers, so we had to learn how to handle this lumbering, heavy jet. Second, the KC-10 had state-of-the-art automation for its time, including an autopilot, which the training aircraft did not have. Part of the nineteen simulator training sessions we flew were spent learning how to use the autopilot to fly the heading, speed, and altitude, or to perform the instrument approach we wanted.

KC-10s boasted a modern cockpit and still were being manufactured and delivered to the Air Force at the time. For this reason, we were dubbed by the Air Force crews flying older aircraft as the "Gucci Boys," but what started as a put-down by outsiders was proudly embraced by the KC-10 community. Our freshly built KC-10s, nicknamed "Big Sexy" by some of the crews, even had airline-style lavatories. No more peeing in a metal tube or pooping in a plastic-lined box.

Randy and I also had to learn the art of air refueling. The KC-10 is officially called "Extender" because its mission is one of force extension. Its air refueling and cargo capabilities greatly increased the Air Force's ability to move fighter and bomber airplanes to a combat zone. The passenger-plane cabin area was transformed into a cavernous cargo hold capable of carrying twenty passengers and twenty-seven pallets of goods on a floor sporting built-in rollers for easy movement.

There also was a passenger configuration available, called the "increased accommodation kit," or IAK. Each kit consisted of seventy-five red-cloth-covered seats, much like those found in the economy section of an airliner. When used, the seats took up the forward third of the cabin, just outside the cockpit door, while still leaving room for twenty pallets of cargo for items such as spare parts or extra engines for fighter aircraft.

In theory, a formation of three KC-10s could escort a squadron of a dozen fighter aircraft, refueling them over the ocean with their maintainers and other support personnel riding along inside the big jets to the deployed location. The KC-10 could both give fuel to receiving airplanes and take on fuel from other tankers, such as the older KC-135 or another KC-10. With that capability, it was said that our GE engines would run out of oil before the jet ran out of fuel.

The simulator training course, therefore, had to teach us not only how to fly and operate the KC-10, but how to run a rendezvous as both a tanker aircraft to dispense fuel or as a receiver aircraft taking on fuel.

Randy and I completed our simulator evaluation and headed to the flight line in late May 1989, with my very pregnant wife about to deliver our first child. I signed into the training division, and a very gracious instructor pilot, Maj. Jerry Babbin, asked, "Isn't your wife expecting a baby any day now?"

"Yes," I answered.

"Then what are you doing here?" he said. "Go home!"

Daniel Joseph Dale was born June 1, 1989, at the Barksdale hospital in Bossier City, Louisiana. His middle name was given in honor of my B-52 friend, Capt. Joe Wolf. In the background, the tiny black-and-white TV in Karin's hospital maternity room showed the major story of the day: the Tiananmen Square standoff in Beijing.

On the day we thought we'd bring our son home, Daniel became jaundiced, and his departure was delayed by three days. As "Tank Man" stood defiantly in front of a Chinese armored column in Tiananmen Square, our tiny son slept in his bassinet by the hospital window. Karin and Daniel stayed another three days at the base hospital, and I went back to the 32 ARS to prepare for my first flight.

On June 7, one week after Daniel was born, I pushed up the three throttles and accelerated down the two-mile-long Louisiana runway. Seven flights later, after numerous takeoffs, landings, and multiple air-refueling rendezvous, I completed my initial qualification checkride on July 10.

One week later, I flew with an instructor pilot, Capt. Pam Melroy, a future Space Shuttle pilot and commander and deputy administrator of NASA. Flying just thirty feet behind another KC-10, I held our jet steady enough to successfully make my first receiver refueling contact as their boom plugged into the receptacle on the roof of our plane. It was an unforgettable thrill. Receiver refueling was not a requirement for copilots to master, but it was both a challenge and confidence-booster to learn to fly in close formation with another large aircraft while taking on fuel.

The next few months were spent becoming mission qualified, flying several missions to overseas bases in England, Germany, Hawaii, and Alaska.

KC-135R (left) and KC-10. The KC-135 is similar to a Boeing 707; this four-engine airframe is also used for the E-3A AWACS, RC-135, EC-135, and VC-137 referenced throughout this book

The Hawaii trip ended on an unexpectedly amusing note. In October 1989 we were tasked to refuel an EC-135 (Boeing 707) intelligence-gathering aircraft over the Pacific as the crew monitored an upcoming Russian missile test. We departed Louisiana on a beautiful fall day for one week of temporary duty (TDY) to Hickam Air Force Base in Hawaii. We planned to come straight back to the mild temperatures of Louisiana—so who needs cold-weather gear, right?

With our week of daily refuelings complete, our task changed to take the EC-135 and its support crews back to Eielson Air Force Base, near Fairbanks, Alaska ... in the winter. Our flight engineer for this trip was a very funny Englishman named Simon Wray. It seems anything said with an English accent was funny, so everyone loved Simon. As a joke, he decided to complete his exterior preflight walk-around wearing only his brightly colored, knee-length Jams swimsuit that was popular in that era. Simon had pasty, white, skinny legs, and we all enjoyed the show.

Hours later, we landed in a driving snowstorm in Alaska, with snowflakes the size of quarters blowing sideways. In between each flight, our flight engineer was required to conduct an exterior inspection, looking for possible fluid leaks or signs of an unknown bird strike. Knowing that Simon was still wearing his Jams under his flight suit, I called out, "Simon! You don't have a hair on your ass if you don't complete that walk-around in your Jams again!"

His first reaction was, "Naaaah, I ain't gonna do that!" But then he thought about it and took on my challenge. He unzipped his flight suit and said, "Well, all right."

I had to get a picture of that, so I headed down the large mobile staircase and into the blizzard with him. He did the world's fastest walk-around inspection, and I met him at the engine nacelle to get his photo. It was a common pose, showing how big our engines were compared to a human. Simon leaned against the engine in his bright orange-and-pink swimsuit, yelling, "Take the picture! Take the picture!"

We returned home to the mild fall temperatures of northern Louisiana in time for the beginning of the holiday season. Around that same time, the evening news began reporting rumblings about some guy named Noriega in Panama.

17
OPERATION DENY CHRISTMAS

Air Force E-3 Sentry AWACS. (Military.com)

IN THE FALL OF 1989, Panamanian dictator Manuel Noriega refused to honor the results of a recent election, and he put down a second attempted coup. Members of the U.S. forces stationed in Panama were attacked and harassed on the streets, and Marine 2nd Lt. Robert Paz was fatally shot in his vehicle as he fled to escape an angry mob. Navy SEAL Lt. Adam Curtis and his wife were detained and assaulted by Panama Defense Forces personnel after witnessing the attack on Lieutenant Paz and his three military companions.

By mid-December, the Defense Department completed plans for an eventual invasion of Panama. The mission would be to safeguard the lives of U.S. citizens in Panama, and to defend democracy and human rights in that country, while also combating drug trafficking and protecting the Panama Canal treaty and its usage.

The KC-10s at Barksdale were placed on "bravo alert," which required the ability to be airborne within two hours of notification. Crews were told to go home, pack a deployment bag and stay on telephone standby. Some crew members returned to the base to stay in the visiting officers' quarters (VOQ). This placed them closer to the fueled and preflighted KC-10s on the flight line.

I headed home in the middle of the day on December 20 and told Karin I had to pack a bag, but couldn't say where I was going or what I was doing. I didn't have any details to give her, anyway.

That night we watched CNN together as the network aired reports from outside of Fort Bragg in North Carolina. The reporter dutifully told the nation that C-141 Starlifter cargo planes were departing from Pope Air Force Base, next to the Army's 82nd Airborne base at Fort Bragg, and were heading south in the direction of Panama. Sitting by me on the sofa, Karin looked at me and said, "I think I know where you're going."

So much for operational security.

Our squadron's crews spent forty-eight hours in the VOQs on bravo alert, ready to depart on a moment's notice. My forty-eight-hour shift began at noon on Christmas Day, which allowed for me to be home Christmas morning and for the off-going crew to get home Christmas afternoon. I was able to spend Daniel's first Christmas at home along with Karin and her parents. After lunch, I loaded my deployment bag into the car and headed for the base.

Baby Daniel Dale and me before a KC-10 flight

Several crew members in the KC-10 had come to the squadron from KC-135s and B-52s, and were used to sitting SAC alert, waiting for a response notification. My aircraft commander (AC), Capt. Willie Waddell, had come to the KC-10 many years earlier as a new second lieutenant right out of pilot training, so he never knew the luxury, thrill, or inconvenience of sitting alert. Willie grew bored sitting around the VOQ, so he headed off to the gym.

Timing is everything, right?

Our number came up to launch, and I received the pager notification for our crew to report to the squadron as soon as possible to take off. I had the flight engineer and boom operator with me, but in the days before cellphones, how would we track down our AC? The crew was assigned one pager, but it was left with me when Willie went to the gym.

After numerous phone calls to the gym, Willie finally was

tracked down in the gymnasium shower. He quickly met us, his hair still wet, at the squadron.

During the mission briefing, we were told we would be refueling the E-3A Airborne Warning and Control System (AWACS) over the Panamanian region. The AWACS is yet another Boeing 707, but with a large, spinning black disk on top that provides radar coverage of an area. They are like air traffic controllers in the sky, designed to help manage air traffic over a war zone, or to vector fighter aircraft toward enemy planes. As described in *Air Force Magazine,* "An AWACS flying over New York City could manage the aerial battle as far north as Boston and south as Washington, D.C., at the same time." In an effort to show leadership by example, the Barksdale wing commander, Colonel Mudd, would fly this Christmas night mission with us.

My first operational combat support mission was quiet and anticlimactic. Military aircrews maintain radio silence during combat support missions to avoid tipping off the enemy with radio chatter. We headed south, toward the eastern coast of Panama, and arrived at our prescribed refueling orbit over the Gulf of Mexico, telling the controlling AWACS over a scrambled radio frequency that we were on station. We set up a long racetrack pattern with thirty-mile legs and U-turns to the left at each end. Everyone on the crew stayed off the radios as Mike, our boom operator, scanned the night sky from his large, aft-facing window in the belly of the plane.

Silently, the large, black-and-white AWACS appeared below us and slowly climbed into the refueling position, stabilizing in a position fifty feet behind us, both airplanes matched at 450 miles per hour. Mike extended the telescoping refueling boom, making contact with the AWACS refueling receptacle above and just aft of their pilots' cockpit seats. Once in contact, Mike told the flight engineer over the aircraft interphone to begin transferring fuel. Within twenty minutes, our AWACS received 9,000 gallons, or roughly 60,000 pounds, of fuel. Once completely topped off, the AWACS headed off to continue his airborne command-and-control mission over Panama, while we stayed in our orbit as an on-call tanker until released to return to Barksdale.

The flight and the refueling went as scheduled, and both were pretty uneventful. My main memory from the flight was that after my copilot duties were complete for the AWACS refueling, I got out of my seat to let the wing commander fly the plane from the right seat. With no other aircraft around us, Willie told him to go into a turn, and Colonel Mudd, a B-52 pilot, aggressively rolled to thirty degrees of bank, slinging those of us now sitting in the red airline seats in the back to and fro. Perhaps he wasn't used to the responsive controls of the KC-10, but it got our attention. We landed twelve hours later, on the morning of December 26.

Officially, the operation was named "Just Cause," because "our cause was just." Among the "crew dogs," as we called ourselves, it was coined either "Operation Just 'Cause" or "Operation Deny Christmas," which would happen over and over throughout the years. After watching the CNN report for this event, and those leading up to Desert Shield and Desert Storm, I began referring to the KC-10 as the "CNN Reaction Force," because if it was on CNN, that's where we were going.

18
SOS

ALL MILITARY OFFICERS take part in professional military education (PME) for career advancement. Leadership training continues throughout our careers, first with squadron officer school (SOS) for captains, followed by intermediate service school (ISS) for majors, and finally senior service school (SSS) for lieutenant colonels and colonels. Each of these schools is a competitive benchmark for those hoping to lead at the next higher level.

By July 1990 I was on my way to attend SOS in residence at Maxwell Air Force Base, located near Montgomery, Alabama. My selection to attend in residence was better than completing the course by correspondence, and it helped pave the way for promotion to my next rank of major. SOS was a six-week course, and I was there until August. Although it was a privilege to attend, when the class was asked to write down our goals for the six-week course, I vowed to not spend a single weekend in Montgomery. It's not a place with a lot to offer, and it's as steamingly hot as Shreveport is in the summer. I failed on my vow once but managed to get out of town on the other five weekends.

On the weekends I spent away from SOS, I played beach volleyball with my ROTC classmate Capt. Robert "Bobber" McMurry near Eglin Air Force Base in the Florida panhandle. I water skied and partied with SOS classmates at our AC-130 gunship classmate's condo near Hurlburt Air Force Base, also in the Florida panhandle, and was lucky enough to attend the Winston 500 NASCAR race at Talladega Superspeedway for free. Just weeks after the course began, I met a classmate who, like me, also was a big NASCAR fan, having been born and raised in Daytona, Florida. After talking about the upcoming event in Lincoln, Alabama, he called my room one night to say that he had won two raceway tickets as part of a local Montgomery radio contest, and he invited me along. For $2 each, we rented two sleeping bags from the morale, welfare, and recreation office, and slept in the bed of his pickup truck the night before the race. The roar of the heavy stock cars shook my feet as the race began with us standing just three rows from the edge of the track. I'll never forget how brightly colored the cars were, with their neon hues so much brighter than shown on television.

The other monumental event involved rendezvousing with Karin and our thirteen-month-old son halfway between Shreveport and Montgomery at a Holiday Inn in Jackson, Mississippi. After a Saturday spent swimming in the pool, we were thrilled to watch Daniel take his first-ever steps in our hotel room that evening. It wasn't a bad way to escape Maxwell, even if for just a few days.

Our SOS class consisted of a dozen captains from various backgrounds: pilots, navigators, engineers, missileers, administrative support, and an Air Force Reserve chaplain named Norris Burkes.

The requirements for the class, in addition to physical fitness and teamwork, were three written point papers (not to be confused with college English papers) and three speeches. Our chaplain's speeches were memorable. This extremely nice Baylor graduate came off as overly polite while talking informally, but when giving a speech he became a different person. It was as if a movie director had yelled, "Action!" Norris would launch into a dramatic and moving speech, but without actually preaching to us, and at the end of his allotted time he would step away from the front of the classroom and resume his meek and mild demeanor. It was an amazing transformation to witness. That man had a commander's voice, and my children would tease me several years later about my own commander's voice.

Daniel's first steps, August 1990, Jackson, Mississippi

The requirements for the class, in addition to physical fitness and teamwork, were three written point papers (not to be confused with college English papers) and three speeches. Our chaplain's speeches were memorable. This extremely nice Baylor graduate came off as overly polite while talking informally, but when giving a speech he became a different person. It was as if a movie director had yelled, "Action!" Norris would launch into a dramatic and moving speech, but without actually preaching to us, and at the end of his allotted time he would step away from the front of the classroom and resume his meek and mild demeanor. It was an amazing transformation to witness. That man had a commander's voice, and my children would tease me several years later about my own commander's voice.

During a class break one day, a female classmate asked an F-15 pilot in our class if he could fly any airplane. His answer was memorable: "If I can start it, I can fly it." Every airplane has a unique sequence for starting either the jet or propeller engine, but once the engine is started, the flying principles remain the same: Add thrust until takeoff speed. Pull back on the stick, and the houses get smaller; push forward, and the houses get bigger again. It helps to know the proper speeds for landing, too, but I've always remembered his quote.

Our SOS class was due to graduate August 10, 1990, but on August 2 Saddam Hussein's Iraqi forces invaded Kuwait, and our world changed forever. His aggression that day eventually led to the first Gulf War, and our deployment to Saudi soil provided the impetus for Osama bin Laden's 9/11 attacks in 2001.

Several students were recalled to their units for immediate deployment, and all of us in aviation hoped to get that recall notification. *Send me back and let me fly!* By this point we had not flown in more than thirty days, so we were all non-current and would need a proficiency flight to regain our takeoff and landing currency.

Some of the F-15, F-16, C-130, and even C-21 Learjet pilots were recalled to their units, but the rest of us had to stay put. We ground out the next week of papers, speeches, and a war-gaming exercise. The aircrew members watched the nightly news reports and called our squadrons, begging to be recalled, but there still were a lot of unknowns. Was the little country of Kuwait worthy of our military protection? We didn't know where all of this was leading.

Growing up, my family attended the local Presbyterian church regularly, and Karin and I attended with our young children in later years. Knowing there was a good chance of deploying to a war zone, I called Chaplain Burkes' room the night before SOS ended, asking if he would give a blessing for our class the next day. After our instructor gave her final debrief of our class performance, we all stood in the middle of the classroom. Bowing our heads, the chaplain asked God to watch over us as we parted ways and prepared for our expected upcoming deployments.

The KC-10's mission is to travel far and wide, delivering military equipment and troops where needed. The thought of deploying was not a scary thought, but it was exciting. If there was a mission to be done, our thoughts were to put us in and let us do it. In our young eyes, it would certainly be better than taking off and landing at Barksdale on training flights each week.

19
DESERT SHIELD

"Big Sexy" in Seeb, Oman

I RETURNED to Barksdale in mid-August to find the ramp empty of its nineteen KC-10s. The planes and crews were busy moving people and equipment all over the world, and the squadron was deployed everywhere, from the Arabian Peninsula, to England, Spain,

Germany, the islands of Guam in the Pacific, and to Diego Garcia in the Indian Ocean. For the time being, I was a non-mission-ready copilot, because I had not flown in more than six weeks—and there were no KC-10s or instructor pilots around to requalify me.

A KC-10 and instructor finally were available August 15, and our four-man crew set out on a mission supporting a B-52 deployment. My requalification flight took place on a three-hour sortie from Barksdale to the B-52 base in Loring, Maine. From there, we flew ten hours to Hickam Air Force Base in Hawaii to spend the night. We then continued the next morning for another seven hours to Andersen Air Force Base, on the island of Guam, about halfway between Australia and Japan. Although thousands of miles from Iraq, this is where some of our B-52 bombers were now stationed. After delivering the bomber support cargo and personnel, we stayed overnight before getting up the next day for the thirteen-hour return flight back to Barksdale. After completing this five-day mission, I was now designated as mission ready for any upcoming missions.

I spent most of September in Zaragoza, Spain, with several other KC-10 crews. We were placed there as an "air bridge," meaning that we were ready to provide air refueling support to any long-range bomber missions in the event the United States needed to strike Saddam's Iraqi forces as our military buildup continued in the desert. American B-52s eventually flew thirty-hour round-trip bombing missions from the States, and these missions were made possible by the refueling tankers over the Atlantic Ocean and Mediterranean Sea.

By October, after I returned from Spain, the ability to fly the KC-10 dropped off again as the planes were already deployed to bases in Oman, Spain, and Italy, along with an adequate amount of crew members. Fortunately, the Air Force had a flying program to allow copilots to gain flying experience when not flying the KC-10. The accelerated copilot enrichment (ACE) program allowed two SAC copilots to sign out a T-37 trainer—the same small, two-seat jet that we first learned to fly in pilot training—and fly around the United States to gain airmanship experience.

At first glance, this might sound like a boondoggle just waiting to be exposed on the CBS news program *60 Minutes.* In reality, it allowed two young copilots the chance to plan flights and make decisions about weather and safety without being overruled by an overprotective aircraft commander. "Cloud dancing" was a favorite activity in the nimble Tweet, as we weaved and bobbed around the cumulus clouds above the Arkansas-Louisiana-Texas region. I spent most of October flying to small airports and grabbing a burger in Ardmore, Oklahoma, College Station, Texas, and New Orleans.

While I was busy supporting the local economy of small airport restaurants, my KC-10 copilot friend (and fellow former Barksdale B-52 navigator) Kirk Shepherd settled into the "tent city" at Seeb Air Base outside of Muscat, Oman, on the eastern edge of the Arabian Peninsula. He was in the second wave of crews dispatched to the threadbare desert base just weeks after Iraq invaded Kuwait. Those first crews arrived at a camp that was built using the prepositioned supplies deployed during the Reagan administration years before.

Quonset huts of materials contained ten-man canvas tents, a chow hall, and even never-used 1984 camouflaged Chevy Blazers with keys inside. Just add oil, gas, and a battery, and they were ready to go. The initial crews rotated home in late November, and Kirk arrived as part of the four new crews manning two KC-10s. Within a few days, he called back and said, "Dave, you've got to get over here. The flying is great!" Our wives were the best of friends, and Karin knew I wanted to be over there helping out.

I asked Kirk and his wife, Colette, if he needed anything; after all, we were bringing a huge KC-10. Remember the part about being a Gucci Boy? Well, Kirk gave me a shopping list—which included power strips, a microwave, a TV, and a videocassette recorder—and he told me what I should pack for the three months. While troops in the Army and Marines deployed with what they could carry, and while smaller Air Force cargo planes arrived with the bare essentials, our jumbo KC-10s made it to the desert with most of the modern conveniences of the early 1990s. The other services would agree: That's pretty Gucci.

My KC-10 simulator partner during initial training, Randy Fopiano, completed his upgrade to aircraft commander on November 1, with me serving as his copilot. His previous flight time as a T-37 instructor counted toward the 1,200 hours required for upgrade, whereas my navigator time didn't count, so I needed to build more hours before I could move up to aircraft commander, and this deployment would provide those needed flight hours. On November 29, Randy and I became a crew, along with our flight engineer (FE), Sgt. Mike McKittrick, and boom operator (BO) Sgt. Eric Thomas. We set off for Mildenhall Air Base in England for an overnight stop before heading downrange to Oman.

Karin and I celebrated Christmas very early that year, and she gave me a striped, blue-and-green-colored long-sleeve rugby jersey. It was the right shirt to wear on a cold November night at the Mildenhall Officers Club. There was a lot of drinking going on that night, as we all knew we were heading for a war zone. I drank a pint of English ale at a table with other Barksdale pilots as a group of loud, staggering-drunk guys from another base started drinking "afterburners," which was a flaming shot of liquor.

I didn't see what happened next, but I saw the effect. A swaying young stud behind me attempted to throw back his flaming shot, but instead proceeded to toss the burning liquid onto his face. In the dark British pub, I sensed a glow behind me and turned to see what looked like a flaming jack-o'-lantern. He was all flames from the neck up.

I jumped out of my chair, tackled the big guy, and started swiping my new rugby jersey sleeves over his face until the flames went out. I held my arms over his face, wondering what I would see when I removed them. I slowly pulled my arms away, and he looked at me with singed eyebrows and a blistered lower lip.

In a low, gravelly voice, he said, "Whoa."

Fortunately, most of the fire was just burning the alcohol; his skin didn't actually burn. Within minutes, the air base medics and police responded to look after the young party animal, and my crew headed to bed.

The next morning, December 1, 1990, we took off for Oman, flying across the Mediterranean region, through Egypt, and across Saudi Arabia. The accents of the foreign controllers were very difficult to understand as we headed eastward.

Suddenly, when we were handed off to Doha Control over Qatar, a perfectly understandable American voice acknowledged my radio check-in. After reporting my altitude and confirming we were in radar contact, I asked, "Are you military, or a contractor brought in for the airlift?"

"Nah," he replied. "I'm one of Reagan's boys."

I found out he was a former U.S. air traffic controller who had gone on strike in 1981. When the government was unwilling to negotiate, he and others like him were fired by President Ronald Reagan for conducting an illegal strike. I told him it was a relief to hear his American accent. As we flew south out of his airspace, he handed us off to the United Arab Emirates (UAE) controllers.

"Good luck to you boys," he said as he signed off. "Be safe."

We landed at Seeb International Airport in the capital city of Muscat, then proceeded to our tent city, named Camp Nacirema, alongside the runway. Not everyone in the international community supported our coalition's buildup and military plans, and there was a bit of contention about Americans being in the region to help one Muslim nation prepare to fight another. It was hard to stay low-key during such a massive military buildup, but we were told not to be too flashy, which included no displays of American flags.

Camp Nacirema was built in late August, soon after the Iraqi invasion of Kuwait, using prepositioned war materials intended for a possible conflict with Iran. The innovative first inhabitants came up with the camp's name, NACIREMA, which was AMERICAN spelled backwards. The name never changed during the entire military operation.

Sgt. Mike McKittrick, Sgt. Eric "ET" Thomas, me, and Capt. Randy Fopiano

Randy, Mike, Eric, and I settled into a large tent along with Kirk's four-man crew. Everyone was assigned a green, folding Army canvas cot, and we each had about four feet by eight feet of personal space, but the tent itself was an open-style barracks without dividers. Our tentmates were happy to see our supply of power strips, large television, VCR, and microwave, just as requested. Karin sent me off to war with a cardboard, powder-blue, fold-out, three-drawer dresser for my clothes, upon which I taped Polaroid family photos. We each brought a sleeping bag, sheets, and a blanket, since the desert could get cold at night.

The camp had showers and lavatory tents at one end, with ten toilets in one tent and eight showers in the other. Because we were advised to stay hydrated in the desert, we initially drank two liters of water per day. After my first 3 a.m. run to the bathroom with a near-bursting bladder, I gave up on the desire to stay overly hydrated.

At the opposite end of the camp was the chow hall, which served cafeteria-style meals. Outside were two large trash cans of hot, soapy water and clean cold water for cleaning out our mess kit after each meal. This was 1990, but the conditions were similar to any TV episode of the 1970s comedy *M*A*S*H*.

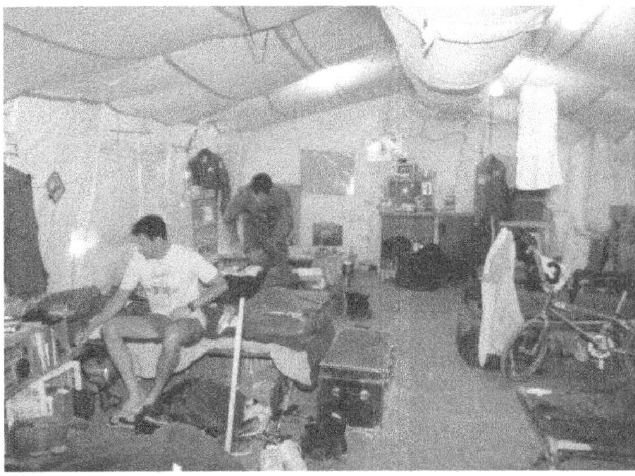

Randy and Kirk in our home away from home, December 1990 to February 1991

Creativity flourished after the basic necessities were addressed. The civil engineering unit out of Travis Air Force Base in California did a marvelous job building the Muscat Rose Saloon, complete with a wooden sidewalk and swinging doors. The benefit of being based in Oman instead of Saudi Arabia was that alcohol was permitted, to a limit. Because of our round-the-clock operation, each crew member was allowed two beers within two hours of landing, and each person had a punch card to track their daily allotment. This didn't prevent the non-drinkers from "loaning" beers, though. Two hours after landing, we were back in crew rest to get ready for the next flight. Beer drinking could start at 10 a.m. if we landed from an all-night mission.

Unused scrap lumber was free game for camp members, and industrious crew members created lounge chairs, tables for card games, and even a mock stockade to chastise offenders of informal camp rules—showering too long, snoring, farting, you name it.

Three days after getting settled into Camp Nacirema, our crew took off on our first five-hour mission. Kirk's aircraft commander, Capt. Pat Heatherman, served as our guide for this orientation to the military operations. Our area ranged from Oman up to Saudi Arabia, just south of the Kuwaiti border, and the skies over the Persian Gulf. This included the area just off the Kuwaiti coast, where Saddam's forces loomed. Our mission that day was to refuel four, four-ship formations of F-16s, for a total of sixteen fighters. We would do this over a one-hour period while orbiting over the northern Saudi desert.

Capt. Pat Heatherman (left) and Capt. Randy Fopiano

With our refueling assignment complete, we headed southeast to Oman at 27,000 feet. Randy needed to take a restroom break and left his seat to use the lavatory, just outside of the cockpit. In the few minutes he was away, the plane suddenly yawed to the left, with the tail swinging abruptly to the right a few degrees. Mike, the flight engineer, and I looked at the three columns of engine instruments. To once again quote that memorable children's song from *Sesame Street*, "one of these things is not like the other."

The engines on any plane are numbered from left to right, so Engine No. 1 is on the left wing, Engine No. 2 is mounted on the tail, and Engine No. 3 is on our right wing. Our engine instruments, in the days before glass displays, were round dials with needles. Each engine had its own column, or stack, of gauges. Engine No. 2 and Engine No. 3 both had their needles pointing toward the right, indicating good rpm, fuel flow, oil pressure, and exhaust gas temperature. The needles of Engine No. 1 were all pointing left, like a fuel tank running on empty. Our left engine had flamed out.

Every KC-10 pilot and flight engineer goes through emergency training in the simulator four times a year, so we knew the procedures inside and out for dealing with an engine failure, and how to land with one engine out. My first step, however, was not in the checklist.

I pushed the PA (public address) button, which was broadcast throughout the empty cabin and lavatory, and calmly announced, "We just had an engine flameout." Randy quickly finished his business, and I turned off the autopilot and autothrottles to manually fly the plane while Randy got back in his seat to assess the situation.

An engine flameout is very rare, and we didn't have an explanation for why it happened. There was never a sense of panic, but rather of a reaction of, "What caused this?" Years earlier, a KC-10 flying out of Riyadh, Saudi Arabia, had contaminated fuel, a result of sand clogging the fuel filters. The crew had one engine flameout but was able to get the airplane back on the ground before the other two engines did the same. That was a real possibility in our case, too, and that incident raced through our minds as we continued back to Seeb Air Base.

Pilots can be described as even-keeled, unflappable, steady, unperturbed, and cool-headed, and the question, "How do you remain so calm?" is one that I and other pilots have heard through the years. Early on in our flight training and aviation careers, situations arise that might be startling at first, but once we see that situation time and again (gusty winds, snow-covered runways, or an amber light on our panel indicating a malfunction), we no longer are startled, so we try to calmly take it in stride.

Throughout training, we learn to remain steady under pressure, and not to become distracted or be a hothead. Crew members who tend to become overly excited, or "ping," during a flight are known as "pingers." One such person was a KC-10 flight engineer I encountered a few years later, with the last name of McClary. In our squadron, he was known as "Scary McClary" for his tendency to fly off the handle. One morning (a few years later), I was taxiing the KC-10 onto the runway for takeoff. As I started to push the throttles up, McClary started yelling, "Shit! Shit! Shit!"

I yanked the throttles to idle, whipped my head around, and asked him, "What's wrong?"

McClary yelled back, "I dropped my damn pen!"

I couldn't believe it. That was not the time or place for his meaningless outburst.

I admit I have lost my cool occasionally—but, for the most part, friends remark about how even-keeled I remain in various situations. One particular time that I got upset was during a Desert Storm air refueling mission. My job was to monitor up to four different radios simultaneously: VHF, UHF, and HF (very high frequency, ultra-high frequency, and high frequency, respectively). The KC-10 had two civilian-style VHF radios, which airliners use daily to talk to air traffic control. One of our two radios was set to an emergency broadcast frequency for potential critical information, or for an unscheduled air refueling request from a desperate fighter. The primary VHF radio enabled us to talk to the E-3 AWACS for traffic separation in the combat arena, and a military UHF radio was used for air-refueling purposes with our receiver aircraft. Copilots had to listen to all of them.

During the combat operations, the frequencies could be jammed or interfered with by the Iraqis. On this day, there was continuous static and a loud squeal coming through my headset from the VHF and UHF frequencies. After two hours of all this constant static and an ear-piercing squeal in my headphones I finally yelled, "Goddamn these fucking radios!"

The cockpit got very quiet for a bit after that. Our flight engineer,

Sgt. Mike McKittrick, told me after the flight, "I've never seen you get mad before."

On this particular day, with one engine flamed out, Randy's crew didn't panic. We weren't startled, but instead just let our training kick in. Some of the questions we wrestled with were: Should we divert to another foreign base without KC-10 maintenance support? Or should we continue over the 8,000-foot mountain range between us and Seeb?

"What could go wrong next? Plan for the worst, but hope for the best," thought the Happy Pessimist.

The No. 2 and No. 3 engines, on the tail and right engine, were operating normally, and Randy and I both remembered our simulator instructor's encouraging words: "This three-engine plane is designed to fly normally on two engines." Knowing that, Randy re-engaged the autopilot and resumed flying, while I declared an emergency with the air traffic controllers.

This was not me shouting "Mayday, Mayday, Mayday!" like we've all seen in the movies, but an advisory call to the Doha air traffic controllers. Hollywood likes to over-dramatize any situation, depicting emergencies with a lot of yelling and excitement, but in reality, when the evening news plays audiotapes from any aircraft incident, people are often struck at how calm the flight crew sounds over the radio. A lot of that is the result of our simulator training. We've seen these emergency situations before; now we need to take the correct actions—and hope we sound cool and collected on the radios.

"Doha Control, Esso 1-0 is declaring an emergency," I said. "We have one engine shutdown and need to proceed direct to Seeb Airport."

"Esso 1-0, Doha copies your emergency," came the reply. "State souls on board and fuel remaining."

This is a routine question during any emergency, for their incident paperwork.

"Doha," I said, "Esso 1-0 has five souls on board, and three hours of fuel remaining."

"Esso 1-0, you are cleared direct to Seeb Airport," came the reply. "We will notify them of your emergency."

Was I nervous? Definitely. I didn't want to make a mistake or be the cause of an accident. But I remained focused on the mission.

There are times in life when I've adopted a technique that I call micro-prayers. Sometimes, when entering a stressful situation, I simply ask, *"LORD, please help me to say and do the right thing."*

Other times, like during an aircraft emergency, I employ Alan Shepherd's astronaut Prayer: *"DEAR LORD, please don't let me screw this up."* Apart from wanting to save my own neck and those of my crew, it's admittedly a selfish prayer to ensure I'm not blamed during an accident investigation.

Our flight engineer, Sergeant McKittrick, read aloud the checklist steps for engine failure in flight, which we completed step by step. Oman was notified of our emergency, and we safely crossed the small mountain range north of the airport. Randy brought our large jet in for a flawless, one-engine-out landing. Welcome to desert flying!

We all certainly enjoyed our two beers that evening.

The KC-10 maintenance crews at Seeb discovered a bad fuel-control unit for the No. 1 engine, but the fuel itself was fine. The control unit was replaced, and the aircraft was put back into service the following week.

Our crew flew again three days later, refueling Navy F-18 fighters and EA-6B Prowler jamming aircraft in Exercise Desert Force, a show of force to let the Iraqis know we were in the region and ready to strike back aggressively if they pushed south from Kuwait and into Saudi Arabia during Gen. Norman Schwarzkopf's military buildup.

A few days later, we closed out our first week of living in the new region by flying a Navy support mission, refueling F-18s and A-6 Intruder attack aircraft from the USS Midway. The carrier was located in the Persian Gulf, across the Straits of Hormuz from Iran.

During Navy refuelings, Eric, our boom operator, extended a long refueling hose from the aft belly of the KC-10 and monitored the refueling as the Navy fighters stabbed our refueling basket with their refueling probes.

One of the dangers of this method of refueling is that if the fighter hits our basket with too much speed, it can create a sine wave with the hose that can whip up and down violently enough to snap off the basket. The KC-10 then has the equivalent of a fireman's hose spewing fuel and wagging uncontrollably, with the risk that it could strike the aircraft's tail. In that event, the boom operator needs to shut off the fuel and sever the flailing hose with a guillotine switch. This clamp-and-sever operation of the guillotine mechanism is like cutting an umbilical cord for a newborn, and it takes only seconds to complete. But this emergency situation requires a boom operator in his boom pod to keep us safe.

A heavily armed Navy F-18 refueling from the KC-10 hose-and-drogue system

By this point, early in our deployment, Eric's stomach was not enjoying international chow hall food. After completing the assigned F-18 refueling, he called over the flight interphone, "Pilot? Boom. I'm not feeling too good. I need to come forward to the bathroom." Randy said he was clear to come forward, and we could hear his flight boots running up the cargo floor. The door to the airline lavatory slammed just outside our cockpit.

A few seconds later, the amber annunciator light on our dashboard lit up, stating "Drogue Engaged." This meant that a Navy fighter had plugged into our refueling basket. In his haste to leave his refueling station, Eric hadn't retracted the hose, and now we had an unknown customer attached. Mike, the flight engineer, was in charge of the refueling pumps that delivered the fuel to our waiting customers. A little unsure, he asked, "What should I do?"

I laughed and replied, "He has to be one of ours. Give him some gas."

Meanwhile, Randy hit the PA button (why do things always happen while in the lavatory?) and said, "Boom! Someone is on the drogue!"

SLAM! THUMP, THUMP, THUMP, THUMP.

We heard Eric dash out of the bathroom and run down the fifty-yard wooden cargo deck and down the stairs to his station. By the time he looked out the large aft window, our mysterious Navy customer had disconnected and was pulling away.

Eric came on the interphone and announced, "Well, it was an A-6."

Chuckling, Randy said, "Boom, if you need to come back forward, please stow the drogue."

Back in Camp Nacirema, the off-duty flight crews, support personnel, and security police gathered at the Muscat Rose Saloon for beers under the cool, black, starlit sky. Kirk and his crew returned from a mission and treated us to a low-altitude KC-10 flyby, using a legal circling approach maneuver.

A circling approach is a landing maneuver used when an airport has an instrument approach to get below the clouds, but not to the runway of intended landing. If the winds are out of the south but the only approach available is to the north, the crew will fly the northbound approach until below the cloud layer, usually not lower than 500 feet above the ground. Once clear of the clouds, the crew breaks off the northbound approach and turns thirty degrees right or left and flies to the north end of the airfield, then begins a U-turn, keeping the field in sight to complete the landing to the south. It's a visual maneuver flown below the clouds once the airport runway and surrounding environment are in sight.

Many crews had accomplished this approach, which conveniently overflew the camp's saloon at 700 feet above the ground. Right on schedule, Kirk's huge KC-10 appeared in the night sky, heading right for us. As they overflew the camp, their boom operator turned on all of their underbelly refueling guidance lights. This is a collection of red, yellow, and green lights in two parallel rows used to tell a receiver aircraft if he was too close, too far, or in the correct refueling position. At the same time, the boom operator lowered the flying boom and wagged it left and right, as Kirk banked the airplane left and right, in a wave to the crowd below. We all cheered and raised our cans of Smithwick Irish Ale, Newcastle Brown Ale, or O'Doul's non-alcoholic beer.

Our wing commander, not amused by the display, announced that Kirk's was the last fly-by to be flown over our camp. We protested, saying they were just flying a practice circling approach, but he was in no mood to change his mind.

"It was a circling approach right up until the wing wag," he said. "Then it became an airshow. No more!"

As the military build-up continued, aircrews routinely monitored BBC broadcasts over the airplane's high-frequency (HF) radio to keep up with the diplomatic efforts, and to ensure we were aware if war broke out in the middle of our eight-hour missions. The HF radio also came in handy for calling our families back home.

The military auxiliary radio system (MARS) is a volunteer organization that uses U.S. amateur (ham) radio operators to complete calls to our military dependents. From our KC-10 flying high over the Arabian Peninsula, we contacted a radio operator in the States, who patched us through to our home telephone in Louisiana. Before beginning the conversation, the radio operator explained that they would be monitoring the call so they could switch a dial from "receive" to "transmit" to carry out the link between the two parties. At the end of each statement, my wife or I had to say, "Over," to let the radio operator know that the other person would now talk. The brief conversations went something like this:

"How are you doing, Karin? Over."

"All is fine here. Over."

"I love you. Over."

"I love you, too. Over."

The touching conversations became memorable for the slogan, "I love you. Over."

We closed out 1990 with an outdoor Christmas celebration, where I sang in the choir on a wooden stage complete with a fake, decorated Christmas tree. I remember thinking that we were in the Middle East, surrounded by dry desert sand, and not far from that "Little Town of Bethlehem."

Operation Desert Shield provided just what the name implied. We provided a protective air shield over the Arabian Peninsula, while ships full of combat personnel and equipment offloaded in ports throughout the region. Our country and allies completed the largest military buildup since World War II in record time.

20
MOGADISHU, PART I

AC-130 gunship. (Military.com)

OUR COUNTRY mainly knows about West Africa's Somalia and its capital, Mogadishu, from the 2001 movie *Black Hawk Down,* which told a story about a downed Army helicopter during the 1993 Battle of Mogadishu and the daring rescue operation that followed. Although I eventually delivered those same Army Rangers into Mogadishu, my first encounter with the capital city started a few nights before Operation Desert Storm kicked off.

While based at Seeb Air Base in Muscat, Oman, our crew was pulled away from our Desert Shield refueling missions as the military buildup in Saudi Arabia continued. We scrambled as an alert tanker to support the evacuation of U.S. Department of State workers in Mogadishu as the city fell to rebel soldiers. Our task was to refuel an AC-130 gunship off the coast of Somalia as it provided air support during the evacuation.

Taking off at 3 a.m., we flew 1,700 miles south from Oman in just under four hours to rendezvous with the gunship as the sun rose on January 4, 1991. The AC-130 had rapid-fire gun barrels and cannon protruding from its side, and it refueled at the very slow speed of 220 knots (roughly 250 miles per hour). In comparison, the relatively slow A-10 fighter refueled at 250 knots, but most of the other aircraft we refueled flew at 280 to 300 knots, so 220 knots seemed quite slow.

The heavily loaded AC-130 pulled up behind us at dawn to start the air refueling process, buts its pilot had difficulty closing the distance between us because the gunship could not penetrate the bow wave coming off our plane. The bow wave is a cushion of air between airplanes, and it requires a little extra power from the trailing aircraft to penetrate and proceed into the refueling position. The heavy AC-130 just couldn't generate enough power to break through this air cushion.

Their pilot asked us to slow to 210 knots, which we did. He soon asked for us to slow some more, so we slowed to 200 knots. We were so focused on helping the AC-130 get onto our refueling boom that we didn't realize we were now flying so slowly that we should have partially deployed our wings' trailing edge flaps. Doing so would create more lift and help to lower our nose closer to a horizontal, level attitude.

We finally realized that our deck angle was abnormally high, so we told the AC-130 pilot to maintain his distance while we deployed our flaps a few degrees and safely slowed to 200 knots. Once our plane slowed, we began a gradual descent, called a "toboggan" maneuver, which allowed the heavy AC-130 to use the descent to gain enough speed to complete its contact and receive the needed fuel.

With the refueling complete, the gunship peeled off to the west, toward Mogadishu. We stayed in the refueling orbit over water for four hours, monitoring the radios to keep abreast of the situation over the crumbling city.

Suddenly we heard the Navy Super Stallion helicopters, which had been sent from the USS Guam to retrieve the State Department workers, calling for air support from the AC-130. There was no reply from the gunship as the helicopters made repeated radio calls. After listening to the unanswered calls, I radioed the AC-130 on the same frequency. Because we were flying at 25,000 feet, much higher than the other low-flying helicopters and gunship, we could hear all of them, but they could not hear each other. I quickly became a radio relay between the two-ship helicopter flight and their gunship support.

The helicopter pilots painted a verbal picture of the situation in the city, saying there were roving patrols of rebels driving around the city in station wagons, with rifles sticking out of the windows. I thought about the dichotomy of our American airborne gunship bristling with cannons and machine-gun barrels, and this Somali "rebel gunship," probably a beat-up 1970s station wagon with AK-47s protruding from its windows. While Randy flew from the left seat, I relayed the position of the roving rebels to the AC-130 crew for them to lend their aerial support to the evacuation below.

By the end of the day, sixty-one State Department personnel were extracted from the U.S. Embassy compound by the two Navy Sea Stallion helicopters and safely evacuated to the USS Guam. Once the AC-130 completed its air support mission over the city, it returned to its air base in Kenya. We flew north late that afternoon, logging twelve hours and forty-five minutes of combat support time. For assisting in the safe evacuation of the State Department workers,

Randy's crew was awarded the Humanitarian Service Medal, and we all felt the immense gratification of being at the right place at the right time.

21
DESERT STORM

KC-10 taking off from Seeb Airport, Muscat, Oman

OUR TIME in the desert took place before cellphones, the internet, or email. I wrote and received a lot of letters, most to and from friends and family in the States, but others were exchanged with kind-hearted Americans writing letters addressed "To Any Serviceman."

These were pen-pal-type letters written by schoolchildren, military veterans, and even another David Dale that was of no relation to me.

Camp Nacirema had one telephone tent, with phones placed in wooden, cubicle-style booths. A camp member could sign up for a ten-minute time slot and call home collect. For me, the trick to holding down the cost was to call my family, give them my international phone number in Oman, and have them call me back quickly at the cheaper rate. I spoke to my mom in Houston on January 15, and I called my dad in Denver at 9:30 p.m. Oman time (10:30 a.m. in Colorado) on January 16. I spoke briefly to him, relaying my number, and hung up to wait for the callback. I sat by the phone for my allotted ten minutes, but it never rang.

Once my time slot closed, I headed back to my cot and off to sleep. Meanwhile, back in the States, my dad couldn't get the call to go through, so he called Karin in Louisiana. They figured out he was dialing the prefix "001" followed by the phone number, but that's for calls going to the States. He needed to dial "011" my number in Oman, but he didn't figure that out before I had gone to bed. Two hours later, the telephone tent was shut down for the next two weeks.

Sometime after midnight, Maj. Jan Swickard, our DO, stepped quietly into our tent of eight sleeping crew members and gently woke up Randy, Eric, Mike, and me. We had been chosen to fly our camp's first mission of Desert Storm. As we slipped on our flight suits and pulled on our boots, I quickly wrote what might have been a "last letter" to my wife and stuck it in my deployment bag. If anything were to happen to me during the war, at least Karin would find this farewell note.

Last Letter Home, January 16, 1991 (fortunately, never mailed)

My Dearest Karin,

This is it. Randy and I were just notified that we will be flying the first real mission in support of the offensive. Everyone has studied, and our crew is one of the best prepared here. Randy has read and asked a lot of questions about tactics. Mike has been a real positive influence on the crew with his "let's do it" attitude. Eric is a good boom operator who takes his job seriously in the air.

Randy and I proofed the flight plans for the operations folks and pointed out pretty useful corrections. Except for our wedding day and the birth of Daniel, this has been one of the most important times of my life. I've been able to make real contributions at a time when they really count.

I'm so sorry we're not together. I honestly have not had a single day in the last forty-nine days when I have not thought of you and our great son Daniel. No matter how mad I've ever gotten at you in the last six years, you have always been one of the most beautiful women I've ever met. I thank you for the fantastic support you've given me, especially in the tough times. Our year at UPT seemed to be our best.
I hope Daniel continues to grow big and strong. He is the pride of our lives. Tell him I LOVE HIM more than anything in the world.

Take care always.
Love Forever,
David,
P.S. Mom, Dad, Lucy, Hannah, and Jack: I LOVE YOU ALL

We gathered in the operations tent for the mission briefing, then signed out the necessary communications gear, enabling our KC-10 radios to make and receive encrypted radio calls without the Iraqis listening in. We piled into the blue Air Force pickup truck and drove out to our waiting KC-10 to begin the preflight. In our rush to get moving, we forgot our bag of protective chemical warfare gear, which would be needed if we returned to a base that had received a chemical attack while we were gone, which was a real possibility. The supervisor of flying, or SOF, quickly brought us the large, green canvas bag of gas masks, black rubber gloves, and green rubber boots.

We took off in the dead of night, heading northwest to refuel F-15s from the 1st Fighter Wing, deployed from Langley Air Force Base in Virginia. Our mission that night lasted seven-and-a-half hours and was all accomplished in radio silence. Other than checking in with the E-3A AWACS providing air traffic control in the sky that night, it was pretty quiet on the radios. The F-15s provided a combat air patrol (CAP), a protective air cover to the warfighters in the desert below. Like hummingbirds returning to a feeder, the four fighter jets came to us two at a time throughout our mission as we orbited in a left-hand, thirty-mile racetrack pattern over northern Saudi Arabia.

Back in the States, Karin went out for pizza with our neighbor, Air Force 1st Lt. Connie Hutchinson. Her husband, 1st Lt. David Hutchinson, was deployed to Lajes Air Base in the Azores with Barksdale's KC-135 squadron. His tanker helped refuel seven Barksdale B-52s that began the bombing campaign of Desert Storm. On their thirty-five-hour, round-trip mission out of Barksdale, those bombers decimated the Iraqi command-and-control centers with air-launched cruise missiles as the war began. The B-52 mission was well underway as Karin and Connie waited for their pizza that evening, the television on the wall relaying news reports of the war beginning. Karin knew at that point I wouldn't be coming home anytime soon. She didn't break into tears and wasn't frightened, but she also knew this was serious, mostly because so much was unknown. She got home in time to talk to my dad about his unsuccessful phone call to me.

By the time Randy and I landed at sunrise in Oman, we weren't really certain that the war had actually begun. We completed our mission debrief with the intelligence officer (nothing significant to report, other than our successful refueling of the F-15s) and turned in our classified communications gear. We then headed to the TV tent to watch CNN's coverage of the beginning of Operation Desert Storm. Like everyone in the States, we watched the reports from Bernard Shaw and Wolf Blitzer, showing the snaking green anti-aircraft tracers arcing over Baghdad, something we would eventually see ourselves. For now, it was time for breakfast—and sleep.

Two missions later, on January 19, there was a miscommunication in the tasking order. Our crew briefing stated that our KC-10 would take off as the fifth tanker behind four of our base's KC-135s. This five-ship tanker package was scheduled to refuel a large number of F-16s before and after their bombing missions. Our mission was referred to officially as "pre-strike and post-strike refueling." Before we departed for our aircraft, word came down that the mission was canceled. The four KC-135s remained on the ground, and our KC-10 was directed to take off and head to an orbit to serve as a back-up tanker. We were on station in case anyone needed emergency refueling.

We arrived on station in the daylight in an area just south of the Kuwaiti border and took up our racetrack pattern of left-hand turns. All was very quiet again on the radios, when suddenly Randy looked over his left shoulder and said, "I have four F-16s closing on our wing."

I looked out my window and said, "I've got four on the right."

Eric, our boom operator, looked out his large window in the bottom of the plane, below the tail, and called out, "I've got eight back here!"

Without warning, our flying gas station was swarmed by sixteen F-16s that had just released their bombs over Kuwait. They came screaming southbound out of the combat area and were now low on fuel. The leader of each four-ship flight prioritized his receivers according to lowest fuel state, and Eric began quickly plugging his boom into the receptacles of the thirsty fighters over the next twenty-two minutes.

I radioed AWACS and said we needed other tanker support in this area, and they quickly vectored other tankers our way. In all, Eric refueled fourteen of the sixteen F-16s, giving them each 1,000 pounds of fuel, or about 150 gallons, in just fifteen seconds per airplane. Two of the sixteen couldn't wait any longer and diverted to another tanker or a nearby runway below us.

It was later determined that only the pre-strike portion of the refueling mission should have been canceled. The strike package of four F-16 four-ship flights either took off with enough fuel to get to their targets, or they refueled from other tankers. Our five-ship tanker package should have been on station for the post-strike refueling. Fortunately, Eric managed to handle most of it by himself. Those fighter pilots were thankful that our boom operator performed so well under pressure.

Me (center), watching Capt. Kirk Shepherd (right) load flight gear and meals ready to eat (MREs) for an upcoming mission. Our intelligence officer is pictured to the left.

Our missions were pretty evenly split between refueling Navy fighters off the eastern coast of Kuwait and refueling Air Force jets south of Kuwait. In an impressive demonstration of the firepower the United States could muster, our crew typically would be one of three KC-10s, flying one mile behind each other, and each plane 500 feet above the preceding tanker. Alongside each KC-10 were eight Navy fighters, four on each wing. The strike packages consisted of F-18s, F-14s, and A-6s. Each KC-10 topped off their eight "chicks" before the entire strike package peeled off northwest toward Kuwait, and then we would await their return.

The Iraqi Air Force soon realized their outdated, Russian-made MiG fighters were outmatched by our F-15s and F-16s, and they began to flee to Iran in the hope of surviving the war. To prevent their escape, we began escorting F-15s deep inside Iraq, where they would chase down the fleeing MiGs. Again, our crew was selected for the first refueling mission into enemy-controlled Iraq.

We were the lead tanker of a two-ship KC-10 flight assigned to refuel four F-15s. As we crossed north into Iraq, we turned off all our external lighting, per our mission directive, so the enemy ground forces 30,000 feet below us couldn't see us. Everything was done in radio silence, with the fighters easing up alongside us in the pitch-black sky.

Ninety miles south of Baghdad, we could see the red anti-aircraft tracers snaking up in four wavy columns into the sky below us but burning out before reaching our altitude. Two interesting facts about tracers: Although depicted on CNN's night-vision cameras as green, they were actually red. And although the tracer rounds burn out at 20,000 feet, the bullets fired as part of the AAA gun burst continue climbing much higher. We were blissfully ignorant of this, not realizing the bullets came much closer to us than the tracers ever did.

Why were we seeing anti-aircraft fire below us? I got my answer as we went into a left U-turn and saw that the second tanker in our formation still had its red anti-collision beacon flashing. It's the same light people see in the night sky as airliners pass overhead. I couldn't believe it.

"Kill your beacon!" I yelled to the second tanker over our interplane formation frequency.

Night missions afforded what I called the "light show" below us in Kuwait. We saw the series of bomb flashes go off as B-52s and coalition fighter-bombers dropped their ordnance on the Iraqi Republican Guard. Many of us in the KC-10 had previously flown the B-52, and although we were happy to be flying the modern KC-10, we also felt nostalgic and missed performing the combat bombing operations for which we had trained.

This five-week air campaign was meant to reduce the Iraqi ground forces before our army moved north. On daytime missions, we could see what looked like long, clawing scratch marks on the Saudi desert floor, as massive amounts of allied tanks and armored fighting vehicles moved into place along the southern Kuwaiti border.

The Army had long-range artillery, known as the M270 Multiple Launch Rocket System (MLRS), and these were fired using either a long-range, low-altitude profile, or a short-range, high-altitude profile. We encountered the latter. After completing our assigned refueling west of Kuwait, our flight plan called for a southbound leg before turning eastward toward Oman. It was a quiet night, and we thought we'd take a shortcut southeast, skirting the border of Kuwait. Our cockpit suddenly lit up as a stream of MLRS missiles came screaming up toward the left side of our cockpit. The only words I could manage were, "Whoa! Whoa! Whoa!" as I pointed across the cockpit to the rising tower of flames. I'm certain the rockets were miles from us, but in a pitch-black sky they certainly looked uncomfortably close. We turned to the right and back to our proper southerly course.

Our base continued these F-15 refueling missions into Iraq for three more nights. We soon realized it's not a good idea to fly the same combat support mission in the same area night after night, because eventually the enemy will detect a pattern. On the fourth evening, a crew was refueling on a partly cloudy night when, suddenly, the clouds around them lit up as bright as day. An enemy surface-to-air missile had been launched and flew through the tanker formation, but fortunately no one was hit. That ended the series of refuelings over Iraq.

The threat came not only from the enemy, though. In the densely packed combat airspace, mid-air collisions were a real danger. One cloudy night we were assigned a Navy refueling mission over the Persian Gulf, refueling eight F-14s that were providing air protection to the carrier fleet below. Our assigned altitude of 25,000 feet was still in the thick of the clouds. The Navy has a smaller version of our Air Force AWACS, called the E-2 Hawkeye, with its own smaller spinning radar. Their mission was to provide air-traffic guidance to the planes in their area. I called the Hawkeye and requested a climb to 27,000 feet to get above the cloud layer so the F-14s could pick us up visually to refuel.

We completed our first set of night refuelings as we skimmed in and out of the top layer of clouds. I started to hear a whining sound from the right, so I looked out my window in time to see a KC-135 pop out of the clouds and zoom right over our cockpit, missing us by 500 feet. I knew it was close when I heard it before I saw it.

I shouted at the E-2, "Who just came through our area?"

He replied, "I'm not painting any targets in your area."

I yelled back, "Well, we almost just got hit!"

Another tanker crew had apparently thought it was a good idea to take a shortcut home.

The support we received from home during Desert Storm was phenomenal. Total strangers and schoolchildren continued mailing us letters by the stack. Organizations big and small sent us care packages, along with a supply of current magazines for our camp's recreation center. Our refueling missions lasted up to eight hours, so I often grabbed a magazine to read on the one-hour return leg home after things calmed down. Before one evening's sortie, I spied a recent issue of *Skin Diver* magazine and threw it in my helmet bag, telling Randy I'd show him an advertisement in it later.

My childhood friend, Larry Leonard, now lived in the Cayman Islands and was the marketing director for a dive shop called Parrots Landing. Larry had finished college during a recession, so he answered a job ad in 1988 for a bartender in the Cayman Islands. His whole family was scuba certified, and now he could bartend at night and dive during the day.

His bartending work had run its course by 1990, though, so with the help of his future wife, Shelley, Larry met Greg Merren, the owner of the Parrots Landing dive shop. Greg was in need of a marketing guy, and Larry was itching to use his business degree and entrepreneurial skills for this small business. Larry realized that the way to fill dive boats was to sell dive packages, so he created one-stop shopping for hotels, airfare, and diving, using a new-at-the-time innovation called the internet. Over the next several years, Parrots Landing grew from a single boat to a fleet of seven offshore diving boats.

To gain exposure, Larry placed advertisements in *Skin Diver* magazine, and I brought along this latest issue to show my crew a small ad for Parrots Landing—and to brag about my friend.

With our refueling complete, we turned southeast for Oman, and I dug the magazine out from my helmet bag. I flipped through the pages, searching for the dive shop advertisement, when I suddenly saw a picture of Larry with a parrot on his shoulder. I couldn't believe it! A random issue of *Skin Diver* that I grabbed from a stack of magazines in Oman had a three-page article about Parrots Landing and its pioneering marketing director, Larry Leonard. The world just kept getting smaller.

One month after the air war began, I completed my twentieth combat support mission on February 16, 1991, during a flight that demonstrated the versatility of our "Big Sexy" KC-10. We were tasked to refuel Navy F-14s and F-18s from the USS America off the coast of Kuwait, and one of my duties as copilot was to monitor several radio frequencies, including an emergency air refueling (A/R) frequency in case there was an urgent need for fuel.

As we continued to refuel the Navy using our hose-and-drogue system, I heard a call on the emergency frequency: "Any tanker! Any tanker!"

I answered the call and discovered it was an F-16 desperate for fuel. He was part of a two-ship hunter/killer F-16 flight, where one wingman would remain at high altitude to spot enemy targets, then guide his wingman down to the target for the kill. The fighters had gotten so wrapped up in their mission that this pilot was now dangerously low on fuel. He asked if we had a boom or a drogue on this mission, since the KC-135 could do one or the other, but not both. I told him, "We're a KC-10. We have both. Come on up."

I gave the F-16s our location and told them we were currently refueling Navy fighters, but they could join our formation. Randy then told the Navy receivers that the F-16s would be joining up soon. I was able to snap a photo of three jets on our wing: two Air Force F-16s, and one Navy F-14. It had to be a pretty cool sight for both services to watch as Eric reeled in the hose and lowered the boom to complete the impromptu Air Force refueling. The F-16s thanked us for the fuel and resumed their mission over Kuwait. As I monitored the refueling frequency, I heard him say, "Hey, if anyone needs gas, there's a real friendly KC-10 off the coast."

Refueling Air Force F-16s and Navy F-14s on the same mission. "Flexibility is the Key to Airpower!"

After thirty days of nearly continuous flying, our crew hit the safe maximum flying hour limit of 150 hours in thirty days. Additionally, our KC-10s still had to undergo routine scheduled maintenance back in the States to maintain FAA certification. Many of these checks had been delayed as long as possible, but the planes still needed to be swapped out. Our base used a first-in, first-out (FIFO) schedule, so Kirk's crew departed a week earlier than our crew, which would be next to head home. Without the ability to fly KC-10 missions because of our excessive flight hours, I decided to go on a "joyride," flying a wartime air refueling mission with a KC-135 crew from our base. That almost didn't end well.

The KC-135 crew made their way up to their assigned Persian Gulf orbit to refuel Navy A-6s with the small hose-and-drogue assembly attached to their boom nozzle, dangling very much like an elephant's trunk. I followed their boom operator back to his station, and we laid on our stomachs, each on a thin bed mattress, our chins resting on a support and looking out of the small, rectangular window. An A-6 appeared from below in the night sky and closed toward the drogue basket. I don't know if the naval aviator was excited or nervous, but he closed at a high rate of speed, undershot the basket, then continued to close on us as the boom operator commanded the emergency procedure: "Break away! Break away! Break away!"

This is the standard command during a botched refueling attempt. The tanker accelerates up and away from the receiver, while at the same time the receiver pulls power and dives below to avoid a collision. Given this A-6 pilot's momentum, the round, bulbous gray nose of his plane rose toward our glass window like a SeaWorld Shamu coming up for a herring treat, and the boom operator and I both backed up as far as we could in the cramped refueling station. Much like the quote from the character Nick "Goose" Bradshaw in *Top Gun,* I could just hear the military telling my wife and mom, "The Defense Department regrets to inform you that your loved one is dead because he was stupid, joyriding in a KC-135 during wartime." Fortunately, the A-6 didn't hit us, and I returned to the base to prepare for the homeward journey.

We landed at Barksdale on the night of February 21, 1991, after an overnight stop in Mildenhall, England. We were home again after eighty-five days of living in the tent city. In total, I completed thirty combat support missions: ten during Desert Shield, and twenty during Desert Storm. On February 27, I rocked our eighteen-month-old son in my lap and listened to President George H. W. Bush tell our nation that the Iraqi forces had surrendered.

Daniel, far right, on the night I returned from Operation Desert Storm.

22

COVERING ALL OF MY BASES

BY MAY 1991, after a long-range mission to Saudi Arabia and back, returning F-117 stealth fighters to Tonopah Air Base, Nevada, I had accumulated the required 1,200 flying hours to enter the aircraft commander upgrade course. All the trips to the desert had accelerated every copilot's upgrade that year. Air Force flight crews typically flew 300 to 400 hours per year, which is much lower than an airline pilot's usual total of 800 to 900 hours per year. I closed out 1991 with 550 flying hours.

Rather than rush into an upgrade course, I swapped with a squadron friend for his fall date and enjoyed a summer vacation and family reunion with my entire family on Table Rock Lake in the Ozarks, showing I sometimes was capable of putting my family first. I entered the upgrade program in September 1991, beginning with a brief academic overview of the KC-10's system and a series of seven simulator sessions. The academics portion was similar to my initial qualification training two years earlier. In 1989 I had absorbed the information, but it was mostly rote memorization and theoretical knowledge. Now I had two years of applying that knowledge, so studying it all a second time really made the details more understandable. I envisioned the knowledge sinking deeper, and not just bouncing off my Teflon brain.

During the four weeks of simulator training, I was paired with another upgrade candidate, Capt. Drexel Kleber, who we all called "Drex." He was a tall young man, with thick, black hair, and I remember him as a nice family man. He shared that he and his wife made it a point to get a baby-sitter once a week and go out on a date. Karin and I took his advice to heart years later, intentionally setting aside time for the two of us without our children.

The hardest part of the upgrade training was physically transitioning from the right seat to the left and retraining my brain to do everything with the opposite hand. It's comparable to the mental gymnastics of an American renting a British car with a stick shift, where the American driver must adapt to driving with the right hand and shifting with the left hand. My transition became a bit of a "rub my stomach and pat my head" exercise for the first few simulator sessions.

Once my brain adjusted to the new control inputs, I began the most physically challenging portion of KC-10 flying: receiver refueling. As a copilot, I was never expected to take on the fuel behind a tanker, but we did practice from the right seat to get used to making the very slight control and throttle inputs required to remain in position. Now it was my responsibility to get into the contact position and stay thirty feet behind the KC-135 or KC-10 as the fuel was transferred into our plane. Although almost everyone mastered this mission capability, the inability to complete the receiver refueling portion of training was grounds for disqualification, and it could potentially lead to a permanent assignment as a "first pilot" in the right seat.

The high-fidelity, full-motion simulator at each KC-10 base featured four hydraulic arms lifting a large white box that contained a life-sized replica of the KC-10 cockpit. It included a viewscreen to project a realistic depiction of the sky and ground, and the training provided extremely realistic scenarios in how to handle KC-10 emergencies, both on the ground and in the air. Although we practiced the normal procedures for our role as both the tanker and the receiver in a refueling situation, the primary focus during each four-hour session was practicing our emergency procedures.

The week of simulator sessions culminated with a stressful two-day evaluation, with each session lasting four hours. During the first four-hour session, I served as Drex's copilot as he handled a loss of electrical generators and a high-speed engine failure on takeoff, requiring that the takeoff continue with one engine inoperative. Drex did a great job performing the required maneuvers and managing the emergency situations.

The second day was my turn in the hot seat. After performing our role as both tanker and receiver, it was time for our evaluator to play "dial-a-disaster." My emergency scenarios (not all at one time) consisted of a dual hydraulic system failure, losing two of our three systems; another high-speed engine failure on takeoff without the ability to abort; and an engine fire at altitude, with a return to the runway with one engine out.

The concentration required was intense throughout the entire session, because I knew my every move and decision was being watched by an evaluator sitting just three feet behind us. After four pressure-packed hours, the simulator box gently settled down on its hydraulic arms as the full-motion sim became still and quiet. I felt a wave of relief, knowing the evaluation was finally over. Our evaluator for both sessions, the chief of the evaluation branch, complimented both of our performances during his one-hour debrief.

With the simulator evaluation completed, it was time to return to the flight line and receive actual refueling practice. I spent the month of October logging six training missions and refueling behind the KC-135 and KC-10. The two most challenging refueling activities were refueling at night behind a KC-135, and receiving my heavyweight onload of 150,000 pounds of fuel behind another KC-10. The KC-10 could carry more fuel (340,000 pounds) than a KC-135 even weighed.

On October 15, 1991, I flew my fourth pilot upgrade (PUP) training flight, a seven-hour sortie that included night refueling over Oklahoma. Up ahead of us, four lights danced in the ink-black night sky: one of them—a red, rotating beacon—pulsed rhythmically, while three small white position lights formed a perfect triangle just above the red beacon. The lights seemed to float in space, drawing us in like a June bug to a porchlight. I was flying a thousand feet below the still-invisible KC-135R, and one mile behind. From that trailing position, I pushed the three KC-10 throttles with my right hand, adding power to climb an uphill slope of 100 feet for each tenth of a mile. From a half-mile behind and 500 feet below, the gray tanker loomed into view, and the roar of its four large CFM56 engines could now be heard.

With my left hand on the control yoke and my right on the three throttles, my hands began to sweat inside my green Nomex flight gloves. The cloth gloves included a small patch of gray leather for the fingers and palms, like the tracing of a ten-year-old's hand, which provided enough traction despite my nervous sweat. I eased the throttles back gently about two inches, stopping the escalator-like ascent to the refueling position. I was now in the pre-contact position, just fifty feet away from the tip of the boom's nozzle, which was pointing at me with a white light, almost like a policeman's flashlight in my front windscreen.

Eighty feet farther ahead, just below the boom attachment point, I could see the face of the KC-135 boom operator through his wide, rectangular window. His face was illuminated by a soft red light inside his boom pod. Inside the tanker, the young airman lay face down on a thin, narrow mattress, his chin resting in a tiny, padded, T-shaped support, taking the strain off his neck. In his left and right hands, he gripped two small black control sticks for the "flyable boom" dangling between us. With his right hand, he controlled the movements of the twenty-eight-foot-long boom. With his left, he could extend the telescoping boom to place it inside our rooftop receptacle once I arrived at the correct position.

I stopped my closure rate and now matched the tanker's speed of 480 miles per hour, or eight miles per minute. From the pre-contact position, I pushed the transmit button near my left index finger and said, "Cajun 2-1. Stable, pre-contact."

"Cajun 2-1, Bolt 3-3," came the reply from the boom operator. "You're cleared to contact."

"Copy," I answered. "Cleared to contact."

I squeezed the three throttles to move them forward a fraction of an inch.

The tip of his boom passed over our cockpit, and the rush of the outside air grew louder as we crept slowly toward the refueling position. The telescoping portion was like the white stick poking from a tire pressure gauge. It could extend from the boom housing and had a "sweet spot" of twelve feet of extension, which meant that I would be sitting about forty feet from the boom operator in the plane ahead of me, but the boom could maintain a contact from as close as eight feet of extension and out to sixteen feet. It also could safely swing left and right eight degrees in each direction. Ideally, the boom dangled at a thirty-degree angle, but could rise up to a twenty-two-degree angle or drop down to forty-five degrees. This was my box of airspace, and it was my job to stay inside that box.

The air rushing over the KC-135's wing spilled downward and encountered the large, blunt nose of our heavy KC-10, creating a bow wave that preceded us and pushed on the tail of the tanker flying above us. I closed in toward the center of the refueling envelope when I suddenly saw the nose of the KC-135 dip down, his fuselage growing larger in our windscreen. His antiquated autopilot was unable to keep up with the changing trim conditions caused by our bow wave and abruptly kicked off.

"Break away! Break away! Break away!" the young boom yelled over the radio, as he recognized that his plane was descending into our huge airplane just outside his window.

I snatched the three throttles back to idle and pushed my yoke forward, beginning an immediate, collision-avoiding descent. Simultaneously, the KC-135 pilot aggressively pushed the power up on his four large engines as he grabbed his yoke and pulled back to climb away from us.

Once we were safely separated below him and drifting aft, I added power to stabilize my position. The KC-135R returned to its assigned refueling altitude of 30,000 feet, and I climbed back to the pre-contact position for another attempt. Such was the thrill of night refueling behind a KC-135R. I really didn't care for it very much.

Refueling behind the KC-135 could be nerve-wracking, but I completed the three KC-135 refuelings of the training syllabus without any problems. I always remained leery approaching the old tanker, not trusting its autopilot to behave. I much preferred refueling behind another, more stable KC-10, and I believe most of my fellow pilots felt the same way.

The heavyweight onload refueling behind a KC-10 was especially challenging because of the long duration of formation flying. It required staying in position for more than twenty-five minutes as the tanker offloaded 23,000 gallons of jet fuel at 900 gallons per minute. This was a true confidence-booster for me to be able to match the other jet's speed and turns for the duration of a TV sitcom. I now knew I could successfully accomplish any overseas airlift mission and not have to divert for lack of fuel.

I passed my aircraft commander flight evaluation on November 4, leading a two-ship formation of KC-10s, then refueling behind a KC-135 for fifteen minutes. The tanker portion involved conducting slow-speed refueling for a C-130, just as I had done as a copilot the previous year off the coast of Somalia. I felt relief and pride as the evaluator closed out my evaluation report, noting, "Captain Dale demonstrated excellent aircraft commander abilities during this complex mission."

There are many milestones throughout a pilot's career, but upgrading to aircraft commander (AC) is a pivotal moment. Our military stresses two factors: leadership and mission accomplishment. I was now entrusted to be the *leader* of my own KC-10 crew, capable of fulfilling our worldwide Air Force *mission*: moving troops, hauling vital military equipment, or escorting fighters and bombers via air refueling to any combat zone around the world in less than twenty-four hours. I thrived on that sense of mission accomplishment. Service members don't earn a lot of money, but they enjoy the gratification of accomplishing a challenging task.

On the evening of November 6, I commanded my first training mission as an AC with a slightly unusual crew complement. In addition to my flight engineer and boom operator, my copilot was a designated squadron safety officer who conducted quarterly briefings on safe aviation principles. As we briefed our nighttime local training sortie, I learned that both the hospital's flight surgeon and the base chaplain needed to log their required quarterly flights and asked to come along. There was certainly no harm in that.

As we proceeded to the flight line for our scheduled five-hour night mission, I was certain I was covered for all eventualities. I had alongside me a safety officer if a mishap occurred, a flight surgeon if it involved injuries, and a chaplain if things really took a turn for the worse. I wondered if all new aircraft commanders were sent out the door in this fashion.

23
TESTIMONY

Shelby Marie's christening, 1993

NEITHER OF OUR children were much for on-time arrivals. Both were due in May, but three years apart. Daniel arrived at 12:30 a.m. on June 1, 1989, and raising him was challenging for us as young parents. He was a colicky baby, battling reflux, breathing issues, and an occasional fever, sometimes as high as 104 degrees.

Shelby greeted us bright and early on April 25, 1992, and with her we completed our son-and-daughter set. Ten days after she was born, we set out with squadron friends, Capt. Scott Mitchell and his wife, Caroline, for a Shreveport Captains minor-league baseball game. We had our newborn daughter with us, wrapped in a blanket, and we coincidentally saw our pediatrician in the stands that night, too.

On Friday morning, May 8, Scott and I, now both aircraft commanders, set off for a weeklong Pacific cargo and refueling mission with our copilot, Capt. Stu Archer. All three of us had begun our careers in the same B-52 squadron: Scott was a copilot, and Stu and I were navigators in the 62nd Bomb Squadron. We now were on a long-range mission that required three pilots (called an augmented crew), enabling us to work up to twenty hours per duty day. The usual two-pilot duty day limit was sixteen hours.

Our first stop was Travis Air Force Base, fifty miles northeast of San Francisco, to upload cargo bound for Hawaii, Japan, and South Korea. From there, we proceeded to Hickam Air Force Base in Hawaii, carrying sixty passengers and 50,000 pounds of cargo. Upon arrival, military airlift crews always checked in with the military airlift command (MAC) command post—often referred to as "Mother MAC"—to see if there were changes to the mission. When we checked in, I was told to call home. This was still in the days before cellphones and email, so important communications could sometimes be really slow.

Before I took off from Hawaii the following morning, I called Karin and found out what the message was all about: She was in the hospital with our two-week-old daughter. Hours earlier, while I was sleeping, Karin had taken Shelby to see our off-base pediatrician because our baby had a fever of 102. (This was the same doctor who was at the ballgame with us just a few nights earlier.) The doctor, alarmed at the high fever in our newborn, quickly admitted Shelby into the hospital, and Karin stayed with her.

The "wives' network" of caring military spouses at Barksdale immediately sprang into action, looking after our three-year-old son until my mother-in-law arrived. When I asked if I needed to come home, Karin said she didn't think so but would keep me updated.

We aviators try to compartmentalize our feelings during a flight, having been taught to leave our problems on the ground. Our job is to focus on the mission at hand and not be distracted by what might be going on with our family or friends back home, so when we share stories with non-aviators, some of them might wonder about our feelings during a given situation. While we aren't robots, we may tend to be a bit emotionally "dead" about concerns for others, or whether a situation should make us freak out. Panic doesn't do anybody any good. Besides just hand-flying skills, pilots learn about positive and negative behaviors and their effects in aviation. In addition to flying lessons, pilots also are taught to avoid distractions and "channelization," which is focusing on one item at the expense of many others. We strive not to fixate on any one instrument or thought, but to scan the cockpit continuously to ensure everything—heading, altitude, airspeed, engine performance—remains as it should.

The military knows there is a spectrum of focusing on the mission versus focusing on people. We have to balance which comes first: are we mission-oriented, or people-oriented? I'm a mission-oriented person, which may strike some as being callous. As the saying goes, "There is a time and place for everything," and I joined the military to carry out Air Force missions. Thankfully, I was surrounded by like-minded team members who enjoyed the satisfaction of getting the job done. With our focus on the flight ahead, Scott, Stu, and I departed Hawaii for Kadena Air Base in Okinawa, Japan, the next morning.

After a night's stay in Japan, we flew sixty-five passengers and more cargo to Osan Air Base in South Korea. Because Karin had reassured me that she didn't think things were that bad with Shelby, I joined the rest of my crew for some power shopping in the district adjacent to the base, where knockoff products were sold cheaply: Adidas and Nike tennis shoes for the guys, Gucci and Dooney & Bourke "duck purses" for our wives.

At this point, we were the farthest point west our trip would go, and I was 7,000 miles—and many hours—from home. That's when Shelby's condition worsened. By Monday morning she was having seizures, and her fever would not go down. It seemed her temperature rose the farther away I traveled. I called Karin from the pay phone in the visiting officers' quarters hallway, and through her tears she told me that Shelby was in the pediatric intensive care unit (PICU) at the Shreveport hospital. Daniel's colicky early years had been a challenge, but we realized this was even more serious. We were both very worried at this point.

The commander of our 32nd Air Refueling Squadron (32 ARS) was Lt. Col. Dennis Dolle, a great leader who I had known for a few years. He had been a major during the 1990-1991 Gulf War, and was assistant director of operations for our small deployed unit in Muscat, Oman. Since then, he had been promoted and given command of 32 ARS, leading one of the best air refueling squadrons.

Dennis and his wife, Suzanne, epitomized what a squadron commander and spouse should be, providing leadership, guidance, and loving care to the members of our squadron. Both served as our role models in the years to come, and both were at the hospital with Karin when I called. He asked Karin to let him talk to me, and in his usual low, calm voice, he spoke to me from halfway around the world.

"Dave, I think it's time to bring y'all home," he said.

Shelby's condition was pretty dire—perhaps a form of meningitis, but still unknown. Dennis assured me that his wife and the other wives were visiting Karin and Shelby at the hospital, while our neighbors, Heather and Joann, were helping my mother-in-law, Barbara, take care of Daniel. He then asked me to put Scott on the phone.

Given my daughter's serious condition, Dennis was concerned about my ability to concentrate during the remaining flights back to the States. He told Scott that I shouldn't fly, and to leave the remaining flying to him and our copilot, Stu. Scott hung up and relayed the commander's directive. I couldn't argue, because I knew Shelby's situation was serious, and there wasn't much I could do to help. That night, I went to bed praying for both Shelby and Karin, hoping the doctors would find an answer.

The crew continued the planned mission the following morning. Scott and Stu flew eastbound, refueling four F-15s en route to Elmendorf Air Force Base in Alaska. At first during the seven-hour flight I alternated between sitting in the red passenger seats just outside the cockpit and lying in one of the four bunks positioned just after of the passenger seats. I came to the realization, however, that being 6,000 miles from home and worried about my baby daughter left me with only one thing I could do: pray. Those prayers had a calming effect on me, and I was able to doze off a few times during the long flight.

Finally, though, I went to the cockpit and told Scott that it wasn't doing me any good to just sit in the back and dwell on the situation at home for what would be a nineteen-hour duty day. He agreed, and I started to rotate into one of the two pilot seats every few hours. As we approached Alaska, he radioed to ask how much cargo we needed to upload for our remaining flight to Louisiana. From overhead Shemya Air Force Base in Alaska, in the Aleutian Islands, he contacted the Elmendorf command post and told them we would like to spend minimum time on the ground, just uploading the required fuel for our next leg home. The command post said that was fine, since there wasn't any cargo scheduled to go with us, so we could "turn and burn" to Barksdale. Meanwhile, an unusual development was taking place at Barksdale.

Unrelatedly, both of our children's births occurred around the same time of some major events in our communist adversaries' countries. For Daniel, it had been the uprising in Tiananmen Square as he lay jaundiced in the Barksdale hospital on June 4, 1989. Shelby was born in April 1992, just after the Berlin Wall came down. Relations with Russia had warmed to the point that there was a visiting Russian Air Force IL-76 cargo plane parked on the Barksdale ramp, visible from Karin's maternity ward window.

One month earlier, in March, two Barksdale B-52s and a KC-10 visited a Russian air base for the first time ever. Now, in May 1992, Barksdale had welcomed two Russian Tupolev Tu-95 "Bear" bombers, an Antonov An-124 "Condor" transport, and fifty-eight Russian airmen. The Russian delegation was visiting our SAC base, home to the Cold War B-52s, KC-135s, and KC-10s. The Russians had been invited to attend SAC's annual bombing and navigation competition (Bomb Comp), which Barksdale played host to each year. Our Louisiana air base was officially closed to landing traffic during this international visit, but all of this was unknown to Scott, Stu, and me as we flew eastward toward Louisiana. Fortunately, once the Barksdale wing commander heard of Shelby's medical emergency, we were granted special permission to land.

The flight from Alaska to northern Louisiana took six hours, and I filled those hours with quiet time for prayer. Each time I prayed, I felt the Holy Spirit provide me with a sense of calm, keeping me from dwelling on negative possibilities. We landed at Barksdale and were directed to park not on our usual cargo ramp near our squadron, but on the old B-52 alert pad near the end of the runway.

Dennis immediately met our crew and released me from any crew duties, and I drove home as quickly as possible. I walked in the door to find Daniel and my mother-in-law having lunch. After giving him the baseball glove, I bought for him in South Korea, I joined Karin at the Shreveport hospital. We shared a long hug and sobbed a bit, then began alternating twelve-hour shifts watching over Shelby, who was now receiving phenobarbital for her mild seizures. Shelby was so tiny, and her pitiful cry so hoarse and scratchy, that it made my heart break.

I took the night shifts, mainly because I can't stand watching daytime television, and slept in a chair next to Shelby's bed. The nurses came in every two hours to check on her, sometimes waking her up from a sound sleep. After seventeen more days in the hospital, our daughter was released to recover at home.

One year later, Shelby was baptized, with Scott and Caroline Mitchell standing beside us as her godparents. She made a full recovery and grew to be a five-foot, ten-inch high school basketball and flag-football player. She's now a college athletic trainer, which combines her compassion for others and her love of sports.

Our family enjoyed a wonderful church life years later in Tampa, Florida, and on some Wednesday evenings a midweek service took place. Our pastor asked for everyone willing to share their testimony, and it was my prayerful Pacific trip that I recounted on one of those evenings. I've always reflected on that weeklong trip as Shelby's condition worsened—especially the nineteen-hour-long day from South Korea, to Alaska, to Louisiana—and my time spent in prayer. As I told my son years later, at some point in life we all may be brought to our knees and realize that, without control over a situation, all we can do is pray.

Scott Mitchell with one-year-old Shelby

24

SOUTHERN WATCH, THE NO-FLY ZONE

NO SOONER HAD Desert Storm ended in early 1991 than Saddam Hussein started making trouble again in his region of the Middle East. After overcoming a failed coup attempt, the Iraqi Air Force bombed, strafed, and gassed Shiite Muslims in southern Iraq. On April 5, 1991, the United Nations passed a resolution "to ensure that the human and political rights of all Iraqis are respected."

By the summer of 1992, it was obvious to leaders in the United States, and the United Kingdom, that Saddam had ignored this U.N. resolution. To prevent any further actions by the Iraqi air force, the United States, the United Kingdom, and France established two no-fly zones to keep Saddam's air force on the ground, stopping his aerial harassment. The northern no-fly zone was relatively small and protected the Kurds in northern Iraq, while the much larger southern no-fly zone protected the Shiites below the 32nd parallel in Iraq.

I was at home on a week's leave (vacation) on August 27, 1992, the official start date of Operation Southern Watch. A squadron scheduler and friend, Capt. Ricky Sobrino, called to ask, "Dave, I know you're on vacation, but we're leaving in twenty-four hours for a deployment to the desert. Want to go?"

"Yes, I do," I answered. "But let me talk to Karin."

"It's the standard, 'Pack your bags for sixty days,' and we'll tell you more in the squadron," he said before hanging up.

Like many of my military pilot friends, I wanted to go where the action was and take part in anything meaningful. I told Karin what was happening, and that I really wanted to be part of it. Admittedly, I volunteered for missions and trips away from home because I enjoyed the adventure, the sense of service, and the fulfillment of mission accomplishment. Back in 1987, on the day I finally found out I was going to Air Force pilot training, I told Karin, "I've wanted this since I was a teenager."

The truth was, I'd wanted it long before any desire to be married. So, yes, I happily said, "Send me," when the request came to fly off somewhere. I left Karin behind to deal with our children, the bills, and life. Perhaps that sounds selfish, and perhaps I got the better part of the deal, but you can't join the military and then say, "I don't want to participate." We made that decision together in 1984.

With her blessing, the next day I was in 32 ARS going through the mobility processing line. The KC-10 crews, in single file, walked down the line of tables in the building across the parking lot from our squadron. Our vaccination records were checked, and any required shots were given on the spot. I needed the dreaded typhoid shot, which made my arm so sore I could barely raise it for two days. The trick was to get the vaccination in the left arm; if given in the right, saluting was very painful, if not impossible.

The legal team was there to update any wills or powers of attorney, if necessary, and the chaplain sat at the last table, passing out little green New Testaments and asking how we were doing. Once the mobility processing line was complete, we carried our fifty-pound green canvas deployment bags to a pallet to be loaded onto one of four KC-10s departing that night. I wasn't piloting it, though; instead, I joined many other crew members in the seventy-five "red seats," which are designated for troop transport and located in the forward section of the KC-10.

We arrived in Abu Dhabi, United Arab Emirates, on August 28

and set up operations on Al Dhafra Air Base. This was a UAE air force base for Mirage fighter operations, as well as a helicopter training base. One hangar was made available for our operation, and we quickly got to work, clearing out unnecessary equipment. We then moved in pallets of our gear: large KC-10 wheels and tires, containers of oil, and maintenance kits, plus bottled water and meals ready to eat (known as MREs) to serve as our in-flight dining.

Sections of the hangar were divided into the necessary offices for the air operations staff and intelligence shop, where we would receive our classified preflight briefings from the intelligence officer. In an odd bit of irony, the intel office was cordoned off with a plywood door. On the door, a gruff, no-nonsense sergeant had misspelled, in thick, black permanent marker, *"OFFICAL BUSNESS ONLY."* Yes, our military intelligence office had two misspellings on their high-security plywood door.

My Southern Watch crew on the day Kreg Lukens pinned on captain bars. Sgt. Curt Hawn (FE), Col. Art Lichte (458 OG/CC), Capt. Kreg Lukens, me, and Senior Airman Jose "Hozer" Martinez

Having completed my upgrade to aircraft commander in November 1991, I now had my own four-person crew. My copilot was 1st Lt. Kreg Lukens, a very good pilot who came to the KC-10 as a second lieutenant three years earlier. He was scheduled to pin on his new rank of captain within a few weeks. Our flight engineer, Curt

Hawn, was a very quiet and reserved sergeant. At the other end of the spectrum (and the airplane, for that matter), was rock 'n' roll guitar-jamming Senior Airman Jose "Hozer" Martinez, our boom operator.

This short-notice deployment for an unknown amount of time to an austere airfield required immediate housing for our aircrews, since a tent city was not yet available at this location. In typical "Gucci Boy" fashion, as any other Air Force crew member can attest, it came as no surprise that our quarters was the twenty-one-story, high-rise Holiday Inn in downtown Abu Dhabi, complete with its own rooftop swimming pool. In an effort not to highlight our presence in the UAE, our group commander, Colonel Lichte, advised the crews to close the curtains of the buses they traveled in to and from the hotel.

This deployment was the epitome of "Gucci Boys in the Desert." The restaurant served any dish imaginable, including twenty-ounce Chateaubriand steaks and other culinary delights, all bought with our government meal allowances. One deployed member from the Air Force Reserve KC-10 squadron was a massive, olive-skinned Cajun boy named Pirough (pronounced "Peer-O"). When not serving as a boom operator in the Air Force, his day job included serving as a heavy equipment operator on construction sites in Louisiana. He was more at home in a sleeveless T-shirt and overalls than a flight suit. Pirough loved to order the Chateaubriand, and was dismayed when we told him it was meant to be shared by two people. He had no trouble finishing the softball-size steak by himself.

We never expected to be staying in a downtown hotel when we packed for this deployment. We assumed we'd be back in a desert tent city, so we had packed casual shorts and T-shirts to wear when not on flying duty. We discovered that Abu Dhabi was a very modernized city, complete with bars and restaurants. Additionally, on the first floor of the hotel was a convenience store, much like a 7-11, and it also housed a barbershop manned by three Pakistani barbers. For a three-dollar cab ride, a crew of four could run down to

JBJ's Bar and listen to live rock bands while drinking beer, but many of us hadn't packed the right clothes.

In a phone call to Karin, I told her what the city had to offer, and that we could buy a flat of two dozen eight-ounce soft drinks in the hotel store, "if only we had booze to make mixed drinks." One week later, another KC-10 arrived with more deployment supplies, as well as care packages from our families back home.

In my opinion, Karin earned "squadron wife of the year" honors by sending me a large box containing collared golf shirts, and a pair of khaki slacks rolled around a large gallon plastic bottle of Seagram's Seven. Now we were in business! I had clothes for downtown, and we could open a small bottle of Coca-Cola or 7-Up, add an ounce of whiskey, and walk around the hotel on our off-duty hours with a mixed drink. That's pretty Gucci, I have to admit.

A few days after our arrival, I decided it was time for a haircut, so I headed downstairs to the barbershop. My Pakistani barber didn't speak English, so I tried to communicate with him using sign language. I always kept my hair within regulation, never touching my ears or collar, but never as short as a Marine's high-and-tight haircut, so I held my finger and thumb a quarter-inch apart and told him, "Just cut off this much." Instead, that was all the hair he left me with after he finished. My blond hair, no longer parted on the left side, looked more like the fuzz on a white tennis ball. I told my friend Scott Mitchell, "I might as well stay here two months. I can't go home 'til this grows out!"

Our refueling missions began a few days later, on September 1, when we refueled an E-3 AWACS, just as I had done over Panama during Operation Just Cause, and also during Operation Desert Shield and Operation Desert Storm. We refueled a wide variety of U.S. and allied aircraft in support of the southern no-fly zone operation. Besides the AWACs, our Air Force customers over the next two months included the air-to-air F-15C Eagle, two-seat F-15E Strike Eagle fighter-bombers, air-to-air and air-to-ground F-16C Falcons,

EF-111 electronic jammer Ravens, RC-135 reconnaissance aircraft, and the F-4G "Wild Weasel" missile-killing Phantom.

The Navy receivers consisted of F-14 Tomcats, A-6 air-to-ground Intruders, EA-6 electronic jammer Prowlers, S-3 anti-shipping Vikings, and the versatile F-18 Hornet. Finally, from the allied coalition, we refueled French Mirage 2000s and British fighter-bomber Tornados, both of which used the same hose-and-drogue system that our Navy and Marine jets used.

Throughout the deployment, the four-person crews were paired off in rooms, with pilots (ACs and copilots) sharing one room, and the boom operator and flight engineer in another. Adjustments were made so that our female crew members (officers or enlisted) could share a room, regardless of their crew positions. On this deployment, we had a female pilot, Michelle, and boom operator, Vivian, that flew on the same crew and shared a room.

Kreg and I shared a two-twin-bed room, and on the early morning missions he would order a cappuccino from room service. On a particularly bleary-eyed 3 a.m. wake-up, often referred to as "oh-dark-thirty," I thought that his choice of beverage sounded like a good idea, so we both ordered double cappuccinos to give us a jolt. As a thirty-one-year-old, I was not yet a coffee drinker, and during the dark and quiet bus ride to the airport the caffeine kicked in on my empty stomach. I had the caffeine shakes for the rest of the morning—a totally new and unusual sensation for me—and I didn't know what to think or how to make them stop. I backed off the double cappuccinos after that.

Our round-the-clock operations continued for the next several weeks. Sometimes our free time was during daylight, so we'd head for the gym or the rooftop pool. Other times crew members had the night off and would head downtown by cab to the local bars, listening to the live bands from across Europe.

25
DEATH OF A FRIEND

Lt. Col. "Dub" Splawn, our deployment commander

MID-AFTERNOON ON SEPTEMBER 18, three weeks into the deployment, I was napping in the hotel room before our tenth mission later that night when Kreg came flying in the door, yelling, "Son of a bitch!"

"What happened?" I asked, startled.

"Ken Reed just died in a crash!" he shouted.

Since I was coming out of a sound sleep, I was confused, because one of our fellow deployed pilots in Abu Dhabi was named Jim Reed. I thought Kreg was telling me a KC-10 had just crashed.

"We lost a plane?" I asked as I jumped out of bed.

"No," he said. "Ken Reed crashed in a T-37 back in the States."

Capt. Ken Reed, a good friend of ours, was a Barksdale KC-10 copilot still back in the States with his family. He had been on a T-37 cross-country trip with another copilot, building up flying time in the ACE flying program back at Barksdale. Because the KC-10 is a non-combat aircraft, we weren't being fired upon by enemy forces, so Ken's death was one of the few times our KC-10 crews experienced the active-duty death of a close friend. At no point in my flying career have I thought, "*I'm going to die.*" It was a shocking reminder that the flying we enjoy and take for granted can be dangerous.

Another good friend, Capt. Lee "Ice" Icenhour, also was in Abu Dhabi and recalled that day, saying: "My mom called me in Abu Dhabi because my Shreveport neighbors, who lived three houses from Ken, had called her in North Carolina to let her know. I remember being down in the hotel lobby, getting ready to go fly, and seeing Ken's best friend, Capt. Greg Ray. He looked so lost. I knew he knew, too. When my crew showed up at the base for our mission, Dub (Lt. Col. "Dub" Splawn, our deployment commander) told us we didn't have to fly that day, but we did anyway."

Dub, our commander for this deployment, was a devout Christian and a very caring leader of his airmen. He posted a comforting letter the following morning notifying everyone of Ken's death, which read:

TO: All KC-10 Crew Members Deployed

On 18 September, Friday afternoon (Barksdale time), Capt. Ken Reed died in a T-37 accident. At times, we are brought uncomfortably close to death, and I am very much grieved by this tragic loss of a close friend. In truth, each of us are but one heartbeat, one breath away from death ourselves. Life is precious, but very fragile, and death is certain. However, there is hope even in the face of death.

It was about 0200 Saturday morning (UAE time) when I received the sad news of Ken's death. I grieved, but I am also comforted by the following scriptures:

"Lord, make me to know my end, and what is the extent of my days. Let me know how transient I am." (Psalm 39:4)
"My times are in Thy hand ... " (Psalm 31:15)
Ken, we'll miss you.

William J. "Dub" Splawn, Lieutenant Colonel, USAF
Commander

A few days later, Dub led a meaningful, somber memorial gathering in a hotel conference room for those of us deployed in the desert. We pulled our folding chairs together in a circle as he read passages from his Bible. After a moment of silence, we shared fond memories of life experiences with Ken—including his ability to crush a golf ball or softball—and we prayed for his young wife and little children. The reality of death was now very sobering. With the exception of Dub, all of us in the room were in our late twenties and early thirties, and Ken's death served to remind us that, regardless of what we previously thought, we are not invincible. Ken's memorial service in that quiet hotel conference room helped us process his death as we continued to fly our missions.

26
THE MISSION CONTINUES

ON SEPTEMBER 23 (Mom's birthday back home), we completed a five-hour night refueling of the intelligence-gathering RC-135, giving them 10,000 gallons of fuel. We returned to Al Dhafra Air Base to find the instrument approach system was out of service. This was not usually an issue, because the nice desert weather usually allowed for a visual approach to the landing runway. This air base did not have an approach control radar facility to help crews line up for a landing.

During flight operations around the world, there normally is a high-altitude controlling sector known as air route traffic control center, and then closer to an airport and below about 18,000 feet there is an approach controller using radar to sequence the planes to a runway for landing. Finally, the crews are handed off to the airport's tower controller for permission to land. In this area of the UAE, there was only the high sector center and the tower, but not a mid-altitude approach controller. Crews were cleared by the air traffic controller to the airfield, and it was up to the crew to establish themselves on the instrument approach in this non-radar environment.

On this particular night, in the days before GPS, there was not an instrument approach available for us to fly because the systems were down. Once we were cleared for a visual approach, I flew toward the runway, hoping we would see it. I descended as low as 1,000 feet, but the runway never came into view. I executed a go-around, adding power while retracting the landing gear and flaps, as we prepared for another landing attempt.

Although there was not a ground navigation aid in service, there were other KC-10s on the ramp undergoing preflight checks for their next mission. I radioed the supervisor of flying (SOF), who oversees ramp operations from a truck equipped with a UHF radio and asked if a KC-10 was powered up on the ground.

"Yes, there is," replied Lieutenant Colonel Splawn, who was serving as the SOF that night.

"Can you bring up their air-to-air TACAN frequency to channel 92?" I asked.

We dialed our TACAN to the inverse, selecting channel 29. This channel pairing gave us a distance and bearing to the plane parked near the runway.

I asked my crew, "Are y'all comfortable flying this as a TACAN approach?"

It would be an unauthorized, makeshift approach down to 400 feet above the ground in the hopes of getting below the cloud deck, but they all agreed that they were. By substituting the stationary KC-10's TACAN for the inoperative ground equipment, we flew the course to runway and broke out of the clouds at 500 feet above the ground and landed safely. This unconventional, ad-hoc instrument approach successfully completed our twelfth mission.

The Holiday Inn had a house-band from Poland, consisting of two women, Anna and Margaret, plus Robert on guitar. The band members performed 1980s rock music (Dire Straits, Fleetwood Mac, and Billy Idol, among others) each night in the hotel lounge, then spent each afternoon sunbathing by the rooftop pool. The aircrews that had a day off also could be found poolside, flirting with Anna and Margaret.

U.S. troops can sometimes develop a reputation of being "ugly

Americans" while serving overseas, and while our deployed crews were mostly respectful and well-mannered, I'll admit we did pretty much take over the hotel's rooftop swimming pool. Despite Colonel Lichte's directive upon arrival, our splashing, whooping, and hollering was not maintaining a low profile. We were just typical brash young Americans taking over a Holiday Inn swimming pool—but in the middle of a major desert city. We took the long blue-and-white nylon rope attached to the lifesaving ring and strung it across the pool to serve as a makeshift volleyball net. With a volleyball purchased from a downtown shop, our water volleyball tournament was born.

Our hotel not only housed American aircrews, but also the flight crews of international airlines, such as those from Singapore and Indonesia. Their crews also enjoyed the pool and joined our water volleyball games. One day, a young, overzealous Indonesian flight attendant went to spike the volleyball with his fist, but the ball careened off his wet knuckles, sailed over the twenty-foot cement wall surrounding the pool, and dropped twenty-one stories to the sidewalk below. Fortunately for all of us, nobody was hit or injured, but the young man had to perform the "walk of shame," riding the elevator down in his wet swimsuit to retrieve the ball from the street below. Undeterred by this little misfortune, the water volleyball tournaments continued.

Our twenty-third mission on October 15 showcased the versatility and capability of the KC-10. Our crew was the third in a three-ship "cell" tasked with refueling F-15C air-to-air fighters and F-15E Strike Eagle fighter-bombers. Other tankers launched with our three-ship tanker package that night, providing us with additional fuel for the eight-hour mission.

Before reaching our assigned refueling orbit in northern Saudi Arabia, I pulled up behind another KC-10 for a heavyweight refueling, just as I had accomplished in upgrade training. This night's mission began with me staying connected to their boom for thirty minutes as our fuel load increased up to 345,000 pounds, or 51,000 gallons. Our KC-10 now weighed 585,000 pounds, just 11,000 pounds shy of our maximum gross weight.

Once the fuel transfer was complete, we continued to our assigned refueling orbit, a large racetrack pattern with thirty-mile straightaways. Our formation leader guided us to our assigned refueling orbit and reported to AWACS that we were on station. My crew took up our position as third in the group. While the lead KC-10 flew at 28,000 feet, the second KC-10 took up a position 500 feet above and one mile aft of the lead KC-10. My crew flew at 29,000 feet, which was another 500 feet above the second KC-10 and one mile behind it. From this cell formation, our receiver fighters, often referred to as "chicks," could safely join the formation.

The fighter pairings arrived in groups of two or four, taking up a position on the left wing of their assigned tanker. Each fighter took turns sipping from our boom, then moved to our right wing once refueled, allowing another customer to take a drink. The formation of F-15Cs and F-15Es waited until everyone had their fill, then departed our formation off to the right. The aerial armada of tankers and fighter jets looked impressive from our "tail-end Charlie" vantage point.

We remained on station as the fighters returned throughout their nighttime no-fly-zone sortie. After offloading 130,000 pounds (20,000 gallons) of fuel, we were released by AWACS for our return to Al Dhafra Air Base. Although this mission was similar to those I had performed as a copilot during Desert Storm, this time I felt the gratification of mission accomplished as the aircraft commander.

On October 17, days before our deployment came to an end, the Holiday Inn was the site of a Romanian fashion show and dinner. Luckily, by including the "and dinner" portion on the ticket, we were able to use our government meal allowance to buy tickets for the event. This high-class affair was held in the hotel's marina club ballroom and was attended by well-dressed Abu Dhabi citizens. Guests included Middle Eastern men sporting white flowing robes, with red-and-white checkered turbans held in place by a coiled black rope.

Our steak dinner was top-notch, and the young Romanian models were gorgeous, in emerald-green, floral-patterned dresses, strutting down the middle of the ballroom along the catwalk dividing the two dozen tables. We Americans, wearing our polo shirts and slacks, were seated at two tables in the back corner.

Romanian fashion show "and dinner" in Abu Dhabi

It was a fitting way to close out this KC-10 deployment. In the previous two months, Kreg, Curt, Jose, and I enjoyed serving our country, flying twenty-five combat-support missions and logging 140 hours over the Arabian Peninsula. But deploying to Abu Dhabi was certainly not a hardship tour. The modern city treated us to such entertainment as jet boat races, televised on ESPN by low-flying helicopters for the folks back home. We were entertained nightly by either the hotel's Polish rock band or the local rock band at JBJ's Bar. Even our boom operator, Hozer, was invited to join them on lead guitar. After two months of desert flying, it was time to turn the operation over to another KC-10 unit.

Our crew departed Al Dhafra Air Base on October 23, stopping in Bahrain to pick up westbound Navy cargo, then proceeded to Naval Air Station Sigonella in southern Italy for the night. The next day we continued a Navy resupply mission, stopping in Rota, Spain, then spent the night in Lajes Field on the Azores islands in the Atlantic. We completed the trans-Atlantic trip, offloading the Navy's cargo at Norfolk Naval Air Station, Virginia, and arrived home in Louisiana on October 26. I now had the required amount of flying time and experience to upgrade to KC-10 instructor pilot.

Senior Airman Jose "Hozer" Martinez in his boom pod, on what must have been "casual Friday."

27

MOGADISHU, PART II

IN DECEMBER 1992 I entered the KC-10 instructor upgrade program, learning to instruct new pilots in the aircraft while performing landings or air refueling from either the right or the left seat. In the program, it becomes a coordination exercise to land and refuel from either seat while also providing instructions to the student in the opposite seat.

I completed my six instructor simulator sessions, with three in the left seat and three in the right. Just before Christmas 1992, Lt. Col. Dub Splawn, our commander during Southern Watch and the chief of our evaluation division, conducted my simulator evaluation, as my partner Greg and I demonstrated slow-speed air refueling for both A-10s and C-130s. I was home for the holidays, but my in-flight instructor training was interrupted by another trip to Mogadishu.

Our mission began on New Year's Eve 1992, flying from Barksdale to March Air Force Base in California. March, located sixty miles east of Los Angeles, was one of three KC-10 bases in the United States. After arriving, we joined the long list of KC-10 crews awaiting our airlift tasking to support Operation Restore Hope, the new international relief mission supporting U.S. humanitarian peacekeeping operations in Somalia after the country's government collapsed during a vicious civil war.

Instead of immediately heading downrange, our crew first was tasked with flying from southern California up to Travis Air Force Base near the Bay Area to retrieve more eastbound cargo. It was an evening flight on January 3, and I had time to watch my Houston Oilers take a commanding lead over the Buffalo Bills—the score was 28-3 by halftime. Houston's lead grew to 35-3 by the time we took off and headed north. Ninety minutes later, we landed at Travis, where I learned that my Oilers were the victims of the greatest comeback in NFL history, losing 41-38.

Once back at March, we resumed our place at the bottom of the list of crews heading eastward. On a foggy January 5 morning, our seven-man "augmented" crew consisting of three pilots, two flight engineers, and two boom operators departed from the base for a sixteen-hour flight to our staging base of Taif in Saudi Arabia. We were the last mission to depart the States for this "wagon train" of supplies heading for Mogadishu. The idea for this procedure was that once a crew arrived in the region and downloaded cargo, that aircrew would begin a rest period. When another plane arrived, the rested crew would then fly the newly arrived plane back to the States. The just-landed crew would then enter crew rest and wait for the next plane.

As we crossed over Kansas, I posed a question to my crew: "If we're the last KC-10 crew, and no one is following us, how will we get home?"

Nobody could think of an answer—so, using the UHF military radio, I contacted our Barksdale command post and was patched through to our squadron. Capt. Ricky Sobrino, the same pilot who told me about going to the UAE for Southern Watch, answered the phone. I posed the same question to Ricky, and he didn't have an answer.

"Well, don't forget about us," I said, and we continued eastward.

The long-range mission required three air refuelings over the United States, the Atlantic Ocean, and the Mediterranean Sea to make it to Taif, Saudi Arabia, near the Red Sea and Mecca. Long before we departed the States, Air Force mission planners drew up our flight routing and coordinated the refueling with KC-135 tankers based on the East Coast and in England to meet us over the Atlantic. Those tankers provided us with additional in-flight fuel for the seventeen-hour trip to the Arabian Peninsula. My crew was exhausted upon arrival at the rundown desert base of Taif. We spent the night in a dilapidated, condemned hotel, sleeping four to a room on old metal bunk beds with worn-out springs that sagged like a hammock.

On January 7, 1993, almost two years after my refueling of an AC-130 gunship off the coast of Somalia, we departed Taif for the three-hour flight to Mogadishu. The country was trying to rebuild after international troops, led by our Marines, helped the Somalis battle the warlords in an attempt to re-establish a stable society. Our missions took place at night, using the darkness and a lights-out configuration to avoid being detected by rebels in and around Mogadishu. It's not easy to disguise a 500,000-pound KC-10, but we took precautions to not announce our arrival. We landed at the Mogadishu Airport with 80,000 pounds of supplies to support Operation Restore Hope.

The runway was an eerie sight as we landed. Much like a scene from the movie *Apocalypse Now,* the runway was lined with fifty-five-gallon drums spewing smoke and flames. We touched down and taxied to our assigned parking spot—and once the door was open, the smell of the camp hit us. We learned that the flaming barrels were full of Marine shit from the camp's lavatory tents. That aromatic runway lighting system made our eyes sting.

We delivered our cargo and returned to Taif with eight Navy personnel who had been waiting for a ride home. The KC-10s originally belonged to Strategic Air Command (SAC), which, along with KC-135s and B-52s, focused on nuclear war during the Cold War.

During that time, cargo airlift operations were assigned to Military Airlift Command (MAC), using mostly the large C-141 and C-5 cargo planes from the 1960s and 1970s. Our KC-10 was a hybrid aircraft capable of delivering large quantities of both fuel and cargo, so we lived in a SAC/MAC world but played mostly by SAC rules.

With the fall of the Berlin Wall and the end of the Cold War, our Air Force reorganized into Air Combat Command (ACC) for all fighters and bombers, and Air Mobility Command (AMC) for all refueling and airlift airplanes. We now had to learn and live by the old MAC rules, as the new AMC largely adopted all of the old MAC policies and procedures at the outset. Fortunately, the flight engineers (FEs) on our KC-10s came from MAC airlifters and knew the rules of this airlift staging operation. My flight engineer said we were on "crew orders," and that enabled us to hitch a ride on any cargo plane transiting the area if there was space available.

On January 8, we tried this idea of hitching a ride out of Taif and boarded a C-130 leaving for Riyadh, Saudi Arabia. The seven of us deplaned in Riyadh, completely unexpected and unannounced, and asked their operations officer when the next flight to the States would be. He was bewildered to see us.

"I don't know who you are or what you think you're doing," he said, "but you need to get off this base ASAP."

We had stumbled into Riyadh just days before a major offensive operation against Saddam Hussein's belligerent forces, who had fired upon our patrolling fighter aircraft.

"You need to be on the next plane out of here," the lieutenant colonel told us, and we were—on a C-130, heading back to Taif.

Well, that idea didn't work!

Fortunately, on January 10 a massive C-5 Galaxy, commanded by one of my former Vance Air Force Base T-37 instructors, came through Taif. I asked Capt. Dave Armstrong, "Can we get a ride out of here with you?"

"You bet, Dave," he answered.

We took up our aft-facing seats in the upper aft level of the C-5 and headed northwest.

Eight months later, my crew traveled back to Mogadishu, this time bringing in the Army Rangers whose exploits became the focus of the movie *Black Hawk Down*.

28

1993 AIRLIFT RODEO

AIRLIFT RODEO IS an annual competition among the squadrons of AMC and our international allies, grading items such as cargo loading, aerial refueling, rendezvous timing, and taking on fuel in midair in an exact amount of time. It's a specifically designed competition for airlift and tanker aircraft to parallel ACC's William Tell Competition among F-16 and F-15 fighter squadrons, and Bomb Comp for squadrons flying B-52 and B-1 bombers.

Our 458th Operations Group commander, Col. Art Lichte, oversaw two active-duty squadrons, the 32 ARS and the 2 ARS. Colonel Lichte selected Capt. Will Nugent from the 2nd, and me from the 32nd, to pilot Barksdale's KC-10 rodeo team. We were joined by boom operators Scott Konieczka and Jeff Sidles, and a flight engineer.

The competition began with a precise, on-time arrival at Little Rock Air Force Base in Arkansas, the site of the June 1993 event. Crews flew an arc-to-radial instrument approach and had to touch down within five seconds of their assigned time slot or be penalized. Out of a complete 360-degree circle thirteen miles from the airfield, the planes only flew about a thirty-degree portion of that circle before joining the final approach, rolling out nine miles from the runway. The trick was to track the timing along the arc.

From my navigator days, I knew about the "Rule of Sixty," because everything in navigation revolves around that number. There are sixty nautical miles in a degree of longitude and latitude, and a compass measures 360 degrees, which is divisible by sixty. Because of this, tracking an aircraft's timing is easier if dealing with a multiple or divisor of sixty. So instead of flying the thirteen-mile arc, I proposed we deliberately fly a twelve-mile arc. Because sixty divided by twelve equals five, we covered one nautical mile in every five radials on the arc. Flying only one mile inside the prescribed arc still kept our airplane within the allowable tolerance for flying the arc-to-radial approach—and it made the math much simpler.

I plotted out the approach starting from our landing time at the runway and worked back along each mile of the approach to the point where we intercepted the arc. By precisely controlling our airspeed, I guided the KC-10 to each mile marker, making small airspeed adjustments to meet the next mark. The other competition pilot, Will, flew our KC-10 from the left seat as I navigated from the right.

During our training approaches at Barksdale, we had this system down to perfection, touching down within the first 3,000 feet of the runway exactly on time. On competition day, though, either I called for the turn to final approach too early or the shifting winds pushed us closer, because we were going to be ten seconds too early with only nine miles to touchdown. Will slowed our plane, and we configured it to a full fifty-degree flap landing to allow for the slowest possible approach speed. He then flew a series of S-turns to kill more time.

I don't think Colonel Lichte, Lieutenant Colonel Dolle and our other passengers in the back enjoyed that part of the flight. I checked my watch as we flew over the approach end of the runway and told Will to land long. Any landing outside the 3,000-foot touchdown zone was a disqualification, so as he glided down the runway, I watched for the 3,000-foot white painted marker stripes on the runway. With 200 feet of legal distance to go, I said, "Put it down," and we touched down five seconds early. Not bad, but not perfect.

Our competitors from Seymour Johnson Air Force Base in North Carolina were flying the newest KC-10s, which now were equipped with GPS. They relied on their newfangled gadget to guide them to the runway—and missed their mark by thirty seconds. Score one for the old B-52 navigator.

Our boom operators, Scott and Jeff, endured several busy days. They were scored on their ability to load 50,000 pounds of cargo, correctly and on time, plus offload the fuel during the aerial refueling competition. For practice, our team flew training cargo missions during the previous months, enabling Scott and Jeff to work with loading various cargo shipments. One of our April training flights was from Biggs Army Airfield, near El Paso, Texas, up to Elmendorf Air Force Base outside of Anchorage, Alaska. We landed in Elmendorf—and, as usual, Will and I made plans to check the weather forecast for the return flight and file the flight plan to get us back to Louisiana. I knew there was a Burger King on base, so I asked the boom operators and flight engineer if they wanted anything to eat.

Scott, in his typical dry humor, said, "Sure. Bring me a cold cheeseburger and a warm Coke."

I tilted my head and asked, "Why do you want that?"

He laughed, then said, "Because that's what you're going to bring me anyway."

We fulfilled his order.

Back at Little Rock during the rodeo competition, the loading portion didn't go as well as the two boom operators had hoped, and they were dinged a few points for their cargo load. We were now in third place going into the aerial refueling competition. This took place over two days, with the KC-10 crews graded on their ability to both give and receive fuel, with the twenty-minute refueling contact beginning exactly on time at the air refueling control point (ARCP).

There were six KC-10 teams in the competition, with one active duty and one reserve team from each of the three bases: Barksdale, Seymour Johnson, and March. For the refueling portion, we were paired with the March active-duty team, piloted by Capt. Milt Jordan and Capt. Mike Hindes. Milt and I knew each other because he had been based at our 32nd Air Refueling Squadron before moving to California. Like me, Milt also was a former navigator.

The competition was overseen by a KC-10 evaluator from March Air Force Base. The evaluator briefed all six teams on the rules of engagement, assigning the rendezvous times to each team and stating that the receiver had twenty minutes to take on the allotted fuel load. The weather forecast showed a small storm further up the northbound refueling track, which would become a factor once the tanker and receiver were in contact and beginning the fuel transfer.

I raised my hand and asked if random refueling was permitted. Random refueling takes place when the aircraft receives permission from air traffic controllers to refuel on one compass heading for a certain distance, and not on a prescribed air refueling track. The evaluator, based at March in the heart of very busy Los Angeles airspace, sarcastically replied, "Sure, if you think you can get it."

That's all we needed to know.

For the first day of refueling, Will and I were the tanker, giving fuel to Milt and Mike, our receivers. We ran a perfect rendezvous west of Little Rock on the northbound track, and Milt's KC-10 pulled up behind us. Milt held his KC-10 in the refueling position as Jeff guided the refueling boom over the receptacle. As we crossed the ARCP at the air refueling control time (ARCT), Jeff plugged his boom nozzle into the KC-10 below him and started the twenty-minute transfer of JP-4 jet fuel.

We were operating in Fort Worth air traffic control airspace, with the small storm looming ahead, so I radioed, "Fort Worth Center, Deuce 48, request."

The Fort Worth controller responded, "Go ahead with your request."

"Deuce 48 requests random refueling on a zero-nine-zero-degree heading for 120 nautical miles."

"Stand by," the controller replied.

To avoid the oncoming cumulus clouds while our planes were linked together during refueling, I was asking to turn east, away from the weather, and complete the twenty-minute contact in clear weather. After a moment, Fort Worth Center responded: "Deuce 48, random refueling is approved on a zero-nine-zero-degree heading for the next 120 nautical miles."

With our boom nozzle engaged, we could now transmit through the boom interphone to the receiver behind us without communicating over an open radio frequency.

"We are coming right to zero-nine-zero," I told Milt as we proceeded in the clear blue sky across Arkansas.

We landed an hour later, hitting all of the required marks and earning 1,277 out of 1,300 possible points. We crossed the control point precisely at the control time, and we had no disconnects during the twenty-minute fuel transfer. Our cocky Seymour Johnson competitors weren't so lucky. They made their refueling contact and then barreled into the turbulence of the clouds, resulting in two disconnects and penalty-point deductions.

The following day, Will guided our KC-10 into the refueling position behind Milt's KC-10. Once an on-time refueling contact was established, we heard Milt say over the boom interphone, "Stand by for a right turn to zero-nine-zero." Our teams again enjoyed random refueling in smooth air, thanks to the obliging controllers at Fort Worth Center. As the receiver this day, we received 1,286 points, just fourteen below the max possible. The rules later were changed so that all refueling had to take place within thirty nautical miles of the prescribed refueling track. The competition officials couldn't believe that we deviated 120 miles off course to remain in smooth air, but it wasn't against the rules at that time.

In the end, our preparation and ingenuity paid off. Our 458th Operations Group active-duty rodeo team flew home on June 12,

1993, under the call sign of Victor 458, with two trophies—Best KC-10 Air Refueling Team and Best KC-10 Aircrew—and we were awarded the General Richard H. Ellis Trophy for Best KC-10 Unit.

29

MOGADISHU, PART III

THE U.S. TRANSPORTATION COMMAND (USTRANSCOM), responsible for the operation of all U.S. military transportation assets, has the ability to task civilian airlines to support military operations by transporting troops through the Civil Reserve Air Fleet, or CRAF. In the 1990s, many international airlines still flew the huge Boeing 747, but an issue arose with the carriers' insurance not covering flights into active war zones. Intelligence agencies reported there was still a threat of small-arms fire and shoulder-fired SA-7s around the Mogadishu airport. The CRAF could get the combat troops to the region, but not into the active combat zone of Somalia.

For this reason, KC-10s deployed to Cairo, Egypt, on Aug. 21, 1993. The Gucci Boys had the hardship assignment of billeting at the Mena House Hotel and Casino, across the street from the famous Egyptian pyramids. This luxury hotel and casino looked like it belonged in a James Bond movie. Life was rough, but somebody had to do it.

The civilian 747s were loaded with Army Ranger combat troops before departing the United States for the Middle East. We timed our departures from Cairo as the 747s flew across the Mediterranean Sea to meet them in the tiny country of Djibouti, just south of the

Red Sea. After the airliners landed, the Army Ranger troops walked down the tall, portable airstairs exiting the 747, crossed the tarmac, and climbed up the stairs of our waiting KC-10s. For this operation, each KC-10 had a temporary FAA authorization to carry 225 troops, triple the amount of our usual load.

My first mission for this operation departed Cairo late at night on Aug. 30, 1993. Capt. Don Barnes flew as the aircraft commander in the left seat. Our copilot, 1st Lt. Dave Denman, flew in the right seat, and a flight engineer sat behind him, facing sideways. As an instructor/evaluator, I could fly in either the left or right seat, but instead I sat in the passenger seats outside the cockpit door as Don and Dave flew the flight into Djibouti from Cairo. We parked on the nearly empty ramp and waited as the large 747 taxied to a stop and the Army personnel deplaned. One hundred and fifteen Army Rangers carrying their combat gear climbed the staircase to our waiting KC-10. Once they were onboard, we departed after midnight for the two-hour flight to Mogadishu, with Don flying from the left seat and me sitting in the copilot seat.

Upon arrival, Don flew a combat arrival, overflying the coastal city at 20,000 feet, then spiraled down over the Arabian Sea to 300 feet. From there, he made a short, right-hand final turn to the runway. This tight approach avoided flying over any nearby buildings, since our intelligence reports stated there could be SA-7 ground-to-air shoulder-fired missiles in the vicinity. Our intense focus was on the short approach, flying the huge KC-10 low over the ocean waves in a right-hand turn toward the seaside airstrip. We had no time to think about possible incoming missiles, and excitement overruled fear in this case.

The Mogadishu runway was long, but it did not have exits at both ends. There was just one midfield taxiway, meaning the only exit was halfway down the 10,000-foot landing strip. If a plane was not traveling slow enough to exit at the midpoint, it needed to go to the end and execute a U-turn, which is very challenging in a large KC-10.

Our flight manual says the KC-10 has a 143-foot turning radius, and on narrow runways crews have been known to drop the nosewheel off the pavement and into the dirt halfway through a U-turn. The Mogadishu runway was only 148 feet wide, leaving just a five-foot buffer—and that assumes the aircraft is starting the turn with its tires against the edge of the pavement.

Another restriction faced by many aircraft is that they shouldn't land with a tailwind greater than ten knots. Pilots always try to take off and land into a headwind to enjoy the benefit of more air moving over the wing, which creates lift. A tailwind landing is fine, but the pilot must carry additional power throughout the landing to prevent dropping the plane firmly onto the runway. The increased groundspeed on landing also increases the stopping distance during deceleration. This would not be a factor when using the whole 10,000-foot runway, but it certainly makes stopping by the midpoint quite a challenge.

Don flew the approach, and I noticed on our short final that we had a thirteen-knot tailwind, slightly above the ten knot restriction. The only other option would have been a circling approach, heading parallel to the runway, out over the water and then turning left for a southwesterly approach over the city. This was riskier than a tailwind landing because of the rebel's shoulder-fired missiles, so we agreed that the tailwind landing was the safer option.

At this point, as an experienced instructor and evaluator pilot, I didn't have a problem with executing a tight U-turn on a narrow runway. But the only steering for the KC-10 nose wheel is for the pilot in the left seat, and I was sitting in the right seat. After Don's landing, I expected him to taxi to the end for the U-turn, but instead he slammed on the brakes to make the midfield taxiway. My shoulders pressed into the shoulder straps as I lurched forward in my seat.

Don and I have always gotten along great, and we've spent many hours laughing at each other's stories, so I wasn't mad at him, but with the roar of the engines' reverse thrust I had to yell to be heard: "Roll to the end! Roll to the end!"

Don yelled back, "No way! I'm not doing a U-turn!"

He brought the beast to a screeching halt in time to turn off at the midfield taxiway, then proceeded to the cargo ramp near the control tower.

Even though we were safely on the ground, we now faced a serious issue. After aggressive braking, the brake temperatures can rise rapidly, and the excessive heat buildup can result in a fire or tire explosion. To prevent the tires from bursting, the wheels have fuse plugs that melt at 400 degrees Celsius, allowing the air from the tires to release at a controlled rate and not explode. Should that happen, the plane would be grounded until another aircraft arrived with parts and equipment to replace any faulty tires and brakes. At an austere location like Mogadishu, Somalia, this would pose a huge problem.

Our KC-10 had a brake temperature gauge, which the flight engineer nervously monitored. The temperatures climbed beyond 350 degrees Celsius, but luckily, we didn't blow any tires.

It was still before sunrise as our Army Ranger passengers filed down the staircase and marched off down the dark tarmac. We talked to our ground-support personnel and gave them our *Stars and Stripes* newspapers and bottles of Stella Artois beer. During this operation, the Barksdale personnel were dispersed to each location from where we operated. Some were in Cairo and living the high life at the Mena House Hotel and Casino, while others were in the former French colony of Djibouti, staying at the Intercontinental Hotel along with airline crews from around the world. One of our maintenance officers had the good fortune of dating a beautiful German Lufthansa flight attendant while proudly serving his country in Djibouti.

The further south our missions went, though, the worse the conditions became. The unlucky third group lived in tents on the dilapidated Somali airfield, surrounded by barbed wire and young Army guards with machine guns. Bringing them free twenty-four-ounce bottles of Stella Artois was the least we could do.

Next to our large KC-10 sat a small Army C-12 King Air turboprop plane, capable of carrying ten passengers. As the sun rose, the warrant officer pilot joined us at the top of the mobile staircase, talking about our planes and mission as we watched a thunderstorm brewing offshore to our left.

In the distance, toward the approach end of the runway we'd just landed on, we heard a low "thump, thump, thump," then saw columns of black smoke rising. Moments later, we heard a repeated "whomp" sound. Curious, we shouted down to a sergeant to ask what was going on. He came up the stairs, reporting that Somali rebels were shelling the far end of the field, and the U.N. troops from Romania were returning fire with mortars. None of this was very loud, and we could only see the smoke rising about a mile away. The explosions were too muffled to cause a panic. We were just idle spectators ... in a war zone.

The flight line became a beehive of activity, as hangar doors suddenly slid open and small, black helicopters on wheeled dollies rolled out of the hangars and into the open. They were MH-6 Little Birds, also known as "Killer Eggs," similar to what Tom Selleck flew in the 1980s television show *Magnum, P.I.* The helicopters, with their blades folded backward, were wheeled to an open area on the ramp in front of our KC-10. Army troops unfolded the blades while their aircrews boarded the helicopters, which were armed with rocket launchers on both sides. Within minutes their rotors were spinning, and I to me it looked like a horde of angry mosquitos as they lifted off. The Army C-12 warrant officer looked toward the departing helicopters in front of us, then at the growing thunderstorm closing in offshore, and said, "Well, I'm out of here."

It didn't take but a few minutes for him to start his engines and taxi to the runway, but it took quite a bit longer for us. I told my crew we needed to get out of there, too, so we verified that our boom operators had completed offloading the Army cargo. We had brought enough fuel onboard for the roundtrip, so we didn't need any aircraft services from the airport. We just needed KC-10 ground personnel to monitor our engine start, as flight crews always had a person manning a fire extinguisher on the ground in the event of a fire during engine start. It was an overly protective requirement of the Air Force, as there wasn't any sense of grave danger and we weren't afraid, but we knew it was better to leave than to stay.

Our crew all quickly got into their assigned positions. It was my leg of the trip to fly in the left seat, with Don now sitting in the right seat, so we started the three engines, and I taxied to the northeast end of the runway and executed the U-turn for a southwesterly departure. The helicopters swept the departure path in front of us, ensuring there weren't any rebel forces under the departure corridor as we lifted off.

Meanwhile, the storm to our left continued to bear down on the airfield, and under normal conditions we weren't supposed to take off with storms closer than ten miles from the field. By this point, the winds and lightning were only five miles away and closing in, but the choices we faced were to remain on the ground—with smoke and mortar fire to our right, and a thunderstorm bearing down on us from the left—or to get the heck out of there. We agreed to disregard the Air Force's storm limitation and leave.

I pushed the power up to maximum takeoff thrust, and we began rolling down the runway. A three-ship helicopter escort consisting of two Army Cobra attack helicopters and one MH-6 Killer Egg flew ahead of us along both sides of the runway. As we gained speed, Don —with his usual inappropriate timing—yelled, "All I know is, the next time I need a checkride, I want you to be my evaluator!"

With the thunderstorm closing in on our left and columns of rising smoke to our right, we retracted the landing gear, and I immediately started a left turn out over the ocean, just 300 feet above the waves. We landed in Cairo four hours later and settled in for three more weeks of round-robin trips, flying three more troop-carrying flights into Djibouti and Mogadishu.

During this deployment, my KC-10 friend, Capt. Kirk Shepherd, was back home in Louisiana reading the latest issue of *Air Force Times,* where he saw a job posting requesting a KC-10 instructor pilot to serve as an exchange officer with the Royal Netherlands

(Dutch) Air Force. When Kirk and his wife, Colette, had Karin over for dinner, he told Karin I should apply for the job.

"Or, better yet," he said, "we can just apply for him and not even tell him!"

Karin liked the idea of living overseas, and during our next phone call she told me about the foreign exchange job. It sounded interesting, so I talked it over with my squadron commander, Lt. Col. Tom Stickford, who was deployed with us in Cairo.

Tom said, "Hmm. Sounds intriguing, but I'm not sure if it would be good for your career. You'd better talk it over with Colonel Lichte once we get home."

30
GOING DUTCH

AFTER RETURNING to Barksdale on September 12, 1993, I called Colonel Lichte, who was now on the AMC headquarters staff at Scott Air Force Base, east of St. Louis. In his opinion, the foreign exchange assignment would have a neutral effect on my career, neither positive nor negative. I would work hard in a foreign country, but none of what I did would be known to our Air Force. In the realm of military promotions, there's a saying that goes, "What have you done for me lately?" Colonel Lichte was concerned that I would basically become invisible to the Air Force while serving with the Dutch. I appreciated his thoughts, but the idea of moving to Europe was too appealing to skip. I had landed in England and Germany many times but had never explored beyond the airfields, and Karin had never been further from home than Hawaii.

I submitted my application to the Air Force Personnel Center and campaigned hard for the assignment. The KC-10 contact at AFPC was Maj. Jim Kotowski, a former 32 ARS KC-10 pilot whom I knew well. I spoke to Jim about the Dutch assignment, and he said my main competition was an instructor/evaluator pilot named Rich from March Air Force Base in California. Rich was the early favorite for the assignment, but by rule the job opportunity had to be advertised for thirty days. During the selection process, I had a few items to bolster my resume, and I continued to update Jim on these events.

On Oct. 13 I flew a VIP mission, showcasing the KC-10 capabilities to the first female secretary of the Air Force, Dr. Sheila Widnall. We picked up Dr. Widnall at Scott Air Force Base in southern Illinois after she visited Air Mobility Command headquarters. She had toured the expansive tanker/airlift control center and received briefings about the command's airlift capabilities from four-star Gen. Ron Fogelman. Fortunately, Colonel Lichte now served as Fogelman's executive officer, and we chatted out on the flight line while waiting for Dr. Widnall, who we flew back to McGuire Air Force Base in central New Jersey on a chilly fall day. During the three-hour flight, I refueled behind a KC-135 over Kentucky, with Dr. Widnall sitting just behind me in the observer's seat. She watched the tanker's boom hover over her head before plugging into our receptacle.

The day after returning to Barksdale, I called Jim at AFPC and said, "Hey, I just flew the secretary of the Air Force from Scott Air Force Base back to D.C. Can you please add that to my record?"

Two weeks later, our base underwent an evaluation from 21st Air Force, the next echelon above our wing. As a squadron evaluator pilot, I received my in-flight checkride from the chief KC-10 evaluator of 21st Air Force, Col. Larry Leturmy. He was highly respected in the community and was one of the original KC-10 pilots when the program began in the early 1980s. My flight evaluation—refueling an EC-130 intelligence-gathering aircraft—went well, and afterward he reported that I was a top-notch instructor/evaluator.

My checkride performance directly helped our KC-10 operations group excel during this major inspection. Within a few days of updating Jim of my checkride performance, I was awarded the job as the first exchange officer for the Royal Netherlands (Dutch) Air Force KDC-10 program. While our KC-10 friends moved on to staff assignments or other flying assignments, Karin and I were moving overseas! We had spent seven years near Shreveport and had made many lifelong friends, but a chance to see real windmills in Holland and learn a new language was too good to pass up.

The Dutch Air Force, officially known as the Royal Netherlands Air Force (RNLAF, pronounced "Ren-laugh") has always supported NATO operations with several squadrons of fighter aircraft. Their aviation fleet in 1995 consisted of numerous F-16s at bases spread across the country, two C-130s, one recently procured G-IV Gulfstream for their Queen Beatrix, and several Fokker F-27 twin-engine turboprop light transports. All but the F-16s were based at Eindhoven Air Base in the southeastern corner of the small country.

When the Gulf War occurred in the early 1990s, the Dutch weren't able to send their F-16s because there weren't enough refueling airplanes to deliver their jets to the desert operation. The United Kingdom participated because they had two varieties of tankers to deploy their Tornado and Jaguar fighters. Having missed out on joining the international coalition, the RNLAF procured two tankers for future refueling and cargo missions.

I spent my remaining six months at Barksdale in the combat crew training school (CCTS) schoolhouse, teaching new students fresh out of undergraduate pilot training to fly the KC-10, upgrading copilots to aircraft commanders, and training aircraft commanders to become instructor pilots. My final Barksdale KC-10 flight took place on April 13, 1994, on a six-hour training mission, helping two new pilots learn the KC-10 mission.

Just three days later, on April 16, we loaded up our silver Chrysler minivan and my Chevy two-door Z-24 with five-year-old Daniel and one-year-old Shelby, plus a cocker spaniel and a beagle, and headed west for Dutch language school in Monterey, California. Because I would be the first Dutch exchange officer for this KDC-10 program, the Air Force considered Karin to also be an ambassador of our Air Force, so she received a seat in the language school course as well.

We set out in our two-car caravan and stopped in Tucson to see my aunt and uncle. My Uncle Jack (Mom's brother) had retired as an

Air Force colonel after serving thirty years, and they returned to the Arizona house they'd owned since he was an A-10 squadron commander at Davis-Monthan Air Force Base in the 1970s. At their suggestion, we booked a cabin near the Grand Canyon for one night and were able to show our children the magnificent colors of the epic canyon landscape at sunset.

We pulled into Monterey, California, on Sunday, April 24, the night before Shelby turned two years old. After settling into our temporary quarters, we bought a small birthday cake for the occasion. We were traveling with clothes but no household goods, so Shelby got her slice of cake on a paper plate. She proceeded to lie face-down on the kitchen floor, eating her cake without a fork or spoon.

The next six months were pivotal for our marriage and family life. Karin and I had been married ten years, and we were busy raising a toddler and a rising kindergartener. We made day-care arrangements at Fort Ord, the Army post where we would live, with a very nice Army wife living two doors down from our base house. In a picturesque family setting, we walked the youngsters down the sidewalk to Susan's house each morning before driving along the Pacific coastline to the Presidio of Monterey and the Defense Language Institute (DLI). It was an idyllic moment—watching the green Pacific Ocean waves crash onto the brown beach, seeing the carved wooden artwork of local artisans along the sidewalk, and observing paragliders adding a splash of color to the blue California sky.

Our multiple-service class of ten consisted of two Army soldiers, two Navy officers, two Marines, me, from the Air Force, and three spouses. The Army personnel included a captain foreign area officer (FAO) specializing in the Netherlands, and a young enlisted woman serving in intelligence. The Navy officers were both lieutenant O-3s, the same military grade as me, a captain in the Air Force. Lt. Tim McElligatt flew the sea-surveillance P-3 Orion, and Lt. Tom Gonzalez was a ship navigator. The Marines were a captain intelligence officer and Gunnery Sgt. Mike Endicott, a hardcore poster child of a Marine who had served on the front lines of Desert Storm as a sniper facing Saddam's Republican Guard. All of us joined Dutch units, with the exception of Lieutenant Gonzalez, who served with the Belgian Navy, just south of us.

Our instructors were a Dutch lady, Mevrouw (Mrs.) Johanna Cornelissen, raised in Indonesia, and an elderly Indonesian man who we called Meneer (Mister) Ron Kwee (pronounced "Quay"). Both had experienced losses at the hands of the Japanese during World War II. Meneer Kwee witnessed gunbattles as a young child hiding under the porch of his house, while Mevrouw Cornelissen lost her Dutch father on a forced labor crew much like that depicted in the movie *Bridge Over the River Kwai.*

Our Monterey, California, Dutch class, 1994

We attended class from 8 a.m. to 4 p.m. each day, learning Dutch vocabulary and grammatical rules. From what I learned, the Dutch language lies directly between German and English, just as the Netherlands lies between Germany and England. We could see and hear a lot of similarities in Dutch and both of the other languages. Each Monday we received a list of sixty to a hundred Dutch words, which we would be tested on by Friday. The first two months were an intensive grammar class, where we conjugated verbs and diagrammed sentences. Once we had the foundations of the language down, we started to practice simple conversations together for two hours each afternoon, with phrases such as, "How are you," "Where are you from," and "Can you help me, please?"

I found it very interesting to observe our progress over the six-month course. Shelby was just beginning to talk, so I could see our Dutch skills evolve from that of a two-year-old up to that of our five-year-old son. As our son learned to read basic "See Spot Run" stories, Karin and I read Dutch kindergarten books about the adventures of two kids, *Jip and Janneke.*

As we had been told might happen, I started dreaming in Dutch, which was a sign that I had internalized the lessons. My listening comprehension was never very good, though, and that frustrated me. Each Friday, in addition to the written test, we had a listening comprehension test, in which a television with a VCR was wheeled to the front of the class, with a bath towel placed over the screen. Meneer Kwee played a short news segment, like those seen on evening news programs. The story would only last two minutes, but we had to decipher what the story was about. To me, the Dutch mumbled a lot, and I rarely got the story right, only catching a few phrases here and there. After we aired our guesses, Meneer Kwee rewound the tape and played it again, but with the towel removed so we could see and hear the story together. That was an aggravating exercise for me and Karin, but she usually understood the story better than I did.

Living on Fort Ord, near John Steinbeck's seaside city of Monterey, California, was a great way to relieve any classroom frustration, and it proved to be a therapeutic turning point for our marriage. Karin and I were together twenty-four hours a day, which for some couples may not sound ideal—but after so many of my extended absences, it was just what we needed. Some married couples say they married their best friend, but that wasn't the case for me; instead, I'd married a hot Texas sorority girl after only dating her for three months. Once married, I'd whisked her away to Sacramento, California, and we'd settled into Air Force life—and only *then* did we start to get to know each other.

In the first ten years of our marriage, I bonded with my fellow crew members, traveling around the world and seeing famous sites, riding camels around the Egyptian pyramids, and snorkeling in Hawaii. When I wasn't on these Air Force adventures, I'd play nine or eighteen holes of golf with squadron friends on weekends. Karin and I went out to eat or to movies, but we didn't *do* many activities together. She had her friends, and I had mine. She had her job (retail management, then tax preparation), and I had my flying. We both were involved in raising our children—feeding, changing, singing songs or reading stories at bedtime—but I was only there half the time. As a couple, we'd been leading parallel lives, but we rarely intertwined. We got along just fine and rarely argued, but we didn't always try to have *fun together*, and the risky part of parallel lives is that they can diverge. California provided a welcome opportunity for our lives to converge and connect.

We now lived on a cul-de-sac of eight houses and could see the ocean from our driveway, but the Army post had recently been slated for closure by the base realignment and closure (BRAC) commission. Its massive 7th Infantry Division was deactivated, and the expansive Pacific Coast base now only had the housing area and commissary open ... plus two eighteen-hole golf courses, one of which was a PGA-qualifying course. Across the street from us lived an Army colonel who was studying international affairs at the nearby Naval Postgraduate School. This family included a fourteen-year-old daughter who became our babysitter.

At least once a week, after class and getting the children home, Karin and I hired our teenage babysitter to watch our children for two hours while we played nine holes of golf for $12 at the post's black or gold golf courses. The setting was picturesque and very similar to nearby Pebble Beach, with views of crashing waves and powered ultralight gliders cruising overhead along the coastline. Some of the golf outings included Daniel and Shelby, and they loved "chauffeuring" us in two golf carts. Two-year-old Shelby steered from my lap, and laughed as the cool wind blew back her wispy blonde hair.

From April through October 1994, we dropped off Daniel and Shelby at Susan's by 7:30 a.m. Susan then walked Daniel and her five-year-old daughter, Allie, to kindergarten before taking care of Shelby and her own small son throughout the day. Karin and I attended language class from 8 a.m. to 4 p.m., and we particularly enjoyed our lunch breaks around the city of Monterey, either with classmates or just by ourselves.

Our favorite spot was eating at the famous Monterey Aquarium while watching seals and otters play in the ocean. The cold sea breeze was trapped by the coastal mountains surrounding the town, so Monterey was cool all year long, with highs typically only in the low sixties, even in the summer. Tourists arrived in their shorts, T-shirts, and flip-flops from the surrounding ninety-degree Golden State and immediately sought warmer clothes. I joked that I could return to Monterey after I retired to sell sweatshirts to the freezing tourists.

Our Dutch fluency progressed to the point that, in the last two months (September and October), our instructors organized Friday debates, and it was an intriguing method to learn a language. The instructors picked controversial topics to discuss, such as gun control, abortion, or the current Haitian immigration crisis unfolding that year. The idea was to become so engrossed in the topic, even arguing at some points, that we wouldn't wait to think in English and translate to Dutch, but instead we'd just blurt out our sometimes-heated arguments in Dutch.

Because our master of the Dutch language was progressing at the same rate within the class, the ten of us could understand each other's sloppy "Monterey Dutch," but the instructors were often bewildered with what we were saying. Our Marine captain was from South Carolina and sounded like Gomer Pyle with his southern accent, and one day as he struggled for the right words to make his point, he asked Meneer Kwee for assistance. Meneer Kwee smiled and said, "I haven't understood a word you've said," to which the Marine replied, in his southern twang, "I'm speakin' Dutch, Muh-neeer!"

People have often asked how fluent we became, and by comparing our skills to talking to Daniel at home, it seemed that Karin and I could talk in Dutch like a five-year-old might. Five-year-olds sometimes make small grammatical errors in past or future tense, or they can't quite find the right word at times. I discovered that I could think quite well in Dutch, but engaging my tongue to speak often made me self-conscious.

Over the six months we were together, our class informally divided by military service into two groups. Each Friday after class, the two Marines and the Army officer changed into their running clothes and ran the eight miles from the Defense Language Institute back to Fort Ord. The two Naval officers, Tim and Tom, left that activity to the "ground-pounders," just like I did. Instead, we drove home with our spouses, changed into polo shirts and shorts, and headed for the golf course just as the sweaty runners arrived on post.

One summer afternoon, though, Tim and I started talking about how we used to be in such good shape. Tim had played lacrosse at the Naval Academy in Annapolis, and I was ten years removed from my last triathlon in college. We decided right then to start running together so we could join the ground-pounders on the last Friday before graduation.

Tim and I tackled the hills of Fort Ord on three- to four-mile runs, and we eventually ran two ten-kilometer (six-mile) runs among the wooded California hills. On the final Friday of class, after the closing well-wishes from Meneer Kwee and Mevrouw Cornelissen, Tim, Tom, and I joined the three ground-pounders and ran eight miles along the coastal town and hard-packed beach for a final trek back to our "seaside village" of Fort Ord.

After six months of forty-hour weeks learning a new language, we graduated with students who were in two other six-month courses, studying German and Spanish, and each class designated a spokesperson to deliver an address in their new language. Of course, only the fellow classmates could understand the address, but Tim gave his short commencement speech in Dutch. We were now qualified to speak the language of a country half the size of South Carolina, with just fifteen million people, but at least that also included beautiful KLM flight attendants and tourists in Aruba.

As an unexpected bonus, Karin and I now had a code language to use around our offspring. We could talk openly about Christmas and birthday gift ideas or weekend plans without them understanding. Our conversations were usually interrupted with yells of, "Stop speaking Dutch!"

31

MOVING ACROSS THE POND

THE CONTRACT TO convert two Martinair DC-10-30s into KDC-10s was awarded to KLM Airlines, with the work conducted at Schiphol Airport in Amsterdam, but the process was tedious, to say the least. McDonnell Douglas engineers in Long Beach, California, drew up the designs for the parts required to create a refueling tanker out of an already produced and functioning passenger jet. Engineering schematics and parts then were shipped from California to Holland, and work began in 1994, but airplane part A didn't always fit into airplane part B, so the project fell way behind schedule while Karin and I were attending our Dutch language school.

After graduating from language school in October, I was told by the Dutch squadron not to report to the Netherlands until January, so our family enjoyed a relaxing Thanksgiving and Christmas holiday with our extended family in the United States. In November 1994 I took a fact-finding trip with another KC-10 evaluator pilot, Maj. Bob Bruton, who also trained Dutch pilots for the first year of our tour.

Major Bruton was selected to lead a four-man KC-10 crew on a two-year contract to train the Dutch crews and help get their operation started. The contract crew consisted of instructor pilot Capt. J.T.

Anderson, flight engineer Master Sgt. Mike Stinson, and boom operator Master Sgt. Steve "Slobo" Slobodnak.

Karin, Shelby, Daniel, and me with the KDC-10

J.T. was a tall, thin, All-American-looking young man, with thick, black hair and a long chin. He had recently married his beautiful young wife, Nikki, who was a trained psychologist and equestrian rider with short, bobbed blonde hair. They began married life together overseas, far from their family back home, which certainly was an adjustment for them both.

Mike was a calm, chain-smoking southern gentleman from Mississippi. He had thinning, swept-back hair, and he often wore a sport coat and a turtleneck when off duty, so he could have passed for a Mafia bodyguard—until he opened his mouth, that is. His southern accent and boisterous laugh didn't fit the bad-guy mold.

Our boom operator, Slobo, spoke in a soft, thoughtful tone, and he literally rounded out the crew, as he was short and round.

Of the five of us, I was the only one who had received language training, and while the contract crew only existed for two years, my position as exchange officer continued for other KC-10 instructor pilots for many more years. Together, the five of us made up the American training contingent that helped the Dutch crew members make their new KDC-10 unit operationally capable.

Bob and I arrived in Eindhoven on a chilly November day to scope out the housing and school prospects for the other American families. Eindhoven is in the country's southeastern corner, not far from both the Belgian and German borders. We stayed at the Eindhoven officer's club, with a twin bed in a small room for each of us. In a scene right out of an IKEA store, the guest quarters were white-walled units, with white dressers and desks, and a white comforter on the bed. It was simple by American standards, but it met our needs.

Every day that week we explored the vast industrial city, which is home to Philips Electronics, as we searched for housing options and schools for our American school-age children. Each weekday afternoon we returned to the squadron bar to enjoy authentic Dutch Heineken beer and plates of Gouda cheese, which prompted Bob to say to me: "We are going to put on so much weight over here!"

On Thursday morning we joined the thirty other members of 334 Squadron at 8 a.m. for their morning routine of drinking coffee, or scalding hot tea, in the same squadron bar, and we were told to be sure to return by 4 p.m. because Crown Prince (now King) Willem Alexander would be in the squadron. The son of Dutch Queen Beatrix was a qualified Air Force pilot, flying the twin-engine Fokker F-27 light transport, so Bob and I made a note to return in time before heading out for the fourth day of our housing tour. At the appointed time, we took our place around the crowded, smoke-filled bar and were introduced to Prince Willem—a very nice, twenty-eight-year-old blond man, five years younger than me.

Friday morning started out the same as the previous few days, with coffee and one last tour of Eindhoven and the surrounding villages. By 3:30 that afternoon, Bob said to me, "We'd better get back to the squadron for beer call." We headed back, assuming the weekend would kick off with more Heineken and Gouda.

We arrived at 334 Squadron to find it open, but dark and quiet inside, so we figured the squadron members were at the officer's club, just like we would do back in the States on Fridays. We hopped in our rented blue Opel hatchback, drove around the runway to the officer's club, and strolled into the bar to find the bartender alone, drying glasses with a rag.

"Where is everyone?" Bob asked him.

"They've all gone home," the bartender replied.

I asked, "Why aren't they here on a Friday night?"

"On Fridays, everyone goes home for the weekend," the bartender told me. "Nobody stays late."

This was certainly a cultural change of events. In the States, aircraft crews go home each Monday through Thursday evening, but stay and drink on Friday nights. In the Netherlands, the opposite occurred, and by 4 p.m. on Fridays the weekends began with their families. Bob and I had a beer with the lonely bartender before flying back to the States the next morning.

In January 1995 I left my family behind and flew to London to in-process for my exchange tour. The exchange program for all of Europe was run by an Air Force colonel based in London—and because of quarantine rules, if our cocker spaniel landed in the U.K., she would be placed in quarantine for six months, even if she was just transiting to the Netherlands. Karin and I agreed that I would head overseas first, followed by Karin, Daniel, Shelby, and then our dog would join me a week later. I certainly got the better part of that bargain.

After a one-night stay in London to complete my paperwork, I flew to Eindhoven and checked into a Center Parcs lodge, which would serve as our temporary housing until we found a house to rent.

One week later, with near-historic rains and flooding throughout the Netherlands, an exhausted Karin arrived in Amsterdam with our children and Dulce, our twelve-year-old cocker spaniel. Jasmine, the beagle, was sold to a California neighbor to make the move a little easier. The nine-hour, international non-stop flight from Houston, via Atlanta, with our children and a dog was a trip Karin said she never wanted to repeat.

I overcame my jet lag in a week, but I now had a confused little two-year-old waking up at 2 a.m. each day as her mom and brother slept soundly, so I took on the night childcare duties while we all struggled with sleep for a few more nights. We were excited to finally be in Europe, but our adventure was off to a rough start.

It took two weeks for our Dutch rental house to become available, so we stayed in a family recreation area complete with fully furnished bungalows, a water park, and bicycles to borrow. This made for great temporary housing while we waited for our household goods to arrive.

In California, Daniel had learned to ride his first bike without training wheels in the grade-school parking lot at Fort Ord. He had struggled with the hilly California terrain, but I told him not to worry because Holland was flat. Now, sitting on his borrowed little Dutch bike, I gave him a push to start him on his way on the Center Parcs paved trail, but after several yards he came upon a speed bump, which the Dutch called "drempels." He hit the asphalt bump, fell over, and cried, "You said there weren't any hills here!"

Welcome to Holland.

32
SMALL COUNTRY, SMALL WORLD

IS IT HOLLAND, or the Netherlands? Well, here's a brief explanation: The Netherlands consists of twelve provinces, two of which are North Holland and South Holland on the North Sea coast. Two-thirds of the country's seventeen million residents live in these two provinces, which encompass the population centers of Amsterdam, The Hague, and Rotterdam. Therefore, for more than eleven million Dutch men and women, it's true that they live in Holland. But the remaining third of Dutch citizens lives outside of those two provinces. While the city of Eindhoven and its air base lie in the southeastern province of Brabant, many have just found it simpler to say Holland rather than "the Netherlands."

To occupy our time during the KDC-10 conversion process, several of us Americans visited some of the F-16 units we eventually would be refueling and toured the military radar facility, called "Dutch Mil." These were the military air traffic controllers who would control the airspace for our refuelings over the North Sea. As we quietly watched the controllers monitoring their radar in the dark control center, I saw an aircraft appear with the call sign of JAMBO 52. JAMBO is the radio call sign adopted by the 62nd Bomb

Squadron at Barksdale Air Force Base in Louisiana, where I was a navigator.

I asked the controller, "Is that a B-52?"

He placed his cursor over the box on the radar to expand the information and replied, "Yes, it is. How did you know?"

"I recognized the call sign," I said. "He's from my old squadron in Louisiana."

The controller pulled up the bomber's flight plan, then shook his head and murmured, "No, he's returning to his base in England."

Knowing the B-52 was taking part in this year's Busy Brewer exercise, just as I had done in 1986 and 1987, I explained, "Well, he's temporarily assigned to RAF Fairford, but he's based in Shreveport, Louisiana."

"Would you like to talk to him?" the controller offered, taking off his headset and handing it to me.

"Sure," I replied as I put on the headset and microphone. I keyed the transmitter, and in my purely American voice called, "JAMBO 52, Dutch Mil."

"Uh, go ahead for JAMBO 52?" he replied in a quizzical voice.

Thinking of the famous Bossier City seafood restaurant, I asked, "How are the mudbugs (crawfish) at Dudley & Gerald's these days?"

"Who is this?" the puzzled bomber copilot asked.

He couldn't see my smile as I answered, "I'm a former navigator from your squadron, living in Holland now," without revealing my name over the open frequency.

It's unprofessional to chatter away on an air traffic control frequency, so we just watched the blip of the B-52 fly west, toward the English Channel. As the bomber proceeded away from Holland, I gave him the radio handoff to England, stating, "JAMBO 52, contact London Mil on frequency 293.5," relaying the contact information for the English military sector. We watched him disappear off the radar scope, and I handed the headset back to the controller. What an amazing, small-world coincidence to have seen the Barksdale B-52 on the Dutch military radar at that brief moment.

By 4 p.m., Bob and I were dutifully back at the 334 Squadron Bar, drinking with other Dutch aircrew members and I relayed the story of the Busy Brewer Barksdale B-52 on the Dutch Mil radar, as well as another story.

Back in 1987, I returned for my second trip to RAF Fairford for Busy Brewer, only this time as a staff navigator. My job was to help the crews plan their bombing runs, using both simulated and live weapon drops over ranges in central Europe. I served as the assistant to the 2nd Bomb Wing's top radar navigator, Maj. Nick Manginelli. The live bomb releases took place on the Vliehors Bombing Range, located on the Dutch North Sea coast, about eighty miles north of Amsterdam.

Using American navigation charts of that area, Nick and I obtained the coordinates of the bomb target, a series of sixteen worn-out military trucks laid out in a "plus sign" pattern on the beach in groups of four, extending north, south, east, and west. Any bombs falling within the plus sign was a hit, or "shack."

The first Barksdale bomber crews took off from England bound for Holland with a load of live Mark 82 500-pound bombs. After crossing the English Channel, the B-52s descended to a low-level altitude of 400 feet above the ground and began their bomb runs. The B-52 copilots radioed their position to the Dutch bombing range controllers, who were monitoring from a nearby metal observation tower.

During any live weapon release in the United States, if there is a problem, the range controllers issue a command, "Withhold! Withhold! Withhold!" at which the bomber crew aborts the weapons release. The radar navigator also disconnects a large cannon plug over his head, which prevents the signals from completing a bomb release.

As our Barksdale crew rolled in on the intended target of old trucks, their position was off by several hundred feet, and they were lined up directly on the control tower instead. The Dutch officer, seeing the large bomber bearing down on him, calmly said over the radio, "I think you might want to withhold."

Onboard the B-52, a few of the crew members faintly heard the word "withhold." Someone asked over the intercom, "Did he say 'withhold?' "

The copilot queried the range controller, "Say again?"

The Dutch officer repeated, "I think you might want to withhold."

The B-52 crew now heard the key word, and someone onboard announced, "Withhold! Withhold! Withhold!" as the radar navigator quickly disconnected the cannon plug.

The massive B-52 roared over the control tower as observers in the tower scrambled down the metal staircase, fearing for their lives.

Once back at Fairford, Nick debriefed the crew and started to investigate why they were dangerously off course. Nick and I were confused, until he remembered that because we were using our U.S. charts instead of European charts, we had not applied a correction for the geodetic datum, a coordinate system (latitude and longitude) used to provide known locations and create maps.

During World War II, it was discovered that the mapping of Germany, the Netherlands, Belgium, and France had incompatible latitude and longitude positioning with the rest of the world, so after the war a correction was established in 1950. That meant that the coordinates Nick and I pulled off an American navigation chart were not the same as those found on Dutch military charts. Conversely, if we were using data supplied by the Dutch, we needed to convert it to make our American bombing system accurate.

The next morning Nick applied the correct conversion factor, and future live bombing missions scored a "shack," placing their bombs not just within the plus sign, but inside the doors of the trucks.

As I finished telling this story at the bar, a Dutch major with a bushy handlebar mustache smiled at me and calmly said, "I was the range officer that day."

"You almost got killed," I told him.

"I know," he said, grinning, as he raised his beer, tapped my glass, and took a sip.

And as for the JAMBO call sign I had seen earlier on the radar screen, that also came into existence during that 1987 Busy Brewer exercise.

One of our B-52 crews took off for their mission with a young second lieutenant serving as their electronic warfare officer (EWO), and their mission included entering an electronic warfare range over northern France. Once within that airspace, the EWO was free to use the powerful electronic jamming equipment in a simulation of what they might encounter over eastern Europe on a Cold War mission.

During this particular mission, the overzealous EWO started his jamming too soon and interfered with European air traffic controllers. The command of "Cease buzzer! Cease buzzer!" was quickly broadcast by ATC, telling any offending crew to stop their jamming of ATC radar.

The crew later reported that the EWO muttered, "Fuck the French," then kept on jamming in the vicinity of Maastricht, a major civilian radar facility. By doing so, he singlehandedly stopped all civilian aircraft departures from Paris, Brussels, and Amsterdam for almost fifteen minutes.

Once back at RAF Fairford, another post-mission investigation ensued, this one conducted by the wing staff electronic warfare officer, who was my roommate on this deployment. It was an in-depth investigation, with reports going all the way to the Pentagon—and apologies made by our Air Force to the European ATC facilities.

The young EWO had to go through retraining and an instructor ride with the staff EWO before being signed off to fly on his own with his crew. For the rest of our deployment, we nicknamed this lieutenant "JAMBO" (a combination of "jammer" and "Rambo"). This became his newly earned call sign.

Upon returning from England, SAC announced that squadrons could adopt their own squadron call sign, instead of picking a revolving call sign out of a pamphlet for each training mission, so the 62nd Bomb Squadron at Barksdale chose "JAMBO" as its call sign.

In a country the size of Indiana, I had just enjoyed two "it's a small world" coincidences in one day. First, seeing a B-52 from my old squadron on the radar during a thirty-minute facility tour, then meeting the Dutch range officer when an American crew almost bombed the observation tower near the North Sea. Small country, small world.

33
REFUELING AROUND THE PERFECT STORM

MONTHS HAD PASSED as the conversion process to create two tankers slowly continued. The five American crew members spent our time behind computer screens, helping the Dutch write their standard operating procedures (SOPs). During this time, we began to learn how life in the Netherlands differed from America, and those differences began right at the front gate of the air base.

The Dutch were just phasing out their era of military conscription, when almost every able-bodied male citizen was required to serve at least two years in the military. Serving in the military was not popular with everyone, and the Dutch had a relaxed attitude toward dress and appearance. There was neither a haircut standard nor rules regarding body piercings and tattoos. The male guard at Eindhoven Air Base who waved us through the gate each morning sported a ponytail extending twelve inches down his back, and a large silver ring piercing his right eyebrow. His appearance certainly differed from that of an American serviceman, who would have close-cropped hair to go along with a salute so crisp it could slice a tomato.

My Dutch counterparts noticed the excessive number of ribbons that Americans wore on their dress uniforms, too. Following all of the operations I took part in, I had four rows of them, consisting of thirteen multicolored ribbons, that denoted various medals and awards. My awards at the ten-year point of my career included:

- Meritorious Service Medal.
- Air Medal.
- Aerial Achievement Medal.
- Commendation Medal.
- Humanitarian Service Medal.
- Expert Marksmanship ribbon.
- Outstanding Unit Award with Valor.
- National Defense Service Medal (which every military member is awarded).

The typical Dutch uniform was adorned with just three ribbons, and I don't know what they signified. My Dutch friend saw mine and asked, "Why do you need to be rewarded or recognized for just doing your job?"

That was a very insightful question. Before arriving in the Netherlands, I had competed unsuccessfully for the coveted "below the zone" promotion to major, when the "fast burners" in the military began to separate from the pack. Over the next two years, I transformed from a hard-charging, "look at me" go-getter to an officer that simply did my best at the job I was given. I became less focused on recognition and instead adopted the attitude that whatever happened in my career, happened. With this newfound perspective, I could not —and would not—be disappointed. I am very thankful for that realization.

The first Dutch KDC-10 finally arrived at Eindhoven in August 1995 after an eight-month delay. Having spent the previous months flying a DC-10 simulator in Brussels, Belgium, or "borrowing" an Air Force KC-10 to keep current, we finally had the first of two jets for the Royal Netherlands Air Force. By the end of the year, all of the Dutch pilots, flight engineers, and boom operators were fully trained and ready for missions.

The Dutch were happy to show off the capability of their new jumbo jets, flying Queen Beatrix's orchestra to concerts around the world, or refueling their RNLAF F-16s on flights over the Atlantic. On one such occasion I did both, flying a KDC-10 loaded with the queen's orchestra while escorting a pair of F-16s from the Netherlands to Curaçao in the Caribbean to celebrate the queen's birthday. On the first leg of the journey, we flew over Iceland and the southern tip of Greenland before stopping for the night in Goose Bay, Canada. During the flight, the pair of F-16s refueled from the remotely controlled refueling boom, which was an advance in technology compared to what we used in the Air Force.

The Dutch KDC-10s incorporated a modified way of air refueling, using a three-dimensional camera system and a boom operator station located just outside our cockpit door. Because the two Dutch KDC-10s had been cargo versions of the DC-10 built in 1976, the McDonnell Douglas engineers decided it was structurally infeasible to cut a hole for the massive refueling window in the back of the large planes for a boom station.

Instead, five cameras mounted under the aircraft belly provided the necessary visibility. Three monovision cameras displayed a 180-degree, aft-facing view of the aircraft from wingtip to wingtip, enabling our boom operators to see approaching receiver aircraft before refueling. Two more three-dimensional cameras focused on the boom nozzle. By wearing a pair of polarized glasses, the boom operators now had the depth perception required to place the telescoping, maneuverable boom into the receptacle of the receiver.

After spending the night in Goose Bay, my Dutch copilot and good friend Freek ("Frake") Vandervaart checked the weather for the next long flight down the eastern seaboard to the Caribbean. What we faced was the "perfect storm," with Hurricane Edouard, a category four storm, and Hurricane Fran, a category three, blocking our southbound path.

From the weather shop in Goose Bay, we printed out the radar depiction of Edouard off the New England coast. I then called the weather shop at Roosevelt Roads Naval Station in Puerto Rico to get a fax of the radar image of Hurricane Fran.

There are many wonderful lessons I've gleaned from aviation. Pilots learn to anticipate problems, so we become proactive rather than reactive. We learn to "take the bull by the horns" and make good, safe decisions, rather than let controllers on the ground or Mother Nature determine our fate. Perhaps this is why pilots have developed a reputation for being cocky or arrogant, but this decisiveness can save not just our lives, but the lives of those flying with us in a metal tube.

Freek and I plotted a zig-zag course between the storms to Curaçao. We planned to depart Canada to the southwest until well west of Edouard, then cut back to the southeast, splitting the two storms, until our path was clear to the Dutch Caribbean islands. We entered the required navigation points on an international flight plan for our altitude reservation (ALTRAV), which was a special air traffic clearance used to block out the airspace required to refuel fighters over the ocean in what we called a "fighter drag." With our flight plan faxed to the Canadian controllers at Moncton Center, Freek and I headed out to the KDC-10 to begin our preflight and ensure that enough fuel was loaded for the long flight.

During the middle of our pre-departure cockpit preflight routine, a Dutch sergeant came on board holding a cellphone, which was a fairly new device in the mid-1990s.

After identifying which of us was "Major Dale," the sergeant handed me the phone and said, "Moncton Center wants to talk to you."

A bit confused, I took the phone and said, "This is Major Dale."

This was certainly a first for me—and I suspect it never happened in the States—but the Canadian controller for our flight said he was looking at our flight plan and wanted to ensure we really wanted to fly a gigantic southbound backward "Z." I explained that we would be refueling two F-16s in the vicinity of two hurricanes and needed to stay away from turbulent air.

The Canadian flight controller understood our logic and filed our ALTRAV. The flight went off without a hitch, and seven hours later we delivered the fighters and orchestra for the weekend festivities.

For the air show itself, we coordinated with the fighters to fly around each of the "ABC islands," which include Aruba to the north, Bonaire to the south, and Curaçao in the middle. Between the islands we flew at 4,000 feet, with one F-16 on each wing. As we approached each island, we descended to a thousand feet and lowered the refueling boom, with one F-16 flying close to the refueling position without actually making contact. The islanders of this Dutch constituent country enjoyed seeing the RNLAF in action.

There are two well-known sayings in the military. "Adapt and overcome" is a popular Army mantra, while "flexibility is the key to air power" is frequently heard in the Air Force. I thrive on problem-solving, so I enjoyed executing a plan to safely deliver two F-16s to the Caribbean despite two major hurricanes obstructing our path.

34
"HAVE YOU EVER BEEN SCARED?"

THE DUTCH GOVERNMENT enthusiastically supported humanitarian causes. Countries in Africa, such as Rwanda and Uganda, needed their assistance when the 1994 genocide wars between the Hutus and the Tutsi minority faction created a humanitarian crisis. The Dutch didn't take sides in this conflict, so they delivered relief goods provided by the United Nations International Children's Emergency Fund (UNICEF) to both countries.

In mid-November 1996 my crew departed Eindhoven Air Base for Copenhagen to upload U.N. water purification equipment, as well as 75,000 pounds of other goods bound for central Africa. We landed in Entebbe, Uganda, at the airport where 106 hijacked passengers of an Air France airliner, all Jewish Israeli citizens, had been detained by dictator Idi Amin in June 1976. The passengers had been in grave danger, and their rescue by Israeli special forces was portrayed in the movie *Raid on Entebbe.*

In college, I enjoyed reading *Self-Portrait of a Hero,* which was based on the letters and biography of Israeli commando leader Lt. Col. Yonatan Netanyahu, the older brother of Israeli prime minister Benjamin Netanyahu. Lieutenant Colonel Netanyahu was killed by Ugandan gunfire while leading his commandos down a C-130 ramp as they crossed the Entebbe airfield. His hundred-man team conducted a surprise raid to liberate the hostages, killing the four hijackers and forty-five Ugandan troops. This book deeply affected me with its description of his sense of duty and leading from the front, and I looked forward to seeing the location of his heroic rescue operation.

After our cargo was offloaded, our taxicab driver drove us around the runway to our hotel. He pointed to a small, dilapidated building near an unused runway and said, "That's where the Israelis kicked our ass." Having read the biography and seen the movie, it was meaningful to see that location firsthand.

The next morning, we took off on a forty-five-minute flight to Kigali, Rwanda, to deliver the U.N. water purification equipment. The Kigali runway is located deep in the jungles made famous by the Sigourney Weaver movie *Gorillas in the Mist,* which told the story of Dian Fossey's work with the mountain gorillas there. During our approach to land, we saw extremely large buzzards circling near our arrival corridor. Those birds could do some damage, even to a KDC-10.

There have been two crashes of E-3A AWACS, and both happened after the planes flew through flocks of large birds. One crashed in Alaska after hitting Canada geese; the other was brought down in Greece by a flock of seagulls. There was no doubt that the large buzzards I saw could take out one or more of our three engines.

It was a calm, blue-sky day, and after landing safely I stood at the top of the mobile staircase, taking in the jungle landscape as the humanitarian cargo was unloaded from our aircraft. With the water purification equipment safely delivered, we closed the cargo door and taxied to the runway to take off, but the buzzards were now everywhere. Dozens lined the runway as we taxied by, and a few took off and glided along beside my left cockpit window. These were the largest birds I had ever seen up close, with wingspans more than six feet across. The massive African buzzards seemed to be taunting me with a look that said, "I can take you out."

As we made our way toward departure, my Dutch copilot, Capt. Bert Pijper, suggested that we get a fire truck to run up and down the runway and scare the large birds away. He called the tower, and our request was forwarded to the fire department located alongside the midpoint of the runway.

I taxied into takeoff position and set the brakes as we watched the red fire truck pull out onto the runway. It drove toward us, then made a U-turn and drove away, scattering the defiant birds—but only for a moment. After the fire truck passed, the buzzards returned to settle on and beside the runway. These really were determined bastards! We finally decided that they might be scared away if they saw our 400,000-pound airplane coming toward them, so we decided to take our chances and take off.

The KDC-10, like all commercial aircraft, was built to fly with the loss of one engine, and we had calculated our maximum takeoff weight should that happen. But the runway was surrounded by dense jungle, and if we hit any of those birds and lost two of our three engines, we would sink into the trees without any hope of surviving. I was so nervous that I had to will myself to stop shaking.

Ernest Gann, in his book *Fate is the Hunter*, describes the difference between fear and fright. To him, fright is the sudden reaction to an event, like the sound of a large bird smacking the cockpit window, while fear is the feeling of looming dread at a situation being faced.

It was fear that I felt.

We agreed to go, and I pushed up the throttles to takeoff power. We gained speed, planning to lift off at 160 miles per hour. As we approached the birds and the midfield fire station, the fire truck driver decided to be helpful, at least in his mind. With our KDC-10 barreling down the runway, Mr. Fireman decided he'd clear our path of buzzards one last time and pulled out onto the runway in front of us. Bert and I couldn't believe our eyes!

I had not yet reached ninety miles per hour, so I aborted the takeoff, pulling the throttles to idle and coasting toward the far end of the runway without overheating the brakes. Once again, the bastard buzzards took off as we came by, then settled back to the runway after we passed. I made a U-turn and taxied the full length of the runway for our second attempt.

Bert told the tower controller to relay to the fire crew that we no longer needed their assistance, if you could call it that. Perhaps our screaming jet noise finally did the trick, because on our second takeoff attempt the flocks of birds finally got out of our way. As we climbed up over the jungle canopy and headed for the Netherlands, I finally stopped shaking.

35

MAJOR DALE, ARE YOU READY?

STARTING IN 1982, NATO allies have taken part in Central Enterprise, a live-fire, realistic military exercise over Europe, and 1996 was the first time the Dutch KDC-10 could participate. In my role as an instructor and evaluator pilot, I needed to attend the coordination meeting at Brize Norton Air Base in England, west of London.

As I thought about transportation to England, it occurred to me that the Dutch F-16 units would also send a representative to coordinate their role with the other NATO fighter forces. I called the Dutch squadron in Leeuwarden, eighty miles north of Amsterdam and near the North Sea coast, and asked if their unit would be sending anyone to RAF Brize Norton. I was told it would be Capt. "Woody" Woodsma, one of their top instructor pilots—and in a few moments he was on the phone.

Woody knew me from my earlier briefings to all Dutch F-16 squadrons about the capabilities of the KDC-10. I had tried, initially, to deliver my speech in Dutch, but everyone knew their English was far better than my Dutch, so I ended up making my delivery in my native tongue instead.

"So are you taking the KDC-10 to England?" he asked.

"No," I replied. "They won't give me the keys to the jet. How are you getting there?"

"I'm taking an F-16," he said. "But, if you'd like, I can see if I can put a B-model on the schedule. Would you like to come with me?"

The Dutch had two versions of F-16s. Most were the single-seat F-16A, but they also had a handful of dual-seat F-16Bs for training purposes, and my phone conversation played out exactly as I had hoped, as Woody arranged for a two-seater to fly us to England.

The following week, I boarded a yellow "fast train" bound for northern Holland, wearing casual civilian clothes and carrying a small duffle bag that held my green flight suit and black flight boots. I also had my green nylon helmet bag for my lightweight flight helmet and oxygen mask. This customized gray helmet and its visor had been molded to my head way back in nav school in 1984, but it still came in handy in 1996.

After the two-hour train ride, I was met by a driver and taken to Leeuwarden Air Base. I changed into my flight suit and boots before stuffing my civilian clothes into the duffle bag. I said no when my hosts asked me if I had flown in an F-16 before, but they also knew that I had flown the T-38 in pilot training. I was fitted with a G-suit, which looked like chaps cowboys wore in the Old West but actually contained a series of air bladders that wrapped around a pilot's thighs and calves. Once these bladders were hooked into the aircraft, air was pumped into them as gravity forces increased, which helped constrict the pilot's leg muscles. This kept the pilot's blood from rushing from the top of the body to the legs during high-G maneuvers, and that helped the pilot remain conscious. The F-16 was known at the time for pulling the most g-forces of any fighter—up to ten times normal body weight—so the G-suit was essential equipment for this flight.

After I was properly outfitted, the life-support personnel led me to a mockup of an F-16 ejection seat, where I was shown how to strap into the seat and told what would happen if I needed to eject. In a matter of just a few minutes, I was deemed ready for flight.

This type of flight is called an "off-station training sortie," so rather than just hopping into an F-16 and zipping across the North Sea to England, we needed to conduct training en route to make the best use of the flying time. Woody and I would be the fourth plane in a four-ship flight of F-16s launching out to meet two British Tornado fighters in a mock engagement over the North Sea.

The leader of the formation, whose name was "Parky" Parker, was an exchange officer, the same as me. He was a red-headed flight lieutenant of the British Royal Air Force—the equivalent of a captain in the U.S. and Dutch air forces—and, as an exchange pilot with the RNLAF, he went by the title of "Captain" to align with his host nation's rank structure.

To me, anything spoken with an English accent is usually highly entertaining, and Parky did not disappoint. In what could have been a comedy sketch from *The Benny Hill Show*, an animated Parky briefed the other three pilots on the timing, formations, and tactics used in taking on the Tornados. To make matters more interesting, our adversaries that day came from Parky's old RAF squadron, and losing was not an option in his mind.

The briefed mission was for a simulated air-to-air missile attack on the first engagement. Once the mission was completed, Woody would then check his fuel status and determine if he and I needed to depart the area for Brize Norton, or if we could remain with the formation for a second mock battle. For this second engagement, the pilot in the third plane, and Woody and I in the fourth, would act as decoys and fly through the Tornado formation in the hopes that they would turn on us, allowing Parky and his wingman to roll in for a gun kill on our attackers. With the mission briefed, we jumped into the small vans for the short ride to our F-16 in a half-moon cement bunker, a holdover from the Cold War.

The crew chief helped me stow my two small bags and strap into the back seat. I remember thinking how hard and stiff everything felt; this plane was built for purpose, not comfort. In very little time, Woody started the jet's engine, and we taxied out of our bunker to take our place behind the other three F-16 Fighting Falcons.

The formation departed two by two, so Woody was slightly offset behind the third plane as we matched his speed and chased him down the runway until we were airborne. The F-16's thrust was beyond intense, and I sank further and further back into the seat as it accelerated. Once airborne, the view from the bubble canopy was incredible, with the glass dome extending below my shoulder height.

After leveling off and heading out to sea, we flew in a loose echelon formation, not very close to the wingmen around us.

Woody then asked me, "Would you like to fly?"

"Sure," I said, placing my hand on the right-hand sidestick controller before announcing, "I have the aircraft."

"You have the aircraft," he repeated.

It was the fulfillment of a childhood dream. I was now flying a fighter aircraft!

The F-16 is a fly-by-wire pane, which was revolutionary during its time back in the 1980s. Rather than a control stick placed between the pilot's legs, this plane had the usual setup of the throttle on the left, but with the control stick just outside the pilot's right thigh. A conventional control stick was the size of a toilet-bowl plunger and could swivel around in a two-foot radius circle, but this sidestick controller barely moved at all. It was so responsive that I practically could just think about the direction I wanted the plane to go.

I was expecting a loose, slippery, responsive feel on the control stick, but it actually was very stiff and hard to move. I didn't go crazy and act like a born-again Thunderbird pilot, though; I just smoothly guided the jet left and right, keeping our distance from the third plane in our formation, which was ahead of us and to our right. After a few minutes, Woody took control of the fighter again, and we prepared to meet the two British Royal Air Force Tornados.

With the Tornados approaching from the west, Woody asked me over the cockpit interphone, "Are you ready?"

I placed my hands on the hand grips just inside the Dutch F-16's canopy, tensed up to prepare for the G-load, and answered, "Yes."

From the backseat, I saw the same display as Woody's, so whatever he selected on his screen was repeated on mine. For the missile engagement, the fighter's eight-inch screen had a large circle, which Woody guided until he was over our adversary. Once he had a lock-on tone, he pulled his trigger, simulating the launch of an air-to-air missile.

Score one missile "kill" for Woody. He checked his fuel, then radioed Parky, the F-16 formation leader, and said, "We can stick around for the second engagement."

The four-ship fighter formation reset for a second mock battle against the two British Tornados. As briefed, Woody and I, flying in the fourth F-16, followed the third jet in our formation as we flew toward the oncoming Tornados. The two British fighters flew past us, but didn't take the bait to turn on us.

"We're through them!" Woody exclaimed. "I'm going back for a gun kill."

He yanked the F-16 into a tight turn, and my vision closed to the size of a half-dollar as the blood rushed from my head. I grunted and strained against the high-G forces, but I didn't pass out or throw up.

Woody switched the display to gun mode, and the eight-inch screen displayed a smaller circle on the green screen. He pursued his Tornado target, placing it within the video-game circle, and pulled the trigger. The tone and screen icon signaled a successful hit. It was the second "kill" of the day for Captain Woodsma.

After our twenty-minute aerial battle between Holland and England, Woody checked his fuel gauge and announced we were at our "bingo" fuel, meaning it was time to depart for our destination. We separated from the F-16 formation and headed to RAF Brize Norton, in central England, fifty miles west of London. I regained my full vision and calmed my breathing, happy to still be conscious and not tasting vomit in my oxygen mask. I chalked those up as my own personal victories.

The coordination meetings were attended by representatives of each unit participating in Central Enterprise exercise, from the F-16s, flown by the Netherlands, Norway, and Belgium, to the older

Jaguars flown by the Brits. Refueling tankers were represented by the U.S. KC-135s at RAF Mildenhall, north of London, and the British VC-10s, an adapted 1960s British airliner. The timeline and airspace were briefed for all participants, and I briefed the refueling capabilities of the KDC-10, stating that we could refuel fighters such as F-16s, F-15s and F-4s, using our boom, but we didn't have the hose-and-drogue capability to refuel the British Tornados or Jaguars. The evening wrapped up at the officers club with ham sandwiches and pints of ale. It was all very English.

The next morning, Woody and I attended a final session of coordination meetings, then prepared for our flight home. At 3 p.m., we headed back to the F-16B for our return flight across the North Sea.

Woody took off from the British base, leveled off at just 3,000 feet, and pointed the F-16's nose east toward the English Channel. As we whistled along at 600 miles per hour, he suddenly spotted a small, red Piper civilian aircraft and quickly banked away from the slow-moving airplane. I'm sure the private pilot got an eyeful as our jet roared by and headed for the coastline.

Once over water, Woody dropped down to a hundred feet above the water, and we cruised smoothly along as I watched the whitecaps just below the canopy railing. Woody suddenly said, "Oops, ship!" and quickly climbed and banked away from a cargo ship that we rapidly overtook. I felt like a youngster on a joyride, smiling from ear to ear.

Once beyond the sea traffic, Woody settled back down to the hundred-foot altitude and asked me, "Do you want to feel the power of this engine?"

"You bet," I said.

Woody then ripped the throttle to idle, and the jet glided along as it quietly lost speed. Though he raised the nose a bit to compensate for the lack of thrust and lift, we never deviated from the 100-foot altitude.

Once he was back to 150 miles per hour, he said, "Ready? Here we go," then slammed the throttle full forward.

Just as in the earlier takeoff, I was pressed back into my seat, and I sank even farther into it as the Fighting Falcon lowered its nose and accelerated toward 500 miles per hour over the ocean waves. The sheer power of that single-engine fighter provided an unforgettable thrill.

After that, Woody asked me, "Do you want to fly again?"

"Yes," I answered, "but not at this altitude."

Since I didn't know how sensitive the pitch of the jet could be, the last thing I wanted to do was get into a "pilot-induced oscillation" (PIO) and splash our sleek fighter into the sea. Woody climbed to 500 feet, and I then took control of the sidestick with my right hand. As I did the previous day, I gently guided the jet left and right, checking out the waves of the English Channel below. Had we been up higher, and clear of other air traffic, I would have enjoyed really flying the F-16 as it was meant, with high-G acrobatics such as loops and rolls, just like in the T-38 over Oklahoma, or like Woody had done in the mock dogfight. It still was an awesome experience.

After a few minutes, I gave the controls back to Woody as the western coast of Holland came into view ahead of us.

I checked my watch and saw that I wouldn't be able to catch the evening train back to Eindhoven, so I told Woody I'd need to get a room at their officers club, which was common at Dutch air bases, and he radioed ahead to his squadron operations room.

"Major Dale won't be able to make his planned train trip back tonight, so can we make arrangements for him?" he asked.

Woody entered the overhead pattern of Leeuwarden Air Base, flying down the landing runway at a thousand feet above the ground, then aggressively rolled into a ninety-degree bank, with a hard left-hand turn. I felt the G-suit activate, the air bladders squeezing my legs like a boa constrictor suffocating its prey. He rolled out after 180 degrees of turn, and after a few seconds he lowered the landing gear and extended the plane's flaps before making a gentle, descending left-hand turn toward the runway. With a "bump, bump," the wheels hit the runway, completing my second F-16 flight in two days.

Woody taxied back into the cement shelter and shut down the engine as the crew chief approached the left side of our canopy with a ladder. I gathered my two bags of gear and exited the cockpit as a van pulled in, just behind the aircraft's tail.

"Major Dale, are you ready to go?" the driver asked.

"Just about," I said, before shaking Woody's hand as I thanked him for two memorable flights.

I expected the van driver to take me to the officers club, which had very spartan amenities for an overnight stay, but that wasn't what they had planned for me.

The van driver continued down the flight line before stopping next to a small, glass-nosed helicopter. It was a French-made Alouette training helicopter.

"We found you a ride home," he said, smiling.

I stepped out of the van as the young second lieutenant helicopter pilot extended his hand and asked, "Are you ready to go to Eindhoven, sir?"

I couldn't believe my luck. I was being treated like a VIP, and this was totally unexpected. I certainly hoped I could luck into a Dutch F-16 flight to England, but I also had never imagined participating in a four-ship dogfight off the coast of Holland, or accelerating to 500 miles per hour just 100 feet above the North Sea. Now I was seated in the left seat of a helicopter with a glass nose that was similar to, but larger than, the Army helicopters seen in *M*A*S*H*. The Dutch lieutenant started the rotor spinning, lifted us off the ground and headed south at 300 feet above the green fields of Holland.

After a half-hour, the lieutenant asked, "Have you ever flown a helicopter before?"

"No, I haven't," I answered with a hopeful tone in my voice.

"Would you like to fly?" he asked.

"You bet," I replied.

I was flying a second aircraft for the first time ever in the same day. I couldn't believe my luck!

I placed my right hand on the control stick that was between my legs and placed my left hand on the "collective," which is the control for pitch and power. My young instructor gave me some pointers, such as keeping the compass case in the windshield even with the horizon to maintain level flight. I didn't make any changes with my left hand, but I did use small inputs with my right hand to make a few turns as I kept the helicopter on course and level.

I didn't start out as a smooth pilot; instead, I often tightly gripped the controls and over-controlled both during pilot training formation flying and my early attempts at air refueling as the receiver behind the tanker. In those years, I was guilty of being a nervous student with a "death grip" on the controls. But ten years after joining our Air Force, I was now a more confident pilot, and I had learned the smooth techniques of a light touch on the controls, and how to make small inputs rather than large, aggressive corrections.

I must have impressed the lieutenant, because he asked, "Are you sure you haven't done this before?"

I accepted his compliment.

"No, but it's a lot like air refueling behind another airplane," I told him.

We continued southbound, flying over green fields surrounded by dikes and channels of water, which kept the fields dry for planting. It seemed that each small, picturesque Dutch town had church steeples poking above the flat horizon. The sun was setting as we approached my home base thirty miles north of the Belgian border.

The lieutenant set the Alouette down on the tarmac near our squadron and wished me a good night. I gathered my two small bags and thanked him for the beautiful sightseeing tour of his country. That was the second of my two best days with the Royal Netherlands Air Force.

36

EMERGENCY AIR REFUELING OVER THE ADRIATIC

BY NOVEMBER 1996 the Dutch were ready to conduct their first combat operations since World War II. The genocide in Bosnia and Herzegovina had been brewing for years and after diplomacy failed, the United Nations began sending troops into the region. The Netherlands provided F-16s and its two KDC-10s for air operations. Our KDC-10s were now certified to refuel NATO F-15s, F-16s, German F-4s, and the NATO E-3 AWACS, all of which were participating in this operation east of the Adriatic Sea.

While coalition F-16s flew missions from Aviano Air Base in northern Italy, the long-range KDC-10 flew its combat support refueling missions from our home base in Eindhoven. Each mission required a two-hour flight over the Swiss Alps and along the eastern coast of Italy to arrive at our assigned air refueling orbit. Once in orbit, we checked in with the controlling AWACS, call sign "MAGIC," and remained in orbit for four hours before heading back home.

Before beginning our support operation, I flew along with a Dutch pilot, flight engineer, and boom operator in a Fokker F-27 to Vicenza, Italy, to receive the intelligence briefing and special instructions (SPINS) that would coordinate the air battle plan. The SPINS in this operation were similar to the tactics we used during Desert Storm and Southern Watch.

At the conclusion of the briefing, the Air Force officer asked if we had a call sign in mind. Normally, our call sign for peacetime missions was "Netherlands Air Force *xxx*" along with a number associated with that day's mission. That was a mouthful to say on every radio call, so we were happy to pick a shorter moniker.

Our boom operator, Bart, suggested, "How about "JUICE," since we're giving them the juice to fly?"

That sounded like a great idea, and the JUICE call sign was born.

It was a surreal feeling to fly the same combat support missions that I flew over the desert, but from "our own backyard." The *Stars and Stripes* U.S. military newspaper ran an article during that period that featured interviews with pilots of the American F-16 units permanently based at Aviano Air Base. With their families living alongside them, those pilots flew daily combat sorties over a war zone. As one of them stated: "It's very strange to be shot at one moment, then get home and your wife asks why you didn't remember to stop to buy milk. One minute you're mowing your grass, and the next minute you're dodging missiles."

My experience was not nearly as dramatic, but I remember Karin and I being invited to our friend's house for dinner with three other civilian couples on an evening after a mission. I completed the eight-hour combat support mission by 5 p.m., then drove to our friend's house still wearing my flight suit and black lace-up flying boots. Karin brought along a change of clothing for me, but I walked in to find everyone gathered around the dinner table, asking me about my "day at the office." They were quite content to have me join them in my work clothes.

We planned our missions the day before each departure, running a computer flight plan that gave us our time en route and the amount of fuel required. One morning at 9 a.m. I was leaning over a map with another pilot, Kees, when there was a large explosion that rattled the windows of our old 1950s wooden building. Kees looked up without much emotion and said, "Oh, yes. They discovered an unexploded World War II bomb yesterday, and they are detonating it this morning at 9 a.m." Thanks for the heads-up, Kees.

Holland was overrun by Germany at the outset of World War II, and Eindhoven had been used as a German bomber base throughout the war—but, in a strange bit of irony, any unexploded munitions discovered each year around Dutch construction sites were bombs dropped from Allied bombers.

Americans living in the States during World War II were far removed from the daily dangers, but for the Dutch it literally was in their backyard. Our KDC-10 flight commander, Maj. Maarten Kuijpers, was born in November 1943. When I discovered this, he told me a family story: As an infant, he was placed in a bassinet outdoors on a sunny day for warmth and sunshine. A German V-2 rocket launcher sat in a neighboring field, aimed at England. One morning, a faulty V-2 exploded shortly after lifting off, and Maarten's family ran outside to check on him. They found rocket shrapnel embedded in his bassinet; he was lucky to be alive.

On December 17, 1996, our crew took off for the Adriatic, and we rendezvoused with two American and two Dutch F-16s that were providing air cover over the region. We offloaded our required fuel load and remained in orbit until our allotted time was up, then called the controlling AWACS requesting permission to return to base, or RTB. With permission granted, we turned northwest and headed toward the Italian coastline.

We were still monitoring the primary air refueling frequency when an excited voice called out, "Any tanker! Any tanker! Cobra 7-1."

I replied, "Cobra 7-1, this is Juice 2-0. Go ahead."

"We are a flight of two F-16s at emergency fuel. Can you refuel us?" he asked.

"Yes," I answered. "We'll turn back toward you. Bring up your air-to-air TACAN."

Two military planes could dial in a reciprocal pair of channels on their tactical air navigation (TACAN) aid to see the distance and bearing to each other. Additionally, the F-16 flight lead could also see our transponder code on his radar. By using those two methods, they completed the rendezvous within minutes.

As Cobra 7-1 pulled up behind us, his wingman, Cobra 7-2, took up his position off our left wing. Meanwhile, our boom operator, Dieter, lowered the refueling boom and prepared for contact.

Once Cobra 7-1 made contact with our refueling boom, his interphone system connected to ours, so we could talk to each other over "boom interphone" and not transmit outside the aircraft over the airwaves.

With contact made, we heard him exclaim, "Oh, man! That feels *gooood!* Brother, I was down to 600 pounds of gas and getting ready to punch out."

Six hundred pounds of fuel is about ninety gallons. This fighter jock had about four minutes of fuel remaining before flaming out his engine and ejecting over the Adriatic Sea. That was definitely running on empty for a powerful single-engine fighter.

The two F-16s had been providing close-air support to our ground forces and engaged an enemy unit attacking our allies. They were so engrossed in their life-saving mission that they had overflown their "bingo" fuel. The lead F-16 on our boom said, "Just give me 1,000 pounds, then get my wingman on for 2,000, then I'll come back to top off."

Dieter obliged his request, making the contacts while the flight engineer activated the fuel pumps to give them their "juice." The entire emergency air refueling took just ten minutes to accomplish. With enough gas to safely fly back to Aviano, the two satisfied customers peeled off to our right. We landed in Eindhoven that evening, logging seven hours of flying time and recording a "save" of two American fighters. To quote our F-16 customer, "Oh, man! That felt *gooood!*"

37

FLYING A DESK

ONE EVENING IN EARLY 1997, our phone rang in Waalre, a small Dutch village just south of Eindhoven. A familiar voice started the conversation: "Hey, what are you doing?"

It was my KC-10 friend, Maj. Scott Mitchell, calling from the Air Force Personnel Center (AFPC) in San Antonio, where he now had a "career-enhancing" non-flying job.

"We just finished dinner over here," I answered. "What's up?"

"We have to find you a job," he said.

"Why's that?" I asked.

"Because you're not going to school," Scott said, delivering the shocking news that I wasn't selected for the next level of professional military education (PME), known as intermediate service school (ISS). This course is designed for mid-level majors—and although I, like all majors, had completed it by correspondence while in Holland, attending the course in person was a steppingstone to becoming a squadron commander. I had not made the latest round of in-school selections, which came as a surprise—and was deflating, too. After riding the high of being selected as a foreign exchange officer, my master plan had hit a road bump. Just as Colonel Lichte had cautioned, I worked hard for two-and-a-half years with the Dutch, but nobody in the Air Force knew or cared what I had accomplished.

According to our plan, we had extended our overseas stay by six months so that a summertime move would put us back in the States in time for a new school year, both for our children and myself. Now Scott was telling me I had to scramble to get another job within the Air Force. At this point in my career, it was time to step out of the cockpit and get a staff job, something known to aviators as "flying a desk." It was a necessary evil for a successful career, but not something I looked forward to doing.

Through our KC-10 contacts, I emailed Maj. Jeff Mintzlaff, a fellow Barksdale KC-10 pilot now serving as an executive officer to a two-star general on the AMC headquarters staff in Belleville, Illinois, east of St. Louis. He lined me up with a job in his plans and programs (XP) division as the KC-10 program element monitor, or PEM, overseeing the fleet of fifty-nine KC-10s for flying hours and modifications. At least I would be dealing with a plane I knew well, and I also would be keeping our beloved KC-10 fleet up to date.

I received a bit of bad advice and good advice before our move to Scott Air Force Base. In a brief conversation with a colonel that I didn't know, he asked, "Are you an alternate for the service school that you missed out on?"

"No," I replied.

"Then you're probably not going to school at all," he said.

The colonel was telling me I likely would never attend ISS, so I should plan on staying at Scott for a three-year tour. For this reason, we bought a house, intending to serve three years on the AMC staff.

Brig. Gen. Art Lichte had been our Barksdale operations group commander colonel in 1994, and he was with me during Operation Southern Watch in Abu Dhabi. He was now based at Scott and had a different, more hopeful perspective. He advised that we should return from overseas in early summer so that, if school became a possibility for me the following year, I would have the minimum one-year time on station at Scott to be released to attend ISS.

In June 1997, my exchange tour with the Dutch came to an end. During that time, our children had attended the year-round regional international school with teachers from England, Scotland, and Ireland. Shelby, now five, spoke with a beautiful English lilt, using phrases such as "Can I have a go?" and "Will we do that straight away?" Daniel, meanwhile, completed third grade with a strict Irish teacher named Ms. McNally, a no-nonsense lady who kept the eight-year-olds in line.

Within the military, service members are allotted thirty days of vacation or "leave" per year that can build up, or carry over, up to sixty days if they don't use all their available leave. I arrived in Holland in January 1995 with a full bank of sixty days, having just completed Dutch language school. Over the next two-and-a-half years I continued to accrue another seventy-five days of leave, for a total of 135 days.

The year-round school schedule for our children in the Netherlands had one-week breaks every five weeks of the school year, so we set out for different family adventures that included southern England, northern Scotland, Bavaria, Germany, Disneyland Paris, the French city of Nice, and Monaco. We even crossed the Austrian border to eat spaghetti in northern Italy.

On Flag Day, June 14, 1997, we arrived back in the States, welcomed by the display of our country's flag everywhere we looked as we left the airport. I returned with a leave balance of just two days, having enjoyed 133 vacation days with my family touring Europe.

After buying a house in O'Fallon, Illinois, I started my desk job at Scott Air Force Base in late June. Meeting my fellow officers in AMC Plans and Programs was a gloomy experience. My predecessor, Maj. Mike Mendonca, introduced me to fellow captains and majors, pilots of the older KC-135, C-141, C-5, and the C-130, plus the newly built C-17 cargo plane. The pilots were responsible for the upkeep of their particular aircraft types, and we all sat close to each other in side-by-side office cubicles.

As I met Maj. Ron Simmons, the C-17 program manager who

was sitting at the desk behind mine, he stuck out his hand and said, "Welcome to hell." The other pilots looked downtrodden, almost like prisoners of war.

I had walked into an office where our boss, a well-meaning, eager-to-please colonel, worked from 6 a.m. to 6 p.m. Monday through Friday—and many weekends, too.

Ron asked me later, "You know what Friday means, don't you?"

"No, what?" I replied.

"Only two more workdays 'til Monday," he said.

This was not going to be fun.

I settled into my office job, building Microsoft Excel spreadsheets to track the millions of dollars necessary for the KC-10 flying-hour training programs and upcoming fleet modifications. The other necessary evil was fielding phone calls from the Pentagon asking about the impact of forecasted budget cuts.

Just as Major Mendonca had predicted when he trained me in our few days of overlap, often a "win" was not losing money. A typical workday started with a call from the KC-10 program manager at the Pentagon running a "drill" after receiving news of potential congressionally mandated budget cuts. The "what-if" scenario often asked the budget impact of cutting my KC-10 budget by five percent to ten percent.

I plugged the numbers into Major Mendonca's Excel sheets. They showed that engine overhauls would be delayed, or that our aircrews would run out of flying hours in September, meaning that the aircrews would be unable to complete their annual training requirements to maintain mission-ready status. This data was forwarded to Lt. Col. Jim Albright (my boss), and to Colonel Snedeker above him, then transmitted to the Pentagon. By the end of a twelve-hour day, the proposed budget cut usually was canceled, and I went home with the same budget I started the day with. It was a whole day's effort just to maintain the status quo. This was the one year of my life when I dreaded Sunday night, because it meant

Monday morning was coming. Karin could tell my mood was more subdued than usual.

On September 13, 1997, an American C-141 Starlifter cargo plane collided with a German Air Force transport off the coast of Namibia in southwest Africa at 35,000 feet. It later was determined the German crew was flying at the wrong altitude for their direction of flight. If you've ever looked out of the window on an airliner and thought you saw another airplane uncomfortably close, rest assured they are separated by a thousand feet from each other.

Airplanes flying any westerly heading will fly at an even altitude, such as 30,000 feet or 40,000 feet. Conversely, any eastbound plane will fly an odd-numbered altitude, such as 29,000 feet. I've always remembered this rule by thinking, "Easterners are odd."

This unfortunate mid-air collision could have been prevented had both airplanes been equipped with the new Traffic Collision Avoidance System, known as TCAS. With this technology, all airplanes emit a code with their transponder system, enabling other aircraft to see their position on a cockpit display—and, if necessary, audible commands are issued to climb or descend to avoid a collision. This technology was available in 1997, but it wasn't made mandatory for military airplanes until after this accident.

My contribution to the KC-10 fleet was the procurement and installation of TCAS, plus updated radios to comply with European airspace requirements. This laid the foundation for a modernized "glass" cockpit, enabling the KC-10 to fly in today's global air traffic management (GATM) modern airspace structure.

The new list of intermediate school attendees was released by December, and thankfully I was chosen to attend the Army's command and general staff course (CGSC) in Fort Leavenworth, Kansas. So, six months after buying a new home in an Illinois cornfield, we learned the good news that I would be leaving the following summer. So much for that unknown colonel's prediction.

As the year on staff progressed, Scott Mitchell called again, telling me of his idea to interview at Andrews Air Force Base in Maryland to fly as a VIP pilot, hopefully on the new Boeing 757 known as a C-32. Scott also had received a school assignment for the following summer to the Navy course in Newport, Rhode Island. His idea was to lock in an assignment at Andrews before going to ISS so he wouldn't have to compete with other school attendees the following year.

"C'mon, Dave," he said. "You should go with me."

We had nothing to lose. If we were turned down, we would simply return to fly the KC-10 after attending the major's course and prepare for a leadership job in our old airplane.

To apply for an Andrews interview, I had to submit a "dream sheet," which is the military's version of a job request. The higher my endorsement on the request, the better my chances of receiving the job. That meant making an appointment with the two-star general in charge of AMC/XP. If I gained his approval, then I had a much better shot of getting an interview at Andrews.

At 10 a.m. on a January morning, I sat down with Major General Hogle in his office, asking for his support. He knew I had just been chosen for school in the upcoming summer. He was not a fan of the "career-ending" (his words) VIP squadrons at Andrews, regarding them as mere flying clubs with fancy civilian airplanes that didn't truly support the Air Force mission.

The whole purpose of attending any ISS, be it Air Force, Army, Navy, or Marines, is to prepare to become a squadron commander or a similar leadership position. In his mind, it would be a wasted opportunity if all I was going to do was move to Andrews to fly their shiny airplanes.

"If all you want to do is go to Andrews, then I don't see why we are wasting a school slot on you," he told me.

I fidgeted nervously, thinking that this two-star general was threatening to pull my school slot.

"I'd like to become a squadron commander," I told him, "and if you're making me choose between ISS and Andrews, then I would choose the school option."

Disappointed, I left his office without his endorsement and called Scott, telling him about the possibility of losing my school slot.

"Dave, he can't do that!" Scott yelled. "The Air Force gave you that school slot, not General Hogle!"

Scott was right. Fortunately for me, my immediate boss was Lt. Col. Jim Albright, who previously served as the CT-43 (Boeing 737) squadron commander, flying VIP missions from Ramstein Air Base in Germany. He said I didn't need Major General Hogle's endorsement, and suggested I forward my dream sheet to Colonel Snedeker, our boss, for his endorsement. Thankfully that turned out to be all I needed to earn an interview at Andrews.

In March 1998, much to the major general's chagrin, Scott and I were selected to interview at Andrews, outside of Washington, D.C. We prepared for the three-day event by going over potential interview questions in our lodging rooms on the base.

The first afternoon kicked off with a social event at the golf course, where the first person I bumped into was my old Vance Air Force Base T-38 instructor pilot, Maj. Larry "Judas" Deist, now a Gulfstream instructor pilot at Andrews. I didn't know he was part of the 99th Airlift Squadron, but I certainly was glad to see a familiar face.

The events during the three-day interview also served as a two-way street of sorts. Andrews personnel would gauge if we were the right fit for their unit, and we would learn through the social times and squadron visits if the Andrews mission was right for us.

Being assigned to Andrews could be very chaotic, with constant mission changes. The conventional wisdom was that if a squadron member had any special event coming up, such as a child's play or a concert with a spouse, then that person should take a day of leave. Otherwise, we were fair game for any missions that popped up on short notice—and there would be many of those.

The afternoons were spent touring both the 99th Airlift Squadron and 1st Airlift Squadron, informally known as the "Little Airplane Squadron" and "Big Airplane Squadron." The 99th Airlift

Squadron flew two types of aircraft: the C-9 (a civilian 1960s-era DC-9), and three Gulfstream varieties, the G-III, G-IV, and newly built G-V. These were known by their Air Force designation C-20B, C-20H, and C-37A. The C-9 often supported the first lady or flew stateside congressional trips, while the Gulfstreams flew cabinet members, service secretaries, and congressmen on longer-range international flights.

The 1st Airlift Squadron flew the 1950s-era VC-137 (a Boeing 707 formerly used as Air Force One) until it was retired and replaced by the new Boeing 757, known as the C-32. Scott's main goal was to fly the new C-32. That had been my desire initially, until I stepped foot on a Gulfstream. This sleek executive jet just oozed "cool" and "high class." All three variants of the Air Force Gulfstreams looked similar inside: a mahogany-lined entryway from the fold-down door that created a small staircase for entry.

The cockpit was to the left of the entryway, while the distinguished visitor (DV) cabin began to the right. Gleaming brown mahogany panels were nicely complimented by dark-blue carpet and a dozen blue-leather first-class seats, six per side, extending to the aft galley, where the flight attendants prepared gourmet meals from scratch. Beyond the galley was a lavatory, also lined in mahogany—and, finally, the small baggage storage room, which was located near the tail. Once I heard about the Gulfstream's ability to fly long range while taking off and landing on just 5,000 feet of runway, I knew this versatile aircraft was the one for me.

The second evening was spent at another social event, where we not only exchanged information, but also gave Andrews pilots a chance to see how the interviewees behaved away from work. Could we play well with others and be good representatives of our Air Force for these VIP missions? They wanted to observe the "whole person," and not just the formal interviewee.

The third day was the sit-down interview in front of a panel of representatives from both squadrons. Both squadron commanders and their deputies, called operations officers, sat in a U-shaped arrangement of tables, along with pilots from the training and evaluation divisions.

I sat in a lone chair, wearing my dress blues of coat and tie, surrounded on three sides by the panel. The 99th Airlift Squadron commander was a KC-10 pilot friend of mine, Lt. Col. Mike Zepf. Mike and I flew in separate squadrons at Barksdale Air Force Base in Louisiana, but we had played intramural softball together four years earlier.

The panel members looked over my flying history from the manilla folders in front of them and asked questions about my experience, as well as questions about how I would handle specific situations. Their purpose was to see how I balanced safety with mission accomplishment. Would I break flying rules to get the job done, or would I keep the passengers safe? The Andrews motto is "safety, comfort, and reliability," so they hoped to determine from among the candidates who would accomplish missions using those priorities.

The final question I got from Lieutenant Colonel Zepf was, "Dave, although we can't guarantee what aircraft you would be hired to fly, if you had a choice, which plane would you choose?"

"Sir, I came to the interview fully hoping to fly the new C-32," I replied. "But after visiting the 99th and seeing the capabilities and versatility of the Gulfstream, that's the plane I hope to fly."

The panel of officers thanked me for my time, and I was dismissed. I stood, saluted crisply, turned, and left the room, hoping for the best.

Four weeks later, Scott and I both learned we made the cut for an Andrews assignment: Scott to the 1st Airlift Squadron, and me to the 99th Airlift Squadron, just as we had hoped. We could now set off for ISS with our follow-on assignment already in hand.

The Army school runs during a normal school year, beginning each August, and is attended by a thousand Army majors, plus sixty officers each from the other services, along with an equal number of international officers. Because we were not familiar with Army tactics, the Air Force, Navy, and Marine officers reported in July to learn how to "speak Army."

Karin and I contracted a local property manager to rent out our one-year-old house, then packed our belongings for a fifth household move in four years. During my going-away party from Scott Air Force Base, I was presented with a small, wooden plaque, on which was mounted a pewter replica of the St. Louis Arch and an engraving that read:

To Major David Dale
June 1997-June 1998
Not here long enough to break anything.

38

FIRST ATP CHECKRIDE

C-20D, a military version of the Gulfstream III. (Air Force photo)

I GRADUATED from the Army's command and general staff course in May 1998, and our family wrapped up what was deemed "The Year of the Family." Although I read and wrote as much as when I earned my earlier master's degree, Karin and I made time to watch Daniel's baseball games and Shelby's soccer matches. I attended Webelos meetings with Daniel, and Karin served as Shelby's Brownie leader. For a year we lived in a rundown 1970s Army rowhouse that had broken linoleum square tiles, no dishwasher, and a leaky septic system in the crawlspace under the floor. Our Army neighbors excitedly said it was the best housing they had ever had, so I realized we had endured an "Air Force appreciation tour" as we packed up our household goods and headed east to a townhouse in Springfield, Virginia.

All Gulfstream pilots at Andrews Air Force Base start off in the G-III (C-20B). For many years the pilots received simulator training from Flight Safety International (FSI) in Savannah, Georgia. The location was ideal because the beautiful business jets are expertly built right across the parking lot from the FSI training center. After completing five simulator training sessions, the Air Force pilots returned to Andrews for their flight training and an initial qualification checkride.

The VIP airlift community was rocked by the crash of a Ramstein CT-43 in Dubrovnik, Croatia, on April 3, 1996, carrying the U.S. Secretary of Commerce Ron Brown. The details of the crash investigation are documented elsewhere, but one of the outcomes of that was Air Force distinguished visitor (DV) airlift pilots now needed an FAA airline transport pilot (ATP) rating to show that military pilots received the same level of training as their civilian counterparts. As a result, my FSI G-III training culminated with a checkride administered by an FAA evaluator.

My simulator partner was a great friend, Keith "Tater" Tatum, with whom I served on the Air Mobility Command staff in 1998. Tater, a funny guy with a great sense of humor, was a Georgia-born comedian. He was Larry the Cable Guy before that persona was created. We studied our butts off for two weeks in Savannah, enjoying a lot of great laughs along the way. The training syllabus called for five four-hour training simulator flights, followed by an FAA-administered simulator checkride on the sixth session. Tater and I worked and flew very well together. The fifth session was known as the "recommend" ride; if we performed up to standard, we would be recommended for the checkride.

Each day we arrived at 8 a.m. for a two-hour briefing, followed by a four-hour simulator session beginning at 10 a.m. In my days in the

KC-10, the instructor attended the evaluation session, running the computer panel, while an additional evaluator was brought along to observe our performance, and that's what I expected to happen in Savannah.

At the end of the "recommend" ride, our Gulfstream simulator instructor said, "Great job, guys. You won't have any problems tomorrow," and signed us off as ready to go.

Relieved, we gathered up our flying gear and books, and as we were leaving the debriefing room, I said, "See you at 8 a.m. tomorrow."

He smiled and replied, "See y'all."

Tater and I showed up at 7:40 a.m. the next morning, coffee in hand, ready to go, twenty minutes early—or so we thought. We walked into our assigned briefing room, where a husky, gray-haired man sat.

"You boys from the Air Force?" he asked, scowling.

"Yes sir," I said, extending my hand. "I'm David Dale."

"And I'm Keith," Tater added, extending his hand.

Our evaluator glared at us and said, "You boys are forty minutes late. I was just getting ready to pack up and go home."

Holy crap. On the day of our first FAA evaluation, both Keith and I missed the fact that it was a THREE-hour briefing, and not the normal two-hour briefing. We apologized profusely, explaining that neither of us caught the 7 a.m. start time.

Our gruff old FAA evaluator (probably my age now) took pity on us and relented.

"Well, we might as well get started," he said.

For the next two hours of our briefing, Tater and I proceeded to verbally build a G-III one system at a time: hydraulics, electrics, fuel, and pressurization. Luckily, we knew our stuff, and finally our evaluator said, "That's enough. Let's go get some coffee."

We leaned against the railing overlooking the simulators, waiting for our sim to become available, because we had to wait for it to settle down on its motion-providing hydraulic lifts from the previous training session. With his anger now subsided, our evaluator asked, "Where you boys from?" with a distinct southern accent.

"I grew up in Houston" I said.

Added Tater: "I grew up in a small town here in Georgia."

"Oh, yeah?" the old guy replied. "Where about?"

"It's a little town called Saint Simons Island," Tater replied. "Only about 10,000 people there."

The old guy raised an eyebrow.

"You're from Saint Simons Island?" he asked. "I'm from Saint Simons Island."

There is a God, I thought.

"You know the Piggly Wiggly on Third Street?" Tater asked him.

"Sure do," Mr. FAA replied.

"That's my uncle's store," Tater said.

The next four hours went amazingly well. In fact, we knew things were going smoothly when our evaluator started to offer advice, asking, "Have y'all ever tried this?" That meant he had seen enough of our evaluation and now just wanted to enjoy the training session for the allotted four hours.

Tater and I earned our first FAA airline transport pilot (ATP) rating, and the day ended on a much lighter note than it began.

39

ANDREWS AIR FORCE BASE GULFSTREAM TRAINING

WITH OUR ATP IN HAND, Tater and I headed back to Andrews to complete the flight training syllabus in the Air Force C-20B, built in the mid-1980s. The beautiful blue-and-white jets had the same interior as most other Air Force Gulfstreams: blue carpet, mahogany wood trim and pullout tables, and a dozen blue, plush, leather swiveling and reclining chairs for our flying guests.

The Air Force operated the plane with five crew members: two officers and three enlisted men. The pilots were officers ranging in rank from captains to lieutenant colonels, all highly experienced in worldwide airlift operations. Behind the two pilots sat a flight engineer, usually a technical sergeant or master sergeant with years of experience in cargo aircraft. Our C-20, or any Gulfstream for that matter, wasn't designed to require a flight engineer, but having one along, with their ability to repair or move the aircraft, certainly aided in our missions.

The flight engineers were not very busy during flights, but they ensured that our high-visibility VIP missions progressed smoothly. They preflighted the aircraft, and were qualified to start the engines and taxi the plane to the red carpet before each flight. This enabled the pilots to plan the flight at base operations and obtain the latest weather information for the route, and to coordinate any changes to the trip with the VIP's liaison officer, known to us as "the contact."

The flight engineer also acted as a third set of eyes when we flew into unfamiliar airfields or austere environments, such as Africa or the former Soviet Union, and was also a certified FAA airframe and powerplant mechanic capable of fixing minor maintenance issues during these international missions.

The communications system operator, or CSO, sat just aft of the cockpit, across the aisle from the entry door, in what amounted to a flying phone booth. He or she gained experience in the E-3 AWACS or C-130 airborne battlefield command-and-control-center mission before serving as the communications link for our VIPs. The CSO placed in-flight telephone calls to the Pentagon, the White House, or battlefield commanders "downrange," and also received encrypted faxes and emails to pass to our VIPs.

The icing on the cake of these executive jets was the in-flight kitchen galley featuring an enlisted, culinary-trained flight attendant (FA). The galley was the size of a recreational vehicle's kitchen, complete with a convection oven and small electrical appliances, which enabled the FA to make gourmet meals from scratch. The meals then were served on porcelain china, with silverware and cloth napkins. One of the main perks of DV airlift was that the crew ate the same delicious meals as the VIPs, and we all gained weight during that assignment.

Our flight attendants came to us from various assignments and included forklift drivers, administrative specialists, and aircraft maintenance personnel. Many of them just wanted the opportunity to fly. If an aircraft maintainer, or crew chief, was not selected to become a flight engineer, that person didn't mind trading in greasy wrenches for a three-piece suit and apron. But he or she still retained their maintenance know-how.

Tech. Sgt. Darrell Armistead, one of our flight attendants, used to be a C-20 crew chief based in Ramstein, Germany. During one mission, the crew was preflighting the aircraft while waiting for the customers, a.k.a. "the party," to arrive in their black Chevy Suburbans. The pilots noticed that one of the engine RPM gauges would not test properly, which was a requirement for the flight to take off. As Darrell prepped the food in the galley, he saw the discussion up in the cockpit as two pilots and the flight engineer hovered over the inoperative gauge. After wiping his hands on his apron, Darrell went forward to ask what was wrong and was told about the dead gauge.

"I used to work on these at Ramstein," he said. "Want me to take a look?"

"Sure," the aircraft commander said.

Darrell pulled out his trusty Leatherman multipurpose tool, unscrewed the offending gauge, straightened a bent wire in the cannon-plug connection, and reassembled the gauge. It passed the self-test, and the crew was back in business.

As he sheathed his Leatherman, Darrell said, "If you boys need me, I'll be in the kitchen."

Before I could enjoy any of these exciting international trips, though, I had to pass my aircraft systems oral evaluation and in-flight checkride. Andrews was known for administering tough, stressful, thorough checkrides, so given the requirements of our mission—taking well-known government officials to unheard-of places—passing a rigorous checkride was essential.

Our aircraft systems knowledge was far beyond that of corporate pilots. We fully understood how the electrical systems worked, from the start of a darkened, powered-off aircraft through engine start and placing the generators online, all the while spouting off enough volts, amps, and frequencies to impress any electrical engineering major.

Similarly, we could describe the fuel system by following a drop of gas from the fuel truck, through the fuel tanks, the engines, and out the exhaust. The same could be done with our pressurization system, following an air molecule from the atmosphere, through the engines, and all the way through our air-conditioning system.

I was not technically oriented when I was growing up, and my dad's idea of home repair was to pick up the phone and support the local economy, so I certainly learned a lot about aircraft systems in those three months of intense training.

On the flying side, each three-hour training mission consisted of multiple practice instrument approaches flown to other airports in our vicinity, from northern Virginia, to Maryland, to southern Pennsylvania. In previous flight training courses, crews only needed to deal with one issue at a time, such as degraded navigation equipment or an aircraft system malfunction, but usually not both. That gentleman's rule did not apply at Andrews. "Compound emergencies" were fair game, so as I flew a single-engine approach (the "dead" engine was operating at idle power, not shut off, so it could be regained for thrust when required), the evaluator could also take away the instrument landing system (ILS), requiring a back-up approach to be flown at the last minute. Tater and I each received our five required training flights before being recommended for our initial qualification checkride.

My evaluator was a well-respected pilot named Maj. Greg Cayon, who also served as a presidential pilot on Air Force One, the mammoth Boeing 747. Greg was easygoing and fun-loving, but he also was a very hard-working pilot. He knew any in-flight evaluation could be a nerve-wracking experience, and I'll never forget his ice-breaking words of wisdom: "Just remember, every checkride is a learning experience. But if you're still learning too much, you fail."

I walked him through all of the aircraft systems, chasing electrons, drops of gas, and air molecules on system diagrams, then we headed out to fly the G-III along with a squadron flight engineer. For the next three hours I concentrated heavily, handling simulated emergencies and degraded navigation equipment. Greg challenged me as I flew numerous approaches to several Delaware airports, including the small New Castle airport near Wilmington, and the huge Dover Air Force Base. By the end of September 14, 1999, I proudly became an ATP-rated, USAF-qualified C-20B pilot.

40

MOSCOW AND THE HOLY LAND IN FIVE DAYS

I STOOD in awe on Moscow's Red Square, posing for a picture in front of the brilliantly colored onion domes of Saint Basil's Cathedral. Fifteen years earlier, I "sat alert" on weeklong tours, trained and ready to drop a nuclear bomb from our B-52 on this very spot. This was both surreal and mind-boggling.

By mid-May 2000 I was serving as the copilot for Lt. Col. Matt Newman on a five-day operational mission evaluation (OME) culminating in Matt's upgrade to aircraft commander. Our evaluator, Maj. Mike Grenke, later served as an Air Force One pilot during President George W. Bush's secret mission into Iraq on Thanksgiving Day 2002. Our three enlisted flight crew members were Master Sgt. Mike Della Valle, Sgt. Andre Florence, and Sgt. Dawn Roberts. The primary passenger for the delegation was President Clinton's national security advisor, Sandy Berger, accompanied by ten of his support-staff members.

Moscow was a seven-hour flight from Andrews, which was plenty of time for Major Grenke to quiz Lieutenant Colonel Newman and observe how he led his crew on an international VIP mission. I was able to sit quietly, listen, and observe, knowing that my OME was just months away. We landed at Vnukovo Airport, on the outskirts of Moscow, on the evening of May 17. The old airport was lined with dozens of Aeroflot Russian airliners, each with a glass nose. We were told this was so they could film and gather intelligence as they flew their commercial flights to various countries.

At Saint Basil's Cathedral on Moscow's Red Square

While the national security advisor conducted his business the day after our arrival, we were free to tour Moscow. Matt hired a tour guide with a minivan, and the six of us set out to see the sights of our former adversary. The most memorable sites were Gorky Park and Red Square outside of the Kremlin. The Soviet space shuttle, a failed attempt at copying our own, sat unceremoniously in Gorky Park. Their version of our Enterprise was now a park attraction that children crawled around on. *Nice try, Ivan.*

Following my remarkable photo op in front of Saint Basil's Cathedral, we drove to a Russian open-air market on a gloomy, overcast, "this must be Russia" day. Like all good tourists, I bought the famous, brightly painted nesting wooden dolls for our daughter, and a Russian bear-fur hat for my dad, which he wore proudly during Colorado winters.

With the delegation's work wrapped up in Moscow after two days, Matt flew all of us to Ben Gurion Airport in Tel Aviv on May 19, landing just before evening. There was so much to see and do that we hardly knew where to start. By the next morning, Matt, Mike, and I were floating in the Dead Sea, caking ourselves with its therapeutic mud. From there, we toured the location of the Dead Sea Scrolls, taking in the sight of the ancient scrolls lying under Plexiglas. We were near the Jordan River, so I scooped up a small jar of water from the location of Jesus' baptism. My younger cousin, Tina, had recently had a baby, and this holy water would be used in her daughter Kylie's baptism. We headed back to the hotel, cleaned up, and prepared for the big event: a tour of Bethlehem and Jerusalem.

By happenstance, of our six crew members, all three pilots still attended church regularly, while the three enlisted personnel had not gone to church since childhood. Major Grenke, a large rough-and-tumble hunter on his days off, surprised everyone, telling us that he still taught Sunday school. Our planned Holy City tour with a guide cost each person more than $200, which was a lot for an enlisted crew member hoping to pocket their per diem to help pay bills back home. Grenke matter-of-factly advised us, "Look, guys, I know people who spend $2,000 to come on a tour of the Holy Land. I'm telling you, we won't pocket any per diem on this trip. There's too much history to see."

He was right.

Our driver, a very nice short, squat Jewish man in his early forties, picked us up at our hotel in his white van and drove toward Jerusalem. We went straight to a market to buy souvenirs, where I bought small crosses and tiny creches (nativity scenes) carved from local olive wood. Space was very limited in our plane, so large items were out of the question.

Maj. Mike Grenke and me, caked in Dead Sea mud

Pope John Paul had visited Israel at Easter, a month earlier, and signs of unrest were already beginning, with the newspaper reports detailing small riots and tires burning in the streets. The town of Jericho and the West Bank were off-limits to us, and I will never forget the tense, quiet seriousness of crossing two heavily armed military checkpoints during our tour. These Israeli soldiers, most likely combat-hardened, were alert and not kidding around.

Placing our gifts on the site of Christ's birth

With our white plastic bags of trinkets and souvenirs, we set out for Bethlehem. What surprised me the most was that 1,000-year-old churches now stood as shrines over sites where 2,000-year-old biblical events took place. A church stood atop the birthplace of Jesus, and we all joined the long line of pilgrims, shuffling along, silently looking up and around the reverently still cathedral. We finally funneled down a circular stone stairwell and into the cramped area of the manger scene. Whether it was truly the location of Christ's birth, I don't know, but I stood quietly in awe. As suggested earlier by our guide, we each took turns placing our plastic bags of gifts on the location of Christ's birth, allowing them to be blessed.

From Bethlehem, we headed toward the Mount of Olives and read quotes of Jesus' Sermon on the Mount from the Gospel of Matthew. These included three-foot-by-five-foot blue-and-white ceramic tile depictions of the Lord's Prayer written in every language imaginable. This took me back to my many days of Sunday school and Bible studies. Suddenly, everything around me was familiar and coming alive.

The next stop was the garden of Gethsemane, where Jesus was betrayed by Judas. Exiting the garden, we could see in the distance Jerusalem's massive protective stone wall, and the gate where Jesus entered the city on what we now call Palm Sunday. So much biblical history! I soaked it all in, my head on a swivel.

Back in the van, our group drove toward the huge gold Dome of the Rock in the center of Old Jerusalem. After parking, our guide advised us to place our gifts under the back seat, and he locked the van. The seven of us walked toward the Western Wall under the shadows of the gold dome; there, our guide told us that this was the holiest place for Jews to pray because it was close to their destroyed temple. Jews would write a prayer on a small scrap of paper and, praying fervently, place it within the cracks of what is also known as the Wailing Wall. We silently took part in that ritual, placing our small, scribbled prayers in the limestone wall.

Thirty minutes later, we arrived back at the van to find the side windows broken out. Our driver's day planner was stolen, and the van had been rummaged through, but all of our "blessed gifts" remained under the rear seat. What a relief! We were thankful to still have our families' gifts intact.

Our guide then led us on a spiritual pilgrimage, walking a portion of the Stations of the Cross. These were the twelve locations identified during the cross-laden procession of "your Jesus" (his words) to Calvary, the site of his execution. Arriving at Calvary, outside the city wall, we once again filed into a thousand-year-old church erected over the site where three crosses once stood.

Not far away was the final stop of our meaningful day and tour: Jesus' tomb. Sadly, the line was extremely long, wrapping around the massive rectangular stone shrine of the tomb, and our time was short. I was struck by the physical proximity between the cross and the tomb. I wasn't certain if these were the actual locations or approximations for the Christian pilgrims. Regardless, our eager-to-please guide led us to a nearby collection of other tombs. One by one, we each took turns getting down on all fours, peeking inside to understand what Jesus' tomb could have looked like. What an ending to this moving day.

I believe religion is an individual choice, and it is not for me to pick or choose which religion is right or wrong. I was raised (somewhat unwillingly) attending the Presbyterian Church and fidgeted through many sermons, and I am not one to evangelize or proselytize. I can only tell those wanting to know what I've seen and heard.

In a remarkable personal journey, just four days earlier, I stood on Moscow's Red Square, a target I was willing to wipe out with a nuclear bomb. Now, standing in Jerusalem, everywhere I looked I was surrounded by many of the events detailed in the Gospels. In a single whirlwind day, we soaked in the sights of Jesus' life: his birth; teaching the Lord's Prayer; his palm-branch-strewn route into Jerusalem; his betrayal; his suffering; his crucifixion; his death; and the tomb from which he rose. This was THE monumental trip of a lifetime.

"For we cannot stop speaking about what we have seen and heard." Acts 4:20

Air Force C-37A parked at Ben Gurion Airport, Tel Aviv, Israel

41

SYDNEY 2000 OLYMPICS

JANUARY 1, 2000. Y2K. How will the world's computers respond? Will our aircraft navigation systems work? Will our country's air traffic control (ATC) system function properly? We were about to find out.

The day before, on December 31, 1999, Maj. Rob Crone and I flew the chief of staff of the Air Force, four-star Gen. Mike Ryan, from Washington, D.C., to Burbank, California. Five years later, Rob was the Lajes command post officer in the Azores for a clandestine C-37 mission, picking up special envoy Paul Bremer in Amman, Jordan.

On New Year's Day, General Ryan served as the grand marshal of the Rose Bowl Parade as everyone hoped their laptops and banking websites still worked. Like the rest of America, we had no idea what would happen to our technology, but just before departure time Rob and I powered up our C-20B. No Y2K bugs! Relieved, we took off from California that evening with a content general on board. Four hours later, we touched down at Andrews at 1 a.m. Sunday, January 2.

By January 2000 I had six months of Gulfstream C-20B flying under my belt and was ready for my second Gulfstream qualification.

Andrews had a diverse fleet of Gulfstream aircraft: the C-20Bs (G-III), C-20Hs (G-IV) and C-37s (G-V). To assist in scheduling the missions using the entire fleet, pilots could be qualified to fly two of these three variants. For safety's sake, the Air Force decided that trying to keep the specifications of two airplanes in our head was OK but did not want to overload us with a third set of numbers and procedures.

The Gulfstream fleet and the separate crew qualifications created a scheduling nightmare. While all pilots could fly the 1980s C-20B, the crew force was split evenly between those who were qualified in the C-20Hs and C-37s, which had different engines and other systems. If, due to a maintenance issue, a mission was switched from a C-20H to a C-37, the scheduler had to find different pilots to fly that Gulfstream.

How were the 99 AS crews picked to fly the early 1990s C-20H or the brand-new C-37? It wasn't by merit, but by Flight Safety International's training calendar instead. Which course did the Savannah training center have coming up next month? G-IV or G-V? Four of us in the squadron were ready for our next Gulfstream type when Savannah said they had four G-V training slots available. I was paired with our squadron commander, Lt. Col. Scott Hanson, a good friend from our days as captains flying the KC-10 at Barksdale. Scott and I worked great together during seven simulator training sessions, and because of our KC-10 background we knew about advanced cockpit avionics. We enjoyed our time in Savannah, learning to fly the beautiful new G-V.

Following a week of G-V academics, we were fortunate to be assigned a respected veteran flight instructor, Homer Bentley. Homer, sporting white hair and a bushy white mustache, spent the second week instructing us as we flew simulated flights into various major airports around the world: Aspen, Memphis, Paris, San Francisco, and Frankfurt. Together, Scott and I learned the intricacies of our new $50 million toy.

Our FAA ATP evaluation day lasted ten hours, starting with a four-hour pre-brief (we showed up on time!). Our morning included walking around a newly built G-V, and Scott and I took turns describing all the systems to our evaluator, pointing to various parts of the right-off-the-assembly-line aircraft.

After a short break, the four-hour simulator session began, which was very similar to the grueling G-III evaluation I took with Tater during the summer. The main difference between the G-III and G-V were the modern avionics and displays, more powerful engines, and a very cool and useful heads-up display (HUD).

The G-V HUD was a round-edge, six-inch-by-seven-inch piece of glass that flipped down in front of the left seat pilot's face. On the glass, projected in green, was all the vital flight information shown on the instruments in front of our chest: airspeed, altitude, heading, and the wind speed and direction. In the distance, beyond this green formation, the pilot also could see the sky or runway, depending on the phase of flight.

The HUD turned flying into a video game. A small circle, called the guidance cue, depicted where I needed to guide the airplane. My actual position was represented by a smaller circle, about the size of a BB. All I needed to do was place my small circle inside the larger floating guidance cue circle, and the plane would fly the headings and pitch necessary to find the runway on a foggy day. The HUD enabled very precise flying, and it came in handy during landings in low visibility, such as when the clouds were a mere 100 feet above the runway. In not-so-technical terms, this was called "PFM," which stood for "pure fucking magic." It's just the way some things in aviation work.

An hourlong debrief session wrapped up our very long day, and Joe complimented both our aviation knowledge and teamwork. Scott and I happily accepted our second ATP rating, now in a G-V, and after hearty handshakes around the debriefing room, we packed up our gear and headed back north to Andrews.

The Air Force C-37 was a joy to fly. Think of driving any finely tuned sportscar, such as a Porsche, Ferrari, or Lamborghini, and that's what flying a G-V was like. The state-of-the-art cockpit itself was ultra-modern and professional-looking, with soft, gray instrument panels, rather than stark, black metal panels. The overhead panel above the pilot seats contained push-button, one-inch, black square capsules, instead of the chunky knobs, switches, and dials of older aircraft. It was designed as a "blacked-out" cockpit, which meant that when everything worked properly, all the capsules were black. If a problem occurred, a capsule would turn blue, amber, or red, depending on the severity of the issue.

The C-37A (G-V) cockpit

The audible tones were gentle to our ears, such as a soft "bing-bong" when the autopilot or auto-throttles were disconnected. Think of the computer voice of HAL in 2001, *A Space Odyssey,* calmly giving the pilot information. This was so much more pleasing than the blaring horns and "quacking duck" audible alarms of other aircraft that loudly declared a change in status or configuration. Our luxury jet also boasted two Rolls-Royce engines, each providing 14,000 pounds of thrust to take us anywhere we wanted to go for up to eleven hours. Squadron pilots often asked, somewhat incredulously, "Can you believe we actually get to fly this plane?"

By September 2000 I was eligible for upgrade to aircraft commander. This required an international VIP mission with a full five-person crew, plus an evaluator, similar to Matt's mission to the Holy Land three months earlier. The mission taskings came to us from the Pentagon's assistant vice chief of staff special air missions division (CVAM), which was in charge of scheduling VIP airlift. CVAM (pronounced "See-Vam") served as the arbitrator for all of the dignitaries vying for any 89th Airlift Wing aircraft. Our 99 AS crews never knew where they might be forty-eight hours later.

On one particular "day-in-the-life" at the 99 AS, I was paged by the squadron scheduler, or seen by him as I walked by his desk (this was known as "line-of-sight scheduling"). During this eight-hour duty day at the squadron, I was on and off five different missions: China, Africa, Israel, Russia, and Japan. "You're going here. No, wait! You're going there!" By the end of the day, I wasn't assigned to any of them and went home instead. Life at Andrews was truly organized chaos.

My upgrade evaluation mission was no different. For three days I planned to take a delegation eastbound to Moscow in an old C-20B. Then, just five days before departure, I was switched to flying the White House delegation, consisting of Secretary of Health and Human Resources Donna Shalala and President Clinton's daughter, Chelsea, westward to the Sydney 2000 Olympics in a new C-37. This was a much better deal, without a doubt, but in a different Gulfstream model to an entirely different region of the world. I was very thankful, however, for the change.

My crew consisted of Maj. Dave Schermer, a qualified AC serving as my copilot; Senior Master Sgt. Dave Rossner (FE), Master Sgt. Kevin McQuay (CSO), Tech. Sgt. Marcy Wright as our flight attendant (FA), and Maj. Trent Bigler as my evaluator.

Trent was a senior member of the Andrews Gulfstream community and worked in the highly respected 89th Operations Group's standardization/evaluation division. He had a reputation for changing his mood from happy to ticked off rather quickly. This variability earned him the monikers of "Good Trent" and "Bad Trent." Fortunately, he was ecstatic to be going to the Olympics for the week.

Maj. Trent Bigler (evaluator), Senior Master Sgt. Dave Rossner (FE), Chelsea Clinton, me, Sgt. Marcy Wright (FA), and Maj. Dave Schermer (pilot). (White House)

I sat in the left seat of the Gulfstream C-37 on September 12, 2000, ready to start both engines, as President Clinton's black limousine pulled up alongside our fold-out staircase, just behind my left shoulder. I watched from the cockpit side window as the president hugged his college-age daughter, seeing her off on this weeklong international adventure. The president and first lady stayed home at this time, as Hillary Clinton was campaigning for one of New York's two U.S. Senate seats.

On a side note, during the summer and fall of 2000 I flew the former first lady twelve times as she campaigned for the U.S. Senate, attended Democratic fund-raisers, or carried out her duties as first lady. I only had one brief, personal encounter with her, and it was quite nice. Normally she would board our aircraft and immediately turn right, taking her seat in the VIP compartment. On a trip throughout California, she returned to our waiting jet in Sacramento, carrying a large green basket of huge strawberries. After climbing our short staircase, she turned left and came into our cockpit. With a big smile, she said, "You have got to try one of these strawberries!" Each red berry was bigger than a golf ball, and my fellow pilot, Lt. Col. Art Smith, joined me in thanking her as we enjoyed the juicy, sweet fruit.

Chelsea Clinton, sporting long, red, curly hair, joined Donna Shalala (all five feet of her) to form the White House delegation to the Olympics. The two were joined by a social secretary for the delegation (known to me as "the contact"), and by Huma Abedin, who served as an assistant to the president's daughter. Security guards and the HHR secretary's support personnel rounded out the eleven-passenger manifest for this trip. Our first leg was a ten-and-a-half-hour flight to Hickam Air Force Base in Hawaii for an overnight stop. Our C-37 whistled along westward at 44,000 feet, chasing the setting sun.

After a good night's rest, I performed the next day's preflight walk-around knowing that I was about to step inside and strap into the left seat for a second ten-and-a-half-hour flight to Sydney. That second preflight has always stuck in my mind as a reminder for why I don't want to fly long-range international flights anymore, because two back-to-back flights of that duration were certainly enough. The long flights also gave Major Bigler ample time to quiz me about how to plan and carry out our high-visibility mission. With a set of Gulfstream flight manuals and Air Force regulations at his fingertips, Trent played "stump the dummy" with me for hours as we cruised over the Pacific Ocean. I held my own, correctly answering or quickly looking up the answers to his probing questions in a stack of five manuals stored in drawers behind the pilot seats.

We landed in Sydney on September 13, and I taxied up to the red carpet for our delegation's arrival. Our VIP guests deplaned and spoke to reporters from a podium as we sat quietly in our seats on a silent aircraft. As our protocol for arrival ceremonies dictated, the engines and auxiliary power unit (APU) remained off so as not to interfere with the ceremony and press conference.

In a crazy "small world" coincidence, my original C-20B mission to Moscow was given to my friend, Maj. Steve "Action" Jackson, for his aircraft commander upgrade evaluation. Steve told me later that he walked into his Moscow hotel room, turned on the television to CNN International, and watched my C-37 taxi to a stop on the red carpet in Australia. It's a funny little world.

We stayed in Sydney for the first week of the Olympics—but with so little advance warning, my six-person crew didn't have tickets for any of the events. We managed to buy scalped tickets to men's gymnastics preliminaries, men's tennis, and judo, which we attended only because the venue was right across the street from our hotel. It was there that I learned some international competitors' Olympic moments could last just four seconds!

On September 18, our crew was watching the Olympics in Kevin's hotel room when my cellphone rang. The device was an international cellphone provided by the U.S. Embassy so we could maintain contact with our delegation while in Australia. Our party's contact, a very nice older lady, said, "We are meeting the basketball 'Dream Team' tomorrow at their practice. Would your crew like to go?"

Without polling my crew, I replied, "Certainly!"

"OK," she continued. "You'll need to work out your own transportation but meet us at our hotel and we'll caravan to their gym."

When I told my crew, "We're going to see the Dream Team tomorrow," there were no objections, so I immediately called our embassy contact, Rodney, and said, "Hey, Rodney! How would you like to meet the basketball Dream Team?"

"That'd be great, sir," he replied.

"Good," I said, "You're in charge of transportation."

"I'm on it, sir," he replied.

The next morning, a caravan of four cars headed out of Sydney to the suburbs and pulled up to a high school gymnasium. Our crew mingled around—but, as a rule of etiquette, we did not approach our VIP party. A large tour bus pulled into the parking lot, and off stepped the tallest men I had ever seen up close: Alonzo Mourning, Kevin Garnett, Steve Smith, Vince Carter, Jason Kidd, and coaches Rudy Tomjanovich and Tubby Smith, the University of Kentucky coach. (To be honest, Tubby was round and not tall.)

We followed them into the basketball court and stood courtside, chatting with Tubby and Rudy T, the renowned Houston player and coach. I told Rudy I was from Houston, where he had played until 1981. In December 1977, while playing against the Lakers, Rudy received a bone-crushing punch to his face. It was a life-threatening, season-ending injury, but fortunately he fully recovered and went on to coach the Rockets—and now he was coaching our country's basketball team.

Many of my crew members grabbed Olympic programs and pens that morning for autographs, but Rodney had the best plan. The night before, he had bought a commemorative Sydney 2000 basketball and a black permanent marker. I don't know where he ended up, but in a glass case somewhere sits Rodney's prize basketball signed by a gold-medal-winning U.S. Dream Team.

We sat among the NBA all-stars on the school's bleachers as they started lacing up their shoes and pulling on their practice jerseys. My copilot, Dave, looked at his watch and realized it was dinner time back home in Washington. He asked me for the embassy's international cellphone so he could call his twelve-year-old son.

Dave sat to my left, telling his son about all the NBA players sitting just a few feet from us when, suddenly, a hand appeared between us and tapped him on his right shoulder. We both turned back to see Jason Kidd asking for the phone. Jason had been listening to Dave's conversation and wanted to surprise his boy.

Dave handed over the phone, and Jason started chatting with his son, who was sitting at his dinner table outside of Washington. From there, Jason started handing the phone around to other players and we just laughed at what his son must've been thinking. Finally, Jason reached toward Kevin Garnett, a total badass, who with a very serious face said, "Man, I ain't talkin' on no phone."

Jason punched Kevin in the shoulder and said, "Hey, it's that man's son. Talk to the boy!"

Kevin took the phone, and in his very deep voice said, "Hello? Yeah, your dad's kicking my ass in one-on-one," and handed back the phone.

We died laughing. What a memorable Olympic moment for us all.

The following morning, I flew the long flight back to Hickam Air Force Base near Honolulu, where Major Bigler finally announced that I had passed my evaluation. As a newly minted Gulfstream aircraft commander, I gladly treated my crew to rum cocktails in a beachside celebration. Good Trent happily took the C-37's left seat for the final ten-hour leg home to Andrews from Hawaii.

Senior Master Sgt. Dave Rossner laughing as Jason Kidd talks to Dave Schermer's son back home

42

DON'T GET COCKY

AVIATION HAS INFLUENCED my life in so many positive ways. As I mentioned before, I grew up shy and lacked self-confidence, and it wasn't until I started taking flying lessons at age sixteen that I ventured out on my own to pursue my own dream. Through aviation, I learned to make decisions, some of which could have life-or-death consequences.

Though I scared myself a few times, I know that from when I started flying in 1978 until I joined the 89th Airlift Wing in 1999, I embodied the slogan "what doesn't kill you makes you stronger."

Completing a challenging instrument approach in bad weather or leading a crew on international missions to austere locations bolstered my self-confidence and decisiveness to the point that I wanted to be a squadron commander. I came out of my shell to become a "people person," happily talking to anyone, anywhere. Karin even remarked that I was now the "social butterfly" of our marriage, and I felt ready for greater responsibility—and a bigger challenge.

According to American psychologist Abraham Maslow's hierarchy of needs, humans are motivated by five needs. From the bottom of Maslow's pyramid to the top, they are:

- Physiological (food and clothing).
- Safety (job security).
- Love and belonging (friendship).
- Esteem (respect, status, recognition).
- Self-actualization (the desire to become the most one can be).

My Air Force flying career fulfilled all of these needs. I moved beyond my childhood friends and set out on a career my uncle had enjoyed. I persevered from my days as a bomber navigator to realizing my dream of becoming an Air Force pilot. I now belonged to a fraternity of aviators, providing both friendship, recognition, and respect. Once I was selected to be an Andrews Air Force Base Gulfstream pilot, I was surrounded by like-minded, highly professional pilots whose main goal was the perfect execution of a smooth flight in support of our very important passengers. We aspired to be the best we could possibly be.

The history of the Andrews VIP air missions dates back to the Harry Truman and Dwight Eisenhower presidential administrations. The early overseas diplomatic missions flown from Washington were designated "Special Air Missions—Foreign," which was abbreviated "SAM-F." In the military phonetic alphabet, the letter F is "foxtrot," so the Andrews missions eventually were dubbed SAMFOX, and everything we did was to the SAMFOX standard of excellence. This instilled a great source of pride.

I never think of myself as "the best pilot," or God's gift to aviation. My aim, however, is to be one of the most conscientious pilots, striving to give my passengers an enjoyable flight experience, flying as smoothly as possible. But beware: With this newfound confidence, cockiness and overconfidence can rise up and humble a person, and sometimes I've been put back in my place.

Each year, every pilot goes through a flight evaluation. These aren't enjoyable, but they are a necessary, albeit stressful, part of our job. According to aviation conventional wisdom, pilots hope the ride before our checkride is less than stellar, so we'll peak at the right moment under the watchful eye of the evaluator. I'd rather make my mistakes on a training flight before an evaluation, because then I'll know what to tighten up when I'm being evaluated. As the aviation saying goes, "Anyone can have a bad day. You just don't want it to be on checkride day."

One year after I upgraded to aircraft commander, I was due for my annual evaluation, to be conducted by a longtime Andrews pilot named Lt. Col. Herb Finch. Herb was a great guy, and we'd flown several fun Gulfstream trips together, so I felt at ease as we prepared for this training sortie.

During the two-hour oral examination, called a "ground eval," I answered all of Herb's questions about airplane systems and how I would handle various aircraft malfunctions. Once I finished verbally "building the airplane" for Herb, we set out for the flight line to begin a three-hour flight.

From Andrews, we flew thirty minutes south to Patrick Henry Airport in Newport News, Virginia. Herb told me which approach to plan for, and I briefed the required items: radio frequency, inbound course heading to the runway, how low we could descend (known as the decision altitude) before committing to land or executing a go-around, and any obstructions in the vicinity. Throughout the approaches, Herb added distractions or restrictions, and I had to factor those into my approach.

One such challenge occurred during a go-around. Once safely above the runway, Herb slowly pulled the right throttle back and said, "OK, you've just lost that No. 2 engine." In actuality, the engine was still running, but only at idle power. Herb told me to fly an antiquated radio beacon (VOR) approach. I flew the procedures for an engine-out approach, followed by Herb's directed single-engine go-around, climbing out on just one engine's power. This required a lot of concentration, adding left rudder inputs to keep the aircraft aligned on runway heading as the powerful left engine tried to push the nose to the right, toward the "dead" engine. The mighty

C-37 performed masterfully, climbing away from Patrick Henry Airport.

Satisfied with my single-engine work, Herb said I could use the "dead" engine throttle again, and from Newport News we flew to Richmond, Virginia. There, I continued my approach work, flying all sorts of instrument approaches the C-37 was capable of performing. These ranged from 1950s-era radio beacon approaches, to the low-visibility instrument approaches using the glass HUD just inches from my face, to the brand-new GPS navigation approaches. That day, each task that Herb gave me I accomplished flawlessly. I remember thinking to myself as we departed Richmond for the last leg to Andrews, *"This is going great today!"* I had flown each approach perfectly, and I was riding high.

I could tell by Herb's lighthearted voice that he also thought things were going well as we enjoyed a beautiful day of flying. As we set up for the final approach to complete the checkride at our home station, Herb said, "OK, I want this to be a 'min run' landing. You need to get off the runway by the second taxiway."

One of the capabilities I loved about the C-37 was its versatility. This sleek executive jet could takeoff at a maximum gross weight of 90,000 pounds and climb straight up to 43,000 feet, cruising above all of the airliners, which were capped at 41,000 feet. It could do this while taking off and landing on runways as short as 5,000 feet. Most airport runways range from 8,000 to 11,000 feet, so a runway less than one mile long is considered short. We had to demonstrate we could land on a short runway during each annual checkride.

The Gulfstream was built with a big, beautiful wing, capable of holding eleven flight-hours of fuel and generating a lot of lift. When coming into land on a short runway, the last thing I wanted to do was float down the runway, with the far end quickly approaching. To avoid this, we trained to point the nose short of the intended landing zone, pull the power to idle at 100 feet above the ground, glide in, and touch down in the first 500 feet of the runway. We wanted to use the minimum amount of runway, so the landings were nicknamed "min run." The second taxiway Herb challenged me to use was just 4,000 feet down the runway. I was up for that challenge.

Swelling with pride from my previous three hours of flying, I distinctly remember thinking to myself, *"I am going to water Herb's eyes and impress the hell out of him."* I picked my aimpoint short of the touchdown zone and headed for the runway, with a strong crosswind blowing from our left to right. I pulled the power to idle and glided over the approach end. The wheels touched, as planned, in the first 500 feet of the runway, and I aggressively applied the brakes to slow the airplane to make the taxiway—but I didn't fully take Mother Nature into account.

By slowing so quickly, the rudder became far less effective in controlling the steering of the aircraft. As a result, my rudder pedals alone couldn't keep the plane from turning into the wind. The nose started pointing left, and we were headed for the edge of the runway as I applied brakes to slow us down. The C-37 has electronic nosewheel steering that is extremely sensitive, and the nosewheel is controlled by a small, V-shaped steering wheel called the tiller. If used at too high a speed, there's a risk of overcorrecting and going on "Mr. Toad's Wild Ride," swerving down the runway. For that reason, we couldn't use the tiller until reaching a slow speed—and because of my rapid deceleration, that time was now.

There's another saying regarding checkrides—"Never scare your evaluator"—but as Herb started yelling, "Tiller! Tiller! Tiller!" it was obvious I had just violated this principle. I quickly moved my left hand from the yoke to the small tiller, straightening the nose to parallel the runway edge, about fifty feet to our left. The cockpit became very quiet as I slowed to ten miles per hour for the turn off the runway, and I taxied in silence to our parking spot. In my effort to water Herb's eyes, I had almost soiled his pants. I hung my head, knowing I had just busted a near-perfect checkride. Back in his office, Herb debriefed me in a low, serious tone and focused on only one event: my botched short-field landing.

Days later, I flew my "recheck" with Maj. Rob Crone. The

prebrief for this re-evaluation consisted of me describing the nose-wheel steering system of a Gulfstream, and how to properly execute a "min run" landing with a crosswind. Rob and I then headed back out to a C-37, where I demonstrated the proper "min run" landing and successfully completed the recheck within an hour.

There is no doubt that my ego and cockiness got the better of me that day. It was certainly a "teachable moment"—and to this day, as I fly instrument approaches in bad weather, I interrupt my intense concentration with this recurring thought: *"Don't get cocky."*

43
TIMING IS EVERYTHING

BY THE WINTER of 1999 I had been promoted to lieutenant colonel and was serving as assistant director of operations, or ADO, of the 99 AS. On one Friday morning, our squadron commander, Lt. Col. Scott Hanson, was out pheasant hunting in his home state of Iowa, and the squadron's director of operations, Lt. Col. Nancy Vetere, was home on convalescent leave following major knee surgery, so that left me "minding the store," sitting at Nancy's desk.

I was answering official squadron emails from the echelons above when one email caught my attention. The wing commander of MacDill Air Force Base in Tampa, Florida, was asking our Andrews wing commander if he had any C-37 instructor pilots who would like to help start up a new squadron supporting the seven four-star combatant commanders across the United States. MacDill was going to receive three new C-37s the following summer and needed a cadre of instructors and evaluators to train the new crews. The email made its way down to the group commander, Col. Dave Fadok, and finally to me at the 99 AS, where I read it with interest.

"Could this really happen?" I asked myself.

I had only been at Andrews for one-and-a-half years of a four-year tour, and I wasn't an instructor yet, but I was due to upgrade at any point.

I called Nancy at her house and asked what she thought of this job opportunity. We knew that the long-range plan was for me to move up to operations officer and eventually become the 99 AS squadron commander. With Scott Hanson out of town on leave, I asked Nancy if I could talk to Colonel Fadok about the assignment, and she said yes. I called the group commander's secretary that afternoon and made an appointment with Colonel Fadok for 10 a.m. Monday morning. I then headed home to tell Karin about this opportunity in Tampa.

When assignments need to be filled, the personnel center runs a matrix of qualified individuals, including factors such as current qualifications, how long candidates have been at the base—known as time on station—and how long they have left to serve in the Air Force. I was coming up on seventeen years in the Air Force, so I had three years to go until my projected retirement. I had been at Andrews almost two years and would be an instructor in a matter of months. According to the matrix, all of the candidates younger than me were not instructors or lieutenant colonels yet; those who were already instructors were too close to their possible retirement to move to MacDill. I was the only willing candidate who met the criteria.

The following Monday morning, I sat down with Colonel Fadok and asked him what he thought of me putting in for the assignment. His reply was memorable, but not exactly confidence-boosting: "To tell you the truth, Dave, we hadn't really thought about you."

Although this sounded like a put-down—and I initially took it as one—what he meant was that I wasn't being considered for MacDill because I already was in the plan to move up within the Andrews hierarchy. He asked me what Scott thought of the idea, and I said I hadn't talked to him because he was out on vacation. Colonel Fadok closed the meeting by saying, "Let me track down Scott and run it by him. Then I'll let you know."

I felt hopeful as I left his office.

Within a few days, the emails reversed course. My name was forwarded up to the Andrews wing commander, then over to the MacDill wing commander for consideration to start up their 310th Airlift Squadron (310 AS).

Once approved by the chain of command, the Air Force Personnel Center in San Antonio had to grant me a time on station (TOS) waiver to move after just twenty-two months at Andrews. Thankfully the waiver was approved, because I was now heading to a leadership position. The cards fell quickly into place.

My next task was to build a cadre of instructors from each crew position who would build up the C-37 crew force at MacDill. Each crew member had an assignment officer in San Antonio, and that person had the overall say as to who would receive the MacDill assignment. For this special, short-notice assignment, this depended upon their aircraft qualifications and the desire to move. The selected cadre consisted of two additional pilots: Maj. Bob Giddings as chief of training, and Maj. Lee "Ice" Icenhour as chief of standards and evaluations. Rounding out the crew were Master Sgt. Kevin McQuay as our communications systems operator (CSO) instructor, Staff Sgt. Allison Miller as flight attendant instructor, and Tech. Sgt. Tony Radcliffe as our instructor flight engineer.

Bob, a tall, quiet thinker, had flown KC-10s and was extremely professional and competent. Working with Bob was the first time in my seventeen-year career where I could delegate a task and the result would exceed my abilities and expectations. Ice was with me in the KC-10 during the Southern Watch deployment when Ken Reed died in a T-37 crash. Kevin was my CSO during the high-visibility Sydney Olympic mission in 2000. Allison was an extremely sharp flight attendant, always impeccably dressed—and, although lower in rank than her colleagues, she performed her job with maximum effort. In my mind, she set the bar for excellent service, always striving to serve the perfect meal. Tony, meanwhile, was everybody's favorite person in the 99 AS. He made everyone's life easier by proactively seeking answers and information to challenges he recognized before us. We were extremely lucky to have this hard-working, life-loving flight engineer on our team.

Four years later, as Tony prepared for retirement, he was diagnosed with stage four cancer. With his wife and young son by his side, Tony fought valiantly for eighteen months before succumbing. It was a heartbreaking moment for everyone who knew and loved this great American.

Although Ice joined us from his C-20 assignment in Ramstein, Germany, the others were at Andrews with me. We gathered in my ADO's office to begin our plans for the move to MacDill and the stand-up of the C-37 operation there. Other members of the 99 AS jokingly referred to us as the "MacDale Crew." As the birds migrated north in March 2001, we headed south to Florida.

44
CREATING A SQUADRON

310 AS patch and name tag

THE PINNACLE of my career began in March 2001 with our move to Valrico, Florida, located thirty minutes east of Tampa and eighty miles west of Disney World. It was the fifteenth address of my seventeen-year marriage to Karin. Moving after just twenty-two months at Andrews didn't go over very well with eleven-year-old Daniel and eight-year-old Shelby. Our family thought I would finish the last five years of my career at Andrews, but instead I was now moving our children for the sixth time in eight years. I will never forget Daniel saying to me: "Why should I bother to make friends? You're just going to move me again anyway."

Ouch. This was vastly different from me growing up across the street from Larry Leonard.

Children also serve, although not always willingly, and they can honestly say, "I didn't sign up for this!" In January 1982, my cousin Tina moved from sunny, hot Tucson, Arizona, to frigid Fairbanks, Alaska, in the middle of her junior year of high school. Her dad, my Uncle Jack, began to operate the A-10 fighter in Alaska, just outside of Russian airspace. Tina took it all in stride, jumping right into her new school's activities, and she was named homecoming queen the next year. The travel and adventure bug seemed to be ingrained in her, as she went on to tour internationally with the music and dance group *Up With People* during her college years.

Our own children experienced a completely different upbringing than I did. I lived in two houses growing up, and I set off to college with the friend I was born across the street from. Daniel lived in three houses by age four, and one day he learned that the only other neighborhood kid—a skinny, blond, eight-year-old boy—was moving away. Daniel sat on the sill of our open back door, facing our grass lawn in humid Louisiana, and without even turning to face me he asked, "Dad, why do my friends always move away?"

Hearing that was heartbreaking. If the military child isn't the one moving, his or her friend is, so everything becomes transient and temporary.

As I grew up, my family enjoyed camping in national parks throughout Utah and Colorado. Conversely, our children experienced life in Louisiana and California, toured Europe from Holland, and lived in Illinois, Kansas, Virginia, and now Florida. They enjoyed adventures from England to Germany, and thrilling Air Force air shows in the United States and Belgium, too. It was a different upbringing than mine, but not bad.

The adventure and travel bug stuck with our children as they grew up. Daniel and Shelby took to heart the advice of Roy Crenshaw, an elderly Black gentleman from our Florida church who had served as a civil servant in South Korea and across our country. He advised our children to become "citizens of the world," and they have. Shelby stepped out of her shy comfort zone and studied abroad in Taiwan, while Daniel's first five years of military service in the Air

Force were spent outside the United States, in Guam, Greenland, and Japan. Roy would be very proud of them, as are Karin and I.

A swimming pool was a major bribe in our move to Tampa. They always were popular with our family, especially since I was a swimmer, and our earlier international travels centered around Karin finding hotels with a pool or swim park nearby. Pools enticed our children's good behavior during the European C-n-C (castles and cathedrals) tours: "If you'll be quiet in this castle, I'll take you swimming," I told little Shelby more than twenty times.

Daniel and Shelby were emotionally exhausted from five previous moves, though, and they groaned at the thought of leaving their Virginia grade school and Scouting friends after only two years. Luckily, the house Karin and I settled on east of Tampa was in the shape of a backward capital "J" that wrapped around a kidney-shaped pool and attached hot tub. Each back wall of the house contained sliding glass doors that "pocketed," or overlapped, each other, opening almost the entire three walls surrounding the 10,000-gallon pool. It was enclosed by a screened lanai to keep out the Florida insects, and was big enough for a glass dining table and barbecue grill.

In a dramatic move, I made sure all of the glass doors were wide-open when our children came through the front door for the first time. Shelby's little face lit up when she saw the sparkling blue water and heard the water lapping over the hot tub's spillway. She and I played many rounds of water volleyball throughout our ten years in that house. We also had church youth group pool parties there, and we loved hearing their laughter with long-term church and school friends.

By late spring 2001, many of the initial core of instructors for the new 310th Airlift Squadron had settled into the Tampa Bay area. Several of the squadron's crew members were already in place, having been assigned to the EC-135 (Boeing 707) and CT-43 (Boeing 737) as part of "D Flight" of the 91st Air Refueling Squadron, the KC-135 squadron at MacDill. These two aircraft flew

VIP missions supporting Central Command (CENTCOM) and Southern Command (SOUTHCOM). CENTCOM's Gen. Tommy Franks, an Army four-star general, flew in the large, four-engine EC-135. The SOUTHCOM commander, Marine four-star Gen. Peter Pace, flew on the smaller, two-engine CT-43. Those two planes now belonged to the new 310 AS while we awaited the three new C-37s.

General Franks' missions departed from MacDill, heading east toward Qatar, Bahrain, and what we called the "Stan-lands" of Kyrgyzstan, Kazakhstan, and Turkmenistan. General Pace, meanwhile, boarded his CT-43 in Miami before continuing south toward Central America and South America. SOUTHCOM missions included regular trips to Bogotá, Colombia, for the ongoing war on drugs.

In the past, all military four-star commanders were entitled to fly on Andrews' Gulfstream fleet. Because of competing demands from higher-ranking civilian leaders, however, these commanders often had to defer to members of Congress and service secretaries in their need for airlift. To solve this, Congress decided to adopt a civilian practice and create a corporate plane-sharing flight department, like NetJets. They authorized the procurement of three MacDill C-37s to be shared by seven U.S.-based combatant commanders. CENTCOM, SOUTHCOM, and Special Operations Command (SOCOM), also headquartered at MacDill, were based in Florida. Those four-star leaders were joined by Transportation Command (TRANSCOM) in southern Illinois, Strategic Command (STRATCOM) in Omaha, Nebraska, Northern Command (NORTHCOM) in Colorado Springs, Colorado, and finally Joint Forces Command (JFCOM), who we nicknamed "JIFFYCOM," in Norfolk, Virginia. There's a musical called *Seven Brides for Seven Brothers*, and in our newly formed squadron we had "Three Jets for Seven Four-Stars," which they had to learn to share. A scheduling office in the Pentagon was the arbitrator and determined which commander got to fly in which C-37.

Many of the crew members flying the EC-135 and CT-43 eventually trained to fly the C-37 or moved on to other assignments. New crew members transferred in to build up our force to twenty pilots, ten flight engineers, ten communication system operators and ten flight attendants. With administrative support included, the new 310th Airlift Squadron boasted sixty-five members. In a novel arrangement, our three C-37 aircraft were leased instead of purchased, and maintenance was provided by contracted Gulfstream civilian personnel.

On a sunny January afternoon in Tampa, the 310 AS was activated under the command of Lt. Col. Eden Murrie in a ceremony inside of Hangar 3. I flew down from Andrews to attend the event and soon became the operations officer (310 AS/DO). We immediately began working to establish our new squadron.

Eden, a KC-135 and EC-135 navigator, had been the operations officer for the 91st Air Refueling Squadron, and she maintained her office in that building until our squadron building was renovated. Next door to Eden's office was a storage room that had been converted to a narrow office for three desks and chairs. How narrow? Put it this way: My desk was the furthest from the door—and when I needed to leave, the other two guys had to get up, push their chairs in and leave the room so I could get out. That's how narrow.

Throughout the spring, Maj. Bob Giddings, our lead C-37 instructor pilot, Tech. Sgt. Tony Radcliff, Master Sgt. Kevin McQuay, and Staff Sgt. Allison Miller helped Eden and me compile a budget request to fund our new flight operation for the remainder of the fiscal year. My time at Air Mobility Command Headquarters, where I had learned about Excel spreadsheets and budget requests, now came in handy. By taking the inputs from our pool of instructors and squadron leaders already at MacDill, we tabulated a request for $214,680. This would fund the remaining four months of the fiscal year for training flights for the incoming crew members and would help procure everything from luggage to clothing to accessories for the airplane.

On a May morning, we walked our request over to the finance

squadron commander, Maj. Randy White, who had worked across the cubicle from me at AMC headquarters three years earlier. Randy reviewed our request, gave it his stamp of approval, and emailed it to the AMC comptroller, our money friend Chuck Mavrogeorge at Scott Air Force Base. We fully expected that we'd have to answer questions to justify our budget request, or to fight for more dollars when less money was eventually allocated.

At four o'clock that afternoon, Eden yelled out from her office, "Dave, come look!"

Bob, Tony, and I shuffled out of our office to look over Eden's shoulder at her computer screen. She had been copied on an email from Chuck to the AMC finance office. It said, "Please fund the 310th Airlift Squadron with an attached request for $214,600." We joked that he stiffed us $80, but we were now fully funded and ready to fly! Now we just needed our first C-37 to arrive on time in July 2001.

Starting up a squadron gave Eden and me the leeway to pick squadron colors for our squadron scarf and nametags, plus a squadron patch—or so we thought. The 310 AS originally was created during World War II as the 310th Troop Carrier Squadron, and its patch was a yellow, spread-wing eagle on a blue background, circled with a white ring. The eagle, drawn in the 1940s, was a very poor rendition and often was referred to as the "dead chicken" or "rubber chicken." One of the EC-135 crew members, Maj. Keith Peloquin, redrew the yellow bird with crisp angles more resembling a rising phoenix.

Since the patch already had a white circle around a blue background, Eden suggested we add an additional outer red circle with the words "Combatant Commander Support" across the top, and four stars at the bottom. This signified that our mission was transporting the four-star commanders of our U.S.-based combatant commands, and it gave our patch a patriotic red, white, and blue look.

Our customers came from the Army, Navy, Air Force, and Marines. Military operations involving multiple services are called joint operations and typically are represented by the color purple. Eden and I discussed replacing the red ring with purple to signify joint/multi-service transportation, but the purple just didn't look right, so Eden suggested burgundy as a color that could pass for either red or purple. Our new burgundy, white, and blue squadron patch looked great with Keith's crisp yellow eagle in the middle. Hundreds were ordered for our incoming crews to wear proudly on their flight suits.

Now we needed two-tone colored nametags and scarves to add to our Air Force flight suit attire. Squadron scarves are a tradition dating back to the first aviation units in World War I. Eden selected yellow lettering and trim for the burgundy nametags, and yellow lightning bolts for our burgundy scarves. Tampa, home of the NHL's Tampa Bay Lightning hockey team, declared itself the "Lightning Capital of the World" with its numerous thunderstorms, so lightning bolts were appropriate.

Our operations group commander, Col. A.J. Stewart, was a KC-135 Strategic Air Command "SAC Warrior" through and through. During our updates on squadron progress, he chided Eden and I about our beautiful Gulfstream executive jet, and our renovated building with brand-new furniture, claiming we weren't real warfighters. We gladly accepted his ribbing, knowing anyone would love to be in our squadron.

Once he saw our new patch with burgundy-and-yellow colors, Colonel Stewart declared, "Y'all are the wine and cheese squadron. Why, even your squadron colors are merlot and cheddar!"

He probably didn't expect it, but we quickly adopted the moniker of "MacDill's Wine and Cheese Squadron." In newcomer orientation briefings, the 310 AS was introduced as the "Wine and Cheese Squadron," while the KC-135 91 ARS was introduced as the "Beer and Bologna Squadron." It was a very fitting description for both flying squadrons.

Eight years later, long after I departed, a new 310 AS commander learned that all squadron patches and colors are governed by the Air Force Heritage Office and could not be changed without approval. Our 310 AS tricolored patch, and wine-and-cheese-colored nametags and scarves, were disapproved. The squadron sadly reverted to its original blue-and-white colors, and the ugly "rubber chicken" patch.

After numerous trips to the Gulfstream plant in Savannah, Georgia, we accepted our first C-37, tail number 10028. The plane touched down at MacDill on July 18, 2001, flown by AMC's four-star commander, Gen. Tony Robertson, with Bob Giddings serving as his instructor pilot in the right seat. The arrival ceremony was a big event, attended by Tampa's mayor, Dick Greco, in front of our new home in Hangar 3. Our second plane was scheduled to arrive on September 13, 2001.

45

FIRST TRIP TO BOGOTÁ, COLOMBIA

IN MAY 2001, as we waited for the first C-37 delivery, I accompanied a CT-43 crew to Bogotá, the capital of Colombia, to learn the ins and outs of the operation down there. We flew into an airfield surrounded by rugged mountains and in a country battling rebel forces called the Revolutionary Armed Forces of Colombia, otherwise known by their Spanish initials, FARC. The guerilla group funded their operation through kidnapping ransom and extortion payments, as well as the sale of illegal drugs. Although not directly cultivating illegal drugs such as cocaine, the FARC raised $60 million to $100 million annually through the taxation of drugs, and the extortion of the drug growers and landowners. Over the previous three decades FARC had conducted roughly 25,000 kidnappings. Our SOUTHCOM general visited Colombia monthly to coordinate U.S. military assistance to the Colombian government.

Our CT-43, piloted by Capt. Joe Brewster and Maj. Dave Knight, landed in Bogotá and taxied to the corporate jet parking ramp. Upon arrival, Natalie warned us of recent intelligence that said FARC was offering a $1 million ransom for any American crew member caught in a flight suit, so now we had a million-dollar bounty on our heads.

The U.S. Embassy provided a van with bulletproof windows, and the driver transported us to a hotel on the outskirts of the city. As my pilot friend Lt. Col. Kevin Oatley pointed out later, our van wasn't a nice, sleek black Suburban like those in Tom Clancy's movie *Clear and Present Danger*. Instead, ours was an old Chevy beater, with three-quarter-inch bulletproof glass bolted on as an afterthought. Homemade brackets on the inside of each window held the additional glass, which was individually screwed over each window. It wasn't very reassuring.

The flight crews were very familiar with Bogotá and had usually enjoyed the overnight stay, with the ability to walk down the sidewalk and have dinner in the city. However, with the new threat of kidnappings and a ransom, this was no longer possible. We were cautioned to stay in the hotel and only dine inside.

At first I thought I'd miss one of the prime benefits of visiting Colombia, which is its beautiful selection of green emeralds. Fortunately, though, one of our two flight attendants, Crystal, contacted a jeweler named Ligia, who arrived in the hotel lobby with a small briefcase of sparkling green-and-gold jewelry. Ligia showed me her beautiful selection, and I picked out a gold ring, a set of earrings, and a heart-shaped pendant, each adorned with small, bright green stones, that I planned to hold onto until Karin's October birthday.

The CT-43 flight crew and I climbed into the U.S. embassy's old Chevy van for the drive back to the airport. We were taking some back roads, but I didn't know where we were to begin with. I noticed Capt. Joe Brewster and Maj. Dave Knight looking at each other before eventually Joe whispered to Dave, "I've never gone this way before. Have you?" Dave shook his head.

Now my mind started to spin. Was this an arranged kidnapping? We drove along a route lined by dense jungle trees and, after forty minutes, we arrived at a rusted back gate of the Bogotá commercial airport. We took a side road around the runway before finally arriving at our aircraft parked near Natalie's office. She coordinated the servicing of military aircraft and took care of our transportation needs. As Dave and Joe began their preflight inspections, Natalie came aboard the plane via its small staircase. Knowing that the longer drive put the crew behind schedule, she quickly explained: "I'm sorry about the longer drive, but two car bombs exploded downtown this morning, so your driver had to take an alternate route."

Natalie's news of the ransom threat, and the morning's car bombing, certainly alerted me to the security situation our Gulfstream crews faced. As a result of the ongoing security threats, 310 AS flight crews never again stayed overnight in Bogotá. They instead dropped the SOUTHCOM commander off before either waiting on the ramp inside the aircraft, or flying to a different location before returning the next day to pick up the general. Bogotá became a monthly high-threat mission flown by our aircrews.

46

9/11

AT 9:42 a.m. Eastern time on September 11, an emergency broadcast came over our aircraft radio: "Attention all aircraft. Due to security reasons, the United States is implementing the national airspace closure program. By order of the Federal Aviation Command Center, all aircraft are directed to land immediately."

That Tuesday morning, I had taken off at 8 a.m. for a planned two-hour flight with Maj. Barry Beavers in the left seat, receiving his initial checkride in our gleaming, blue-and-white C-37, complete with its "new car" smell. Onboard were flight engineer Master Sgt. Ken Griffith and a third pilot, Maj. "Ice" Icenhour. The four of us departed on a routine training flight so I could give Barry his qualification flight. Ice, an evaluator pilot like myself, came along to watch me conduct the checkride so he could take over our evaluation division in the squadron as we certified more new pilots.

We set out first for the Fort Myers airport, about a thirty-minute flight south of MacDill. I sat in the right seat as Barry flew a series of approaches that either ended with a touch-and-go landing or a go-around before we went back into the pattern for more approaches with simulated emergencies.

Around 9 a.m., as we flew a practice approach to the Fort Myers runway, the tower controller asked if we had heard about a plane hitting some buildings in New York (which happened at 8:46 a.m.). Not wanting to be distracted, I quickly replied that we had not heard about it before I resumed giving the checkride. My first thought was that perhaps two airliners had collided over the city, and one of them had fallen into downtown New York.

We finished our approach work at Fort Myers and headed north toward Lakeland airport, about thirty miles east of MacDill. Barry continued flying his required instrument approaches while Ice went back to the passenger cabin and tuned in a local radio station. As we were completing the checkride, Ice came running up into the cockpit, leaned over Ken's shoulder, and said, "The radio just announced there's a terrorist attack underway on the United States!"

I thought Ice was purposely trying to be a distraction to see how Barry could operate under pressure, so I replied, "That's not funny, Ice."

Ice replied, "No, Dave. I'm serious."

Barry was one of our strongest pilots in the squadron, and he had flown very well that morning. I looked over at him and said, "You passed. Qual 1 (the highest grade). Now take us to a holding pattern."

While Barry set up an oval holding pattern over Lakeland airport, I contacted the MacDill command post on a second radio. MacDill already had broadcast over the military UHF radio that the base was closed. I didn't want to land this military airplane at a civilian airport, especially since we could see MacDill from our holding pattern at 4,000 feet. The command post relayed our request for permission to land to the wing commander, Brig. Gen. Wayne Hodges, and within minutes he granted our request to land.

Our cockpit was silent as Barry exited the holding pattern over Lakeland and we returned to MacDill, landing at just after 10 a.m. As we taxied toward our parking spot, we could see the president's backup aircraft, the blue-and-white C-32, on our ramp. At that same moment, President George W. Bush was just down the road from us in

Sarasota. In a now-famous video clip, he was reading a book to young schoolchildren when the message was passed to him that America was under attack. From our cockpit, we watched the Andrews aircrew quickly head out to their Boeing 757 to join President Bush's Boeing 747 "Air Force One" in the skies over the Gulf of Mexico.

Barry parked near Hangar 3 and shut down the engines. Normally, a checkride ended with smiles and handshakes as the tension of a stressful flight subsided, but that didn't happen on this day. We quietly packed up our flight gear and began walking across the tarmac toward our squadron.

One of our Gulfstream civilian contract crew chiefs had been a C-37 flight engineer while on active duty at Andrews with Tony, Bob, and me. His last name was Bacca, so naturally, we called him "Chewy" (as in the *Star Wars* character Chewbacca). Chewy had grown out his hair and now had a thick, bushy mop of wavy gray hair. With America under attack and knowing that we would pick up our second aircraft in just two more days, Chewy looked stunned and asked, "What do I need to do?"

"Get a haircut," I said as I headed back into the squadron. "We might need you soon." (In actuality, Chewy remained a Gulfstream contract employee until I retired.)

Once inside our second-floor squadron operation center, the flat-screen TV hanging in the corner relayed images of the smoking towers of the World Trade Center. At 10:28 a.m., everyone stood, stunned, as we watched the north tower crumble to the ground. There were about thirty of us packed in the room that day, all staring in disbelief. We knew our lives had changed forever—and that we were about to become very busy.

The squadron's manpower divided into small groups that day as we transitioned to an around-the-clock duty schedule. One of my assistants, Lt. Col. Keith Kreeger, along with a handful of others, volunteered to take the first night shift. This began weeklong, twenty-four-hour operations throughout all military bases. Our military, like everyone else in America, was still trying to determine if more attacks would occur.

Like many Americans, I got home late that evening and relived the horrible news with my family. We found out much later through Daniel's friends at his junior high that when he heard of the terrorist attacks, he started sobbing and told his teacher, "Now my dad will be leaving." I'm certain many young military dependents had the same realization. It's not just the active-duty members that serve our nation, but our spouses and children as well.

I'll never forget my drive to work on September 12. I listened to my usual classic rock station as the hosts tried to comprehend what happened the day before. They announced a blood drive taking place at the Tampa Bay Buccaneers' Raymond James Stadium. When I got off the freeway and onto MacDill Avenue leading into the back gate of the base, traffic came to a standstill. All U.S. military bases had implemented searches of all vehicles, and MacDill was a base with 5,000 employees.

I inched along for more than two hours through a tree-lined neighborhood. In a heartwarming, patriotic gesture, the people living along that avenue opened their houses for emergency bathroom breaks. They also graciously offered drinks, pastries, and cookies to the line of military commuters.

Because of the horrendous driving conditions leading to the base, I decided that day to stay at MacDill for the next few nights.

As if the terrorist attacks weren't enough that week, Mother Nature decided to join in, too. Tropical Storm Gabrielle was making its way up the western coast of Florida, presumably heading for the Florida panhandle. On September 13, I was still in our 310th Airlift Squadron building with Lt. Col. Eden Murrie, who had returned with Gen. Tommy Franks on the EC-135 from Greece, flying across the eerily quiet Atlantic Ocean the day before.

Karin called me from our house and asked, "Are you going to evacuate your planes for the hurricane?"

I replied, "No, it's heading for Pensacola."

"No," she answered. "The news just said that Gabrielle is now a category one hurricane and made a right turn. It's coming right toward Tampa Bay."

That was certainly timely information to get from my wife.

Eden and I immediately went down the stairs from our squadron office and crossed the large, cement hangar floor before entering the weather shop on the opposite side of the hangar, where a technical sergeant was looking down at his weather charts as we approached his desk.

"Do we need to start thinking about evacuating our aircraft?" I asked.

He looked up and stuttered, "Y-y-yes."

Eden chimed in: "And when do we need to do that?"

"Now would be good," he replied.

"When were you going to tell us?" I asked.

"I was just about to pick up the phone to call you," he said.

Thanks to Karin's warning, we quickly assembled our crews to evacuate the EC-135, the CT-43, and our one Gulfstream C-37 before gale-force winds exceeded their takeoff limits. Our commander, Lieutenant Colonel Murrie, flew out on the EC-135, and I remained behind to watch over the squadron.

A lighthearted moment during these stressful days was provided by a British tanker crew. They had landed their Royal Air Force VC-10 refueling tanker at MacDill on September 10. Three days later, a call went out directing the Brits to fly their tanker to a safer location. The VC-10 aircraft commander, in his distinct British accent and a bit of a slur, replied, "Right, mate. That's goin' ta be a bit o' a problem. Me and me mates have been drinking quite a bit. Do you have a hangar you can put our airplane in?"

This was passed along to Brigadier General Hodges, and he directed that their tanker be placed inside one of our American hangars to ride out the storm. It was a bit of levity during those gloomy days.

Our 310th Airlift Squadron was on the second floor, and the

forecast called for major flooding of our low-lying airbase, which stood just thirteen feet above sea level. I remained in the squadron building for three nights, sleeping on a blue cloth sofa I pulled into the operations center. From my second-floor perch, I figured I'd stay well above any potential flooding as the parking lots below took on water.

On September 14, I sat alone watching a rebroadcast of our nation's memorial service led by President Bush and the Rev. Billy Graham from the National Cathedral in Washington. It was a very somber but meaningful ceremony. Sitting alone in the silent, dark squadron, I quietly soaked it all in.

That evening, Karin finally broke down in tears, telling me over the phone: "I can handle a terrorist attack and a hurricane, but not both in the same week!"

Sympathizing with her, I said, "Go into our bedroom and look under my nightstand."

As I waited, Karin retrieved the box of jewelry from Bogotá. As she opened it, I told her, "I was saving those for your birthday, but I think you need them right now."

She opened the box to find the gold ring with four green emeralds, matching earrings, and a heart-shaped pendant of sparkling green emeralds. My gift was much appreciated and provided a loving moment between us, which was just what we needed.

47
BISHKEK, KYRGYZSTAN

BY OCTOBER 2001 we had our full fleet of three C-37s, and the majority of our crews were qualified and ready for missions. The first international mission was flown by Maj. Barry Beavers and me. We flew the transportation command (TRANSCOM) commander, Gen. John Handy, to the Middle East to begin setting up military base agreements with Qatar and Kyrgyzstan.

Our first stop was an overnight stay in Incirlik, Turkey. before proceeding to Doha, Qatar. After staying at the Intercontinental Hotel in Doha, our crew departed for a relatively new air base out in the desert named Al Udeid, where we had a bit of an embarrassing security issue on that flight.

The morning of departure from Doha, a sergeant working for General Handy rolled a baggage trolley down the hotel hallway, collecting the luggage of the military party to be transported on our Gulfstream. With our passengers and their baggage on board, we departed for the austere desert location. The brown, drab air base was so hard to spot in the desert that Barry and I built our own approach using GPS coordinates to guide us to the runway.

After landing, we proceeded to download our party's luggage from the cramped baggage compartment in the back of our jet.

Everyone had nearly identical black suitcases, and they were all piled in a circle. Among the luggage sat two large, blue suitcases. The general departed for his meeting with the base leadership, and everyone else reached into the circle of luggage to claim their bags. After all of the black bags were claimed, the two powder-blue suitcases still remained in the center, untouched. We looked around and asked if anybody knew whose luggage this was, but nobody stepped forward to claim them.

A sergeant on the general's staff took the luggage aside and checked the luggage tags. After some phone calls, he discovered that they belonged to two Brits from the Intercontinental Hotel. When the vacationing couple opened their hotel door that morning, they saw the baggage trolley and thought that a nice doorman was providing excellent service. They happily placed their two blue suitcases on the trolley of military luggage when the sergeant was gathering luggage across the hall. While this would have been funny under other circumstances, this certainly violated our strict security protocol, and it happened just a month after 9/11. We were lucky there was nothing sinister inside their luggage.

After the couple was contacted, the couple's luggage was placed on the next C-130 transport flight returning to Doha.

After departing Al Udeid, we flew General Handy further east to Bishkek, Kyrgyzstan. We landed in this former Soviet republic in central Asia using a challenging approach flown at night, surrounded by mountains. Kyrgyzstan flew by Russian aviation rules and used meters instead of feet on their altimeters. Fortunately, our advanced aircraft could switch the altimeter from feet to meters with the push of a button. We also had to be on our guard as we flew an unfamiliar nighttime approach over the mountains, using procedures we rarely saw other than during our simulator training.

The language barrier made it very difficult to understand the air traffic controllers in their broken English, as they also used non-standard terminology. Deciphering the controller's instructions took intense concentration from Barry, me, and our flight engineer, Tech.

Sgt. Jake Piascik. During the flight, Barry and I became distracted while trying to understand the controller's confusing instructions and looking at our navigation displays and flight-management system. Our third set of eyes, Jake, finally tapped Barry on the shoulder, pointed out the left window, and said, "Why don't we just land on that runway right there?" Following his gesture, we saw the lit-up runway on this dark night. Barry completed a safe nighttime landing and taxied our business jet to the enormous ramp, which was dimly lit by sparsely spaced light poles.

What I remember most about Bishkek was how dry, gray, and dusty the area was. We stayed at a nice international hotel, but everything looked colorless and drab as we drove through the city. When we checked into the hotel, the clerk requested to see our passports, then left the room carrying a stack of them. I'm certain they were being copied in their back office, and that we now had the beginnings of our very own Russian dossier.

We stayed in this location for two nights while General Handy completed the coalition basing agreements, giving the United States the right to use this airfield in any upcoming conflict. Air operations supporting Operation Enduring Freedom began a few months later, in December 2001.

The night before our departure, I was sound asleep when I heard a rustling at my door. I got out of bed and walked in the dark toward my hotel door when I saw a large manila envelope being pushed underneath. Nobody knocked on the door, and no words were exchanged. I turned on the lamp in my room and saw the note attached to the package, which read, "Lieutenant Colonel Dale, please deliver this package to Andrews AFB intel."

I thought I had been dropped into a scene from *Mission Impossible*. One of my main concerns about this envelope was that it arrived during the same few weeks that America was being terrorized by anthrax-laced envelopes circulating around Washington. In my movie-fed imagination, I wondered if I was about to deliver an anthrax-laden package to the intelligence office at Andrews. The

"Happy Pessimist" might now have a supporting role in his own spy movie.

Our flight departed Kyrgyzstan and headed west, stopping briefly in Incirlik, Turkey, for a refueling stop before proceeding to Ramstein Air Base in Germany for an overnight stay. The next morning, we flew across the Atlantic to Andrews, where I left the airplane to deliver the thick, sealed package to the intelligence office. I explained my midnight courier assignment to the captain accepting the package. I have no idea what the envelope contained, but I suspect it was an intelligence assessment of the air base and its surrounding area.

Shortly afterward, our coalition's large air operation began. Eventually, the air campaign included refueling tankers, cargo aircraft, and B-1 bombers flying from Kyrgyzstan's Manas Air Base, and all of this was in support of Operation Enduring Freedom, the war in Afghanistan against the Taliban and al-Qaida.

48
PROVIDING FIVE-STAR SERVICE TO THE FOUR-STARS

THE CEREMONY NARRATOR read the order relinquishing Lt. Col. Eden Murrie of her command and passing that command to me. The sergeant handed the guidon (a small, blue flag on a wooden pole) to Lieutenant Colonel Murrie, who passed it to Col. Rob Kane, stating, "Sir, I relinquish command." She then stepped to her right and two steps backward as I stepped forward. Colonel Kane passed the guidon to me, holding it out for me to take. After I accepted this symbol of taking command, I then passed it back to the sergeant on my right. I turned and saluted Colonel Kane sharply, stating, "Sir, I assume command."

At 3 p.m. on July 22, 2002, Lieutenant Colonel Murrie passed the command of our 310th Airlift Squadron to me in a ceremony based on an age-old military tradition dating back to Frederick the Great of Prussia in the eighteenth century. At that time, organizational flags were developed with color arrangements and symbols unique to each unit. The soldiers of the unit would proclaim their loyalty and trust to the commander and the unit, as represented by the flag. When a change of command took place, the flag was passed from the outgoing commander to the individual assuming command.

This ceremony took place in front of the unit so that each soldier could witness the new leader assuming command.

Colonel Kane, the commander of our 6th Operation Group, presided over the event and thanked Eden for her excellent work over the previous year and a half. In that time, she had built a cohesive team and molded the 310 AS into the Air Force's newest squadron. From what had once been a two-airplane flight of the 91 ARS, Eden established a sixty-five-member DV airlift squadron on par with any flying squadron at Andrews.

Eden gave her parting remarks, thanking the squadron members she led and the chain of command above her. She wished us all the best of luck as she departed to attend senior service school (also known as the "colonel's course"). Lieutenant Colonel Murrie eventually became a one-star brigadier general and commanded the 100th Air Refueling Wing in Mildenhall, England.

Following Eden's remarks, the two of us stood at the front of the stage, with Colonel Kane standing to her left and me to her right, as viewed from the audience. When Colonel Kane gave the order, Eden and I made a right-face, ninety-degree turn to face our commander. The squadron guidon was brought forward by our ranking enlisted member, Senior Master Sgt. Ray Ikone. The guidon was a small, dark-blue flag on a wooden pole, with bright yellow letters depicting "310 AS" above a yellow eagle with outstretched wings.

After assuming command, I thanked the base leadership for placing their faith in me, and I assured the 310 AS members in attendance that we would continue to excel at our DV airlift mission. Knowing that we were continuing a high-visibility, no-fail mission, I challenged the squadron to "earn their Ph.D. in air mobility."

Our squadron had endured some growing pains throughout the previous year as we merged the established crews dedicated to serving just the CENTCOM and SOUTHCOM commanders with the large number of inbound personnel. All of our crews were highly capable, but not all stayed at MacDill to transition to the C-37s. For some, it was the right time in their career development to move to another assignment for advancement.

One major stressor for our squadron was that General Franks, the CENTCOM commander, did not want to lose his large EC-135. Thanks to its inflight refueling capability, the EC-135 could transport thirty-four people (sixteen aircrew members and eighteen passengers) non-stop to Doha, Qatar, or Bishkek, Kyrgyzstan. As the commanding wartime general in the Middle East region, he was in no mood to fly in a twelve-passenger executive jet that required a refueling stop in Germany or Italy before proceeding to the desert. The CT-43 retired as scheduled to the Arizona desert on September 30, 2001, but the EC-135 was extended after General Franks appealed directly to Secretary of Defense Donald Rumsfeld. The EC-135 crews needed to stay with us for the time being.

Every three months for the next year, the Air Force extended the operation of the EC-135 for another quarter. These quarterly extensions canceled assignments for outbound EC-135 crew members who thought they had another Air Force job lined up, and threw turmoil into families trying to make decisions to sell a current home, buy another, and decide what school their children would attend the next year. My heart went out to these families, but it was our mission to continue supporting the CENTCOM commander in his EC-135.

Six months before the change of command, I wanted to ensure everyone focused on our squadron's mission. As the 310 AS/DO, I wrote a memo and read it to the available aircrews at a gathering in our squadron.

The portion below reflects the message I repeated at my assumption of command on July 22, 2002:

What does it mean to be a part of the 310th Airlift Squadron? To me, it means being a part of THE BEST C-37/CT-43/EC-135 combatant commander support unit in the Air Force. It means working with people that want to study every bit of useful information about the aircraft, want to showcase their talents in every meal served, and want to provide the commanders with the finest communications platform this Air Force has to offer. In short, we will provide five-star service to the four-stars.

We can also have fun performing our mission. For me, the Harlem Globetrotters have always been an inspiration. They master their talent first, then go out and have great fun doing their job. That's how I approach my job in the Air Force, and that's how I hope you approach your job in the 310th as well.

Being a lieutenant colonel is as far as I want to go in the Air Force. Building the 310th is the pinnacle of my career. We are going to be the premier C-37 flying unit in the Air Force.

The 310th Airlift Squadron: Providing five-star service to the four-stars.

That motto remained the squadron's motto until it closed September 30, 2019.

Once the Air Force decided to deactivate the 310 AS, the three MacDill C-37s were dispersed to Hawaii, Belgium, and Andrews Air Force Base to continue supporting warfighting commanders from those bases.

49

"THANKS FOR KEEPING ME SAFE"

ON A SNOWY DECEMBER MORNING, our C-37 (call sign SPAR 29) was more than a half-hour late as I began the approach to Runway 19L, the left of two parallel southbound runways at Andrews. In the cabin not far from our cockpit sat CENTCOM's commander, Gen. Tommy Franks, and a Marine Corps major, an F-18 fighter pilot, who served as the general's aide. The right-side runway at Andrews was closed, perhaps for snow removal, so we could not fly a Category II instrument landing system precision approach down to a hundred feet above the ground. Because of the less-precise instrumentation on the left-side runway, we were instead restricted to using the approach to Runway 19L, which could only be flown to 200 feet above the ground. That hundred-foot difference was important on this snowy winter morning.

According to our C-37 policies, I flew the approach using the heads-up display (HUD) while my copilot peered through the clouds, hoping to spot the runway lights by the time we reached the 200-foot decision altitude. My copilot, Don Axlund, an excellent officer and pilot, had just completed his check out in the C-37 the day before. This was his first operational VIP mission, which he got to fly with me, his squadron commander. No pressure, Don.

I briefed the ILS approach and lined up for the approach. I emphasized to Don: "If you don't see the runway, it's OK. Just call the 'go around,' and we'll try it again."

As we approached 300 feet AGL, Don announced, "Approaching minimums." At 200 feet, with nothing but white in front of us, Don commanded, "Go around." I applied full power, and our C-37 rose quickly through the dense, white clouds.

Two hours earlier, Don and I had departed Tampa International Airport with General Franks onboard, bound for Andrews. It was time for him to present another Operation Enduring Freedom update to the president and the secretary of defense.

During this timeframe, our MacDill runway had been closed for repair. We were forced to operate out of Tampa International Airport, which was a half-hour drive north of our air base. This mission got off to a poor start, with a delayed takeoff, after the general and his party arrived at our C-37 well past the planned takeoff time. The flight north to Washington, D.C., took two hours, but we knew we were flying into a major snowstorm. There is a tendency in Distinguished Visitor Airlift to do anything to please the customer, and this led to some crews pressing the corners of the safety envelope to accomplish their mission on time.

On April 3, 1996, Secretary of Commerce Ron Brown and 34 other passengers died in an Air Force CT-43 crash into a mountainside near Dubrovnik, Croatia. The crew had departed five minutes early—but, because of the wartime routing into Croatia, they were assigned a route that took fifteen minutes longer than planned. In their attempt to provide an on-time arrival, the crew flew faster than normal on their approach to the airfield. Additionally, they were flying a primitive, non-directional-beacon instrument approach into a cloud deck that was just 400 feet above the ground. The combination of a non-precision approach flown in bad weather while trying to make up time resulted in a tragic accident. The crew strayed off course in low visibility, and the plane slammed into the side of a hill, killing all onboard.

At the time of the accident, I was flying NATO troops into Split, Croatia, in the Netherlands Air Force KDC-10. As a commander of a DV Airlift squadron, I was constantly aware of the pressures our crews faced to press the limits of safety to please our customers. As I had learned during my two years at Andrews, it's OK to say no.

There were two important safety lessons I brought with me to this new Florida squadron: First, if the VIP gets mad because you didn't think it was safe to land, just let it flow like water off a duck's back. They'll get over it, but you will all still be alive. Second, don't bend over backward to set a precedent that your fellow squadron pilots can't meet. In other words, don't be the reason that the general or his staff could say, "Well, the last guy did it." I passed these lessons on to our new pilots just learning about the pressures of VIP airlift.

As I made our approach with General Franks onboard, I was unable to see the Andrews runway. I applied go-around thrust, and the powerful C-37 pitched up and climbed quickly to 2,000 feet. Just seconds before the go-around, we could see snow-covered trees directly below us, so the vertical visibility was almost 200 feet, but the forward visibility in front of us was still low. That restricted forward visibility kept us from seeing the runway, or even the bright white approach lights once we reached the decision altitude.

Knowing we were so close to breaking out, Don requested vectors for a second approach attempt. Ten minutes later, we were on final approach and descending again into the blowing snow. Nothing improved on this second attempt, so rather than "ducking under" the clouds in the hope of seeing the runway, Don again correctly called for the go-around, which I performed.

Part of the thrill of instrument flying is intense concentration while flying an approach. Pilots are not concerned with the people riding along in back. We are focused solely on our instruments, the runway, and Mother Nature. Whenever I jockey the throttles to maintain airspeed during gusty winds, I am constantly reminded of my teenage days with Mr. Lovell barking, "Stay on speed!" or, during buffeting crosswinds, "Fight for centerline!" before commenting if I was one or two feet off centerline after I touched down.

Throughout my year at the Army's command and general staff course, we were the hosts for several guest speakers, from Vietnam fighter aces to Medal of Honor winners, all relating their stories of combat and leadership. I served as the escort officer for a World War II P-51 Mustang pilot credited with the first shoot-down of two German ME-262 jets, a revolutionary aircraft of that era. The white-haired man in his late 70s told the tale of completing his bomber escort mission over Germany, then turning for home and seeking "targets of opportunity." While we assumed this was going to be a tale of the powerful Mustang dogfighting with two new jets over the skies of Germany, the old pilot admitted that he destroyed the first one as it taxied toward the runway, then banked around and shot down the second jet as it lifted off the ground—historic, but a bit anticlimactic.

During the question-and-answer period that followed, an Army major became very philosophical with her questions, asking him about his moral touchstones and motivations during this engagement.

The old fighter pilot stood on stage, confused.

"My what?' he asked.

She forged ahead: "What did you feel inside? What motivated you to carry out your mission?"

He brought the microphone to his lips and said, "Hell, I just didn't want to die!"

I've often thought about that straightforward reply when people ask me how I handle the pressure of landing a plane with passengers on board. How do I cope with the responsibility? Quite honestly, I'm just very selfish. I enjoy the challenge, the intense focus, and the rush of adrenaline that takes place during a gusty or stormy landing. However, I am solely focused on the runway in front of me and not the people behind me. Pilots concentrate on two things during a landing: aimpoint and airspeed. It was drilled into us during pilot training, and many pilots repeat these words over and over in their head: "*Aimpoint. Airspeed. Aimpoint. Airspeed.*" When people say they are afraid to fly, I just tell them their safety is a direct result of my selfishness.

As that WWII pilot said: "Hell, I just didn't want to die!"

We pilots take on Mother Nature's challenges, but we also strive to keep everything within safe limits. If it's not safe to land, we can always go into a holding pattern and wait, or divert to a better location. The priorities are safety first, then comfort, then reliability. Keeping them in that order saves lives.

The winds were very light that particular day, only blowing five knots out of the south. Most airplanes can handle landing with a ten-knot tailwind, so I asked Don to request an opposite-direction approach from the south to the north. There were no other planes in the area to create a conflict, so permission was granted, and we lined up for the northbound right-side runway. Fortunately, the weather south of Andrews was clearing. As I approached 300 feet, the white approach lights and the runway came into view through the low clouds. At 200 feet, Don announced, "Runway in sight." Staring through the HUD, I transitioned my focus from the green instruments on the glass to a visual aimpoint a thousand feet down the runway.

On this gloomy winter day, Don and I safely delivered General Franks to Washington, but forty-five minutes behind schedule. President Bush and Secretary of Defense Don Rumsfeld were kept waiting for their warfighting general.

How would the general react? Some uppity VIPs are known to not give a hoot about excuses and only want to remain on schedule at all costs—and several of those ranting celebrities or businessmen have paid for that attitude with their lives.

We parked the jet on the red-painted cement "carpet" near base operations, and our flight engineer opened the door, allowing the brisk winter breeze to blow through the cabin. General Franks and his aide, the Marine F-18 pilot, prepared to exit, and having a fellow aviator onboard turned out to be a godsend. Although the general and his fellow passengers could see the snow-covered pine trees directly below us on approach, the Marine pilot explained to the other passengers that forward "slant-range" vision is often restricted, and considerably less than looking straight down.

People that knew I flew Gen. Tommy Franks often asked me, "What is he like?"

My reply: "Loud! He can be really happy or really pissed off, but he's always loud!"

As General Franks departed our Gulfstream on that white winter day in Washington, he stepped into our cockpit, popped me on my right shoulder with his large fist, and said in his deep baritone Texan voice, "Thanks for keeping me safe!"

I could not have asked for a better aviation lesson than that for my new copilot.

50
HIGHS AND LOWS

My Last Overseas Mission

ON APRIL 14, 2004, I set out for my final overseas trip in the C-37, and the last one of my Air Force career. I had interviewed with Southwest Airlines one month earlier and was hoping to hear some results any day. Our eight-day trip retraced a lot of the same cities and bases I had visited in October 2001, but this time our customer was Army Gen. Doug Brown, the new commander of Special Operations Command.

We made stops in Doha, Qatar, and Bishkek, Kyrgyzstan, before flying over the mountain range into Bagram Air Base, forty-five miles north of Kabul, Afghanistan. Employing a combat arrival technique, we overflew the air base at 20,000 feet, then spiraled down, staying within the confines of the airfield to limit our potential exposure to shoulder-fired missiles or anti-aircraft gunfire. The base was a major installation for our Air Force and numerous coalition forces, with American F-16s and A-10s flying daily combat missions. After spending the night at Bagram, we departed the next day heading south toward Pakistan, before turning west toward Muscat, Oman, where I had flown KC-10 missions during Operation Desert Storm in 1991.

As we flew over Pakistan, a datalink message arrived from our squadron telling me that someone from Southwest Airlines had called looking for me. I knew that had to be a good sign. With our satellite phone on the aircraft, I called the squadron and spoke with Lt. Col. Steve Kowalski, who was manning our squadron operations center that day.

"Hey, Dave, I thought you'd like to know that a lady named Mary called for you and asked you to call her back," he said, passing along her Dallas office phone number.

I thanked him for the message and told him that I'd return the call as soon as possible.

After hanging up, I told my copilot, Lt. Col. Steve McAllister, the news. Steve grinned and told me, "You should call her back right now."

"You really think so?" I asked.

"Sure," he replied.

I picked up the satellite phone and dialed the number, and a lady from the company's personnel department answered the phone. I told her who I was, and she replied that it was time for me to schedule a drug test. She couldn't commit to the fact that I was hired, but this was the next step—and that meant that I had passed the interview process. Southwest was now wrapping up the final details before the airline offered me a job.

"I'm currently out of the country, but I'll take care of that as soon as I get back home," I said.

"Where are you right now?" she asked.

"Well, I'm currently flying over Pakistan," I told her. Yes, I was showing off.

"Oh, that's so cool!" she exclaimed.

That was the end of a very happy, but short, conversation.

Steve was grinning at me as I hung up.

"Congratulations," he said.

This was the fulfillment of the second part of my teenage dream. I told myself as a high school senior that I wanted to serve twenty years as an Air Force pilot, then fly for Southwest, my home-state airline. This was the same airline that launched when I was in junior high that was famous for its flight attendants in hot pants and go-go boots.

An hour later, we landed at Seeb Airport in Muscat, Oman, for a night's stay. The base had come a long way since the tent city of 1990 to 1991. The desert military installation now had hard-sided buildings—a vast collection of tan, rectangular single-story portable shelters, each with window air conditioners and generators humming away.

Our communications system operator for this mission was a twenty-three-year-old enlisted crew member named Abbey Skinner. The next day, as we walked on the crunchy gray gravel paths of the small base, I told her that when she was eleven years old, I lived for three months in one of fifty canvas tents alongside the runway.

We made our way over to the new chow hall where we saw General Brown's aide, an Army major. As we joined him at a table, he told us, "This has been the greatest trip ever."

"Why's that?" I asked.

He told us he now was able to see the camps that had come into existence after his clandestine efforts back in the fall of 2001. This major had a very mild-mannered appearance, looking like any big-city accountant walking down a sidewalk. In actuality, he had been a special operations forces captain after the 9/11 attacks and had parachuted into the mountainous regions of Afghanistan with CIA agents carrying suitcases full of hundreds of thousands of dollars. Their mission, detailed in a lengthy *New York Times* article, was to buy the allegiance of the warlords within the area so we could have safe passage in our upcoming fight with al-Qaida and the Taliban in Afghanistan. The groundwork of Army outposts that he helped create back in 2001, riding horseback and carrying suitcases of money through the mountains, had now come to fruition.

That afternoon, on April 22, we departed for the westbound trip back to Florida. A few hours into the trip, in the dark skies over the Atlantic, the Army major came back up into the cockpit, yelling, "Son of a bitch!"

"What's wrong?" I asked him as I turned around.

"Pat Tillman has just been killed," he said.

This was the night a firefight took the life of NFL star Pat Tillman, the Arizona Cardinal player who walked away from millions of dollars to become an Army Ranger immediately after the 9/11 attacks. The unfortunate deadly shooting later turned out to be from our own troops, but on this still night over the ocean, nobody knew the details of his death. Everyone assumed it was an enemy ambush on our forces.

This was the low point of a roller-coaster two-day period. What had started with the excitement of my potential hiring with Southwest Airlines now concluded with somber news of the death of a true American hero. Our cockpit was very quiet as we flew westward over the dark ocean.

51
COMING FULL CIRCLE

ONE OF THE final trips of my twenty-year career was to take Air Force Gen. Ed Eberhart, commander of Northern Command (NORTHCOM), on visits to the Air National Guard and Air Force Reserve bases in the southeastern and south-central United States. Our first stop was Homestead Air Force Base near Miami to see the Jacksonville Air National Guard F-15s, whose pilots were maintaining their alert rotation. We then headed north to Jacksonville Airport, where the former F-15 fighter pilot took a flight in one of the National Guard F-15s.

The next morning, we set off for New Orleans, visiting yet another F-15 fighter unit. Our planned final stop was Ellington Field, just south of my hometown of Houston. As we flew toward New Orleans, I told the other pilot, my good friend Maj. "Ice" Icenhour, that I learned to fly at LaPorte Municipal Airport, not far from Ellington.

"That's cool," he said. "You should call up your old flight instructor."

I told him my instructor, Richard Lovell, was a Korean War Navy veteran, and I wasn't sure if he was even still alive. I had last seen him and his wife, Sylvia, in 1990, when Karin and I took our baby boy,

Daniel, to visit them in Pasadena, Texas. Ice told me I had to call him, and to tell him we'd be at Ellington tomorrow. I really dreaded making that phone call, fearing Sylvia might answer and tell me that Mr. Lovell had passed away. But with Ice's continued prompting, I got up my courage and dialed his number. On the second ring, he answered the phone. What a relief!

I told him we would be flying a new Gulfstream V into Ellington the next day with a four-star general onboard. Without me prompting, Mr. Lovell asked, "Can we get together for dinner?"

"That would be great," I told him. "And I'd like to show you the aircraft after we land."

Ellington Field is a joint civilian and military air base open to the public, allowing visitors to park near base operations. We taxied our C-37 up to the painted cement "red carpet," where an entourage of colonels were waiting to greet their visiting four-star general. The group whisked General Eberhart away to visit the F-16 squadron that had escorted President Bush's Air Force One on 9/11.

Once the passengers left, I walked along the red carpet to find the Lovells sitting on an outdoor wooden bench, looking like Ma and Pa Kettle. Mr. Lovell's once-curly hair was now thin, and he leaned forward on the bench, supported by his wooden cane.

I owe my flying career to Mr. Lovell, and I never called him or knew him as Richard, only Mr. Lovell. It had been twenty-six years since he took over as the leader of our Aviation Explorers post in the southern part of Houston. Twenty-four years had passed since I last flew with the former Navy boxing champion with a permanently crooked nose. The tough old cuss no longer dipped and swallowed Copenhagen chewing tobacco, but he still sucked on the inside of his lower lip out of habit.

As was the case with a lot of teenagers, my training stagnated in the late 1970s. Sometimes it was because of family vacations; other times it was because I had to put my restaurant paycheck into car repairs instead of flying lessons. The result of my poor consistency led to retaking lessons to regain flying proficiency, a common occurrence in private flying.

The FAA requires students to have twenty hours of flight instruction and twenty hours of solo time, including cross-country flights, to take their private-license flight evaluation. By the summer of 1980, after my high school graduation, I was approaching sixty hours of flying time and was set to leave for college by mid-August. Mr. Lovell was the one who kicked me in the pants to complete the rating, telling me, "If you don't finish it before starting college, then you'll never finish it."

I am a pilot today because of that caring, tough old man.

"Would you like to see our jet?" I asked him.

"I suppose so," he answered quietly, smiling, and we walked slowly out to the beautiful blue-and-white C-37 with "United States of America" painted above the line of six oval windows. We climbed the short fold-out staircase and turned left so he could see the modern glass cockpit of six screens in front of the pilot seats, and the panels overhead consisting of only black push-button squares. It was a very smooth, clean cockpit.

I then guided the Lovells down the blue carpeted hallway and into the VIP cabin, with its mahogany wood and twelve blue-leather, first class-sized chairs, each with its own spacious window. The Lovells each took a seat and looked around the cabin.

"What do you think?" I asked my old mentor.

Trying not to sound impressed, Mr. Lovell replied, "Well, they all fly the same. Keep the shiny side up and the wheels on the bottom."

After they finished their quick tour of our jet, I changed clothes, and the three of us went out for seafood along the Kemah Boardwalk, between Houston and Galveston. We spent the evening catching up over dinner. I told them all about Karin, Daniel, and Shelby, and my international flying exploits since September 11.

I gladly treated the Lovells to dinner that night as a very small repayment for Mr. Lovell's patience and graciousness during my teenage years. After dinner, he brought their large four-door Ford sedan up near the restaurant door as I waited with his wife. I held the passenger door open for Sylvia, and as she started to climb in, she squeezed my elbow, leaned in close to me, and whispered, "You'll never know how much this means to him."

My flying career had come full circle. As I prepared to retire from the Air Force and join the ranks of commercial airline pilots, I happily thanked the gruff old guy who taught me to fly.

Relinquishing command of the 310 AS

My shadow box, expertly crafted by Staff Sgt. Keith O'Steen, 310 AS flight engineer. Awards: Five Meritorious Service medals, Air Medal, Aerial Achievement, Commendation, Combat Readiness, National Defense Service, Armed Forces Expeditionary, Southwest Asia Service, Humanitarian Service, Kuwaiti Liberation medal. Other awards: Outstanding Unit with Valor, Expert Marksmanship

EPILOGUE

Air Force C-37A at MacDill Air Force Base. (Robin Parrish)

JUNE 2004, MacDill Air Force Base, Tampa, Florida

On a muggy Monday morning in June 2004, I was standing in the hallway just outside my office when my office phone rang. Hustling around my desk, I grabbed it and said, "310th Airlift Squadron, Lieutenant Colonel Dale."

"Dave, this is Colonel Zepf at CVAM. Do you have a STU-III in your squadron?"

"Yes, sir, we do," I answered, still standing over my phone.

"OK, please call me right back," he said.

Col. Mike Zepf was the division chief of CVAM at the Pentagon. CVAM scheduled the highest-ranking civilian and military distinguished visitor travel itineraries on military aircraft. They were the scheduling agency for both Andrews Air Force Base in Maryland, supporting the Pentagon and Washington-based DVs, and also for my squadron at MacDill, just outside Tampa. Our STU-III telephone was used only for encrypted classified conversations, so Colonel Zepf's request meant that the topic had to be extremely sensitive.

I wasn't concerned about this call when I answered, because I was very familiar with Colonel Zepf. He and I had been friends for fifteen years, since our days flying the KC-10 air refueling tanker at Barksdale in Louisiana. We not only flew together, we also played intramural softball on the KC-10 team when he was a major and I was a captain.

Since July 2002 I had been the squadron commander of the 310 AS at MacDill. Our squadron took up the entire upper left side of a huge 1950s-era hangar along the flight line of the Florida air force base. At the opposite end of our long, skinny squadron from my office lay the sensitive compartmented information facility (SCIF), a locked room containing the STU-III telephone and files of classified information. I rarely spoke to Colonel Zepf directly, so walking down the hundred-foot-long hallway to the SCIF, I wondered if we had a seriously ticked-off four-star general following one of our squadron's recent trips.

I quickly called Colonel Zepf back.

"Dave, what I'm about to tell you ... only you, me, and five people in the White House know about."

As an opening statement in a presentation, that's called the "attention step"—and he had my attention now.

"I need your squadron to plan a classified mission to Amman, Jordan, for two weeks from now," he said. "It will probably take two crews. I can't tell you much more but work the details directly through me."

I now had my marching orders, as the military saying goes.

I knew it would be a challenge keeping everything a secret. Because of the highly sensitive nature of this mission, we would need two five-person crews, plus mission planners to get the ball rolling on putting this mission together. We had to get this done without letting the news slip outside of our squadron. Our online flight scheduling program could be seen by other units and was color-coded for training missions, operational missions, and aircraft that may require downtime for maintenance. We needed to handle this carefully so as to not raise attention outside of the squadron.

After the call, I walked back down the long hallway to the squadron operations center (SOC) desk, the hub of all activity in the middle of our squadron. There, I briefed a handful of squadron members who would be involved in planning and carrying out this mission. After talking with Lt. Col. Keith Kreeger, my director of operations, we decided to block out a weeklong "off-station training mission" for one of our three C-37s. It would last from Friday, June 24, to Friday, July 2. The mission appeared as a long blue line on the scheduling program created by our pilot, Maj. "Arnie" Palmer. It wouldn't raise any suspicions, because these off-station training missions often were used to qualify a group of new crew members in our special airlift mission.

As planning continued, we faced a couple of questions. Who were we carrying? At this point, Saddam Hussein had been captured and was still confined in Iraq. Were we bringing him to the United States to face justice? That definitely would be a high-priority mission, and our mission was being monitored directly from the Pentagon and White House.

We also realized that although the C-37 could fly eleven hours before stopping for fuel, to get in and out of Jordan quickly we would need to "pony express" the airplane—i.e., have a fuel stop and crew swap at some point during the mission. As the plan unfolded, the first crew, piloted by Lt. Col. Kevin Oatley and my eventual replacement, Lt. Col. Monty Perry, would depart a day early and overnight at the U.S. Naval Air Station in Sigonella, on the island of Sicily. They then would depart for Amman, Jordan, the next morning, quickly pick up the unknown passenger, then depart for the westward flight home.

Our five-person C-37 crew, consisting of two pilots, a flight engineer, communications system operator, and flight attendant, could work a sixteen-hour day, but the trip from Sicily to Jordan to the States would exceed that time. This meant a second crew and a fuel stop on the way home was required. Our planners suggested Kevin's crew stop for fuel at Lajes Air Base, an Air Force/Portuguese airfield in the Azores Islands off the coast of Portugal in the Atlantic. The first crew would be met by Lt. Col. Pete Martin and Lt. Col. Dean Metz, who would take over the mission with a second full crew for the trans-Atlantic flight to Washington.

To ensure a quick gas-and-go at Lajes Air Base, I knew that Maj. Rob Crone, working in the Lajes command post, could be of great help. Rob had been a Gulfstream evaluator pilot when I was based at Andrews, and Colonel Zepf knew him well. I hoped to brief Rob over a STU-III telephone on the mission, and the need for a quick refueling and crew swap. He would fully understand the need for secrecy, and this would help keep the mission under wraps.

A bit selfishly, I thought this mission came at a critical point in my life. After twenty years in the Air Force, I was set to retire on July 27. My final family vacation was planned for the same last week of June as this classified mission. I wondered how this mission might affect my family's plans to visit Larry and Shelley Leonard in the Caymans. I also wondered when I'd be allowed to tell my boss, Col. Brian Kelly at MacDill's 6th Operations Group, and his boss, Brigadier General Snyder at the 6th Air Mobility Wing headquarters, about this secret mission.

As I updated Col Zepf on the planning progress, he agreed that I could brief Major Crone in the Azores on our quick-stop fuel requirement for the return leg. He also said I could tell my chain of command about the mission the day before I left for vacation. Finally, he dispelled any notion that our crews were bringing Saddam

Hussein to the United States when he said to make sure the flight attendant had a selection of beer and liquor for the return flight home.

Well, *that* was certainly different.

The mission details all fell into place. The crews obtained their required visas and diplomatic clearances, the food and beverages were procured, and Rob assured me that Lajes Air Base would be ready for the crew swap on the trans-Atlantic flight home. On my day before starting vacation, I stopped by the operations group to see Colonel Kelly to make sure my leave form was processed.

"Sir, do you have a minute?" I asked him.

"Come in, Dave," he said." What have you got?"

"I need to tell you about that mission that is blocked out next week as an off-station trainer," I said. "It's not really training. It's a classified mission to Amman, Jordan."

"And you're just now telling me about this?" Kelly remarked, tilting his head.

I could tell he wondered why a lieutenant colonel was keeping a secret from a colonel.

"I couldn't before," I said. "It came down directly from Colonel Zepf at CVAM to our squadron."

"Who is the passenger?" he asked.

"We don't know," I said. "But they have to get in and out of Jordan quickly, and back to the States."

On June 28, 2004, just ahead of the June 30 deadline, Paul Bremer, the presidential envoy to Iraq, formally transferred sovereignty of Iraqi territory to the Iraqi interim government. The U.S. and Iraqi governments wanted to accomplish this before the deadline to prevent any civil unrest during the transfer of power. Intelligence reports suggested that terrorists were coming into Baghdad from the west and the south to conduct car bombings and other attacks on June 30. Additionally, reports on June 26 indicated that the insurgents planned to capture a city—perhaps Ramadi or Baquba—on June 30 to cripple the new government before it could take power. I later discovered these details after reading the ambassador's memoir, titled *My Year in Iraq*.

The ambassador, wearing a business suit and desert-brown combat boots, departed Iraq for Jordan on June 28, and he boarded our 310th Airlift Squadron C-37 for his flight back to Washington, complete with cocktails. The entire mission, including the quick turnaround and crew change at Lajes Air Base, all went off smoothly. I could not have been prouder of our flight crews and squadron personnel as they provided five-star service to the president's envoy.

Thankfully, my vacation with Larry and my retirement from the Air Force also happened just as planned. On July 27, 2004, I handed over command of the 310 AS to the next squadron commander, Lt. Col. Monty Perry, and retired from the Air Force that same day. Five days later, on August 2, I realized my second dream as I became a Boeing 737 pilot for Southwest Airlines.

Ten years later, while visiting the George W. Bush Presidential Library in Dallas, I came across a notecard written by national security advisor Dr. Condoleezza Rice to President George W. Bush on June 28, 2004. Her message stated: "Mr. President, Iraq is sovereign. Letter was passed from Bremer at 10:26 a.m., Iraq time.—Condi"

The president's handwritten reply in red felt-tip marker read, "Let Freedom Reign!"

Beaming with pride, I snapped a photo of the index card to share with the 310 AS alumni.

APPENDIX 1: THANKS MOM AND DAD

"I'd like to introduce you to my mom and dad," I said to my Southwest Airlines crew. Mom *and* Dad. This may not seem like an unusual thing to say, but for those who grew up a child of divorced parents, it's a statement many of them long to say—and I relished that for three days in November 2006. Like many marriages in the 1970s, my parent's union dissolved when I was in grade school. I'm not exactly sure when, since it was a long, drawn-out process, but I believe I was about ten or eleven years old. I can't speak for my brother or sisters, but I think we were fortunate in some aspects, because I don't remember our parents fighting or squabbling in our presence. Many marriages end with bitter feelings—but, from my perspective, my parents' marriage fizzled out instead of exploded. Nonetheless, my siblings and I joined the ranks of the many children of divorced parents and then moved on with life.

My parents both went through the marriage/divorce cycle one more time before my dad married a great lady willing to put up with him, and my mom remained close with lifelong friends, but single. The best part of their relationship is that they remained cordial and friendly over the years. Many children may not be able to say that of their married or divorced parents. My mom lived in the Houston house I was raised in until the mid-1990s. By that time, my sisters were raising families in the Denver area, and my dad, stepmom, and stepsister lived south of Denver. Mom's house was too big for her and was a lonely, empty nest, so my dad suggested to her, "Why don't you move out here to Denver, since this is where most of the grandkids are?"

So Mom sold the house and moved to Denver to prepare for her retirement years.

When some marriages crumble, the former couple can't bear to be in the same room together, and my heart goes out to them and their children. We were fortunate that when our family gathered for holidays or birthdays, Mom and Dad were both there, usually at one or the other's house.

Still, though, any child of divorce goes through struggles. At a younger age, it can be, "Do I *want* to go to Dad's house this weekend just because it's 'his turn?' " Then, in the teenage years, it might be, "Which house do I want to live in?" As an adult, young or old, there can be the dilemma of which parent's house to visit first on trips, and where to stay. Maybe it's a self-imposed guilt trip, but the thoughts were there for me year after year. I admired my stepmom, and I'm very grateful to have had her and my stepsister in our lives, but I suspect many children would wish their parents were together again. I got to enjoy that feeling, and I am forever thankful.

I thoroughly enjoyed flying as a first officer for Southwest Airlines, and I was extremely excited to see a three-day trip with overnights in Denver and Washington, D.C., when my November 2006 schedule came out. My stepsister and my cousin Tina (Mom's niece) both lived in the D.C. area, so I first ran my proposal by my stepmom, Karen, because Dad refused to use email. Dad and Karen could fly with me on the second day from Denver, through Chicago, to D.C., and visit their daughter and son-in-law. Then, on the third day, I could fly them from D.C. to Florida, and see my family before the Thanksgiving holidays. Karen had a conflict and couldn't go, but she wanted Dad to go, and that presented some challenges. Dad hadn't traveled much in the post-9/11 world, and not at all as a standby passenger on our airline. Mom, on the other hand, spread her wings in retirement and cruised through airports like a pro. Well, a slow pro.

I wrote back to Karen to ask if it would be OK if I offered the trip to my mom as well, so that she could visit her niece and help Dad through the travel wickets. Karen replied, "Are you asking if it is proper? Hell, I don't care! We're all one big, happy family, aren't we?" We discovered that Karen had mastered the art of yelling through email, but at least I had her blessing.

The weekend adventure got off to a gratifying, yet stressful, start. The gratifying part was introducing the flight crew (captain and flight attendants) to Mom AND Dad. It had been more than thirty-two years since I had stood solely with my parents and said, "I'd like you to meet my mom AND dad." It was a pleasure I hoped to repeat over the next three days. First, however, we had to get out of Denver. Let me just say that when trying to get septuagenarian parents through Denver International security and the terminal, it can be anything but *The Amazing Race*. Mom breezed through security, while Dad struggled to get out his ID, set off the screener with his cellphone and was sent back again to take off his Velcro shoes. Sorry, Dad. I could have forewarned you—but, like the lessons of my youth, some things you just have to figure out for yourself. Try telling that to the eye-rolling, rat-racing fellow passengers.

We strolled to the gate to find that 136 of the 137 seats had sold. Hmmm. Dilemma time: Which parent goes, and which parent stays behind? That self-imposed guilt trip started to surface again. I was not about to pick, so since they had worked out their divorce amicably, I figured they could work this out, too. They each insisted the other go—talk about selfless and considerate! In the end, their kindness was rewarded when just 134 passengers checked in. The "Mom AND Dad" adventure was underway.

The skies over the Midwest and Appalachian Mountains were clear, and the air was smooth throughout the whole trip, which added to the sense that all was right. I landed in D.C., and we began the one-mile trek to the curb, where my cousin was picking us up. *AARP Magazine* would not rank Dulles Airport highly, as my dad struggled with the long walk, stopping to rest along the way, with my mom offering what assistance she could. Cousin Tina had to "go around" at the curb and went back out to the "holding pattern" in the cell-phone lot until we got closer.

That evening we split up for dinner, with Dad dining with his daughter and son-in-law, and Mom and I visiting Tina and her family. I rejoined Dad at the crew hotel later that night, and Mom spent the night with her niece.

The next morning, I started my typical airline morning at 5:30 a.m. and flew two legs before returning to Washington for the final trip to Florida. That allowed my parents time to sleep in, and gave Tina time to swing by the hotel with Mom and take Dad back to the airport. Tina had the forethought to arrange two wheelchairs to help them traverse the airport. When I found them at the top of the jetway, Mom told me about their "wheelchair race" to the gate. I piloted them down the East Coast, making sure to point out the sights via the P.A. system: Charleston, South Carolina, then Savannah, Georgia, and St. Augustine and Cape Canaveral in Florida. The flight attendants doted over them and told me how nice they were. On final approach for my landing, the captain told me, "Buddy, you can land as long as you want, but it better be smooth. Your parents are on board." I treated them to a smooth landing.

Once home in Florida, our children enjoyed the rare treat of having my parents visit without other family members present. Large family gatherings can be fun, but this was special, at least for me. That Sunday was Thanksgiving and Christmas morning rolled into one, regarding my relationship with my parents. After church, the three of us sat on our sunny lanai enjoying ham-and-cheese sandwiches by the pool. We took advantage of the "Chamber of Commerce" weather and drove over the Sunshine Skyway Bridge to Fort DeSoto Beach. What followed was a memory of a lifetime.

Under blue skies and with a temperature of seventy degrees, we slowly walked along the beach as my mom searched for seashells and they told stories of their lives, together and apart, over the past fifty years.

That evening my wife joined us for a "Mostly Pops" pre-holiday concert at our Brandon church. It was a perfect way to cap a memorable visit and begin the Thanksgiving and Christmas season. The orchestra played everything from classical Mozart, to Louis Armstrong's perfectly appropriate *What a Wonderful World,* to holiday medleys, and sing-along Christmas hymns. Life does not get any better than to hold your wife's hand, listening to Mom's soprano voice sing *O Come, All Ye Faithful* as Dad taps his foot. As we left the performance, I took the opportunity to say to friends, "I'd like you to meet my mom AND dad." Thanks, Mom and Dad.

APPENDIX 2: FIND YOUR MOUNTAIN

Appalachian Mountains, June 2003

My wife and I woke up in our little pup tent happy to have survived the night. It was our second night in the Appalachian Mountains, and a storm had blown through, its heavy winds buffeting the pine tree limbs over our tiny two-person tent. We were camping with nine Boy Scouts in June 2003, on the second day of a fifty-mile Appalachian Trail hike. Our goal was to finish fifty miles in one week, and we were setting out for the third day with a ten-mile hike. After breaking down the tent and our camp, we hoisted our fifty-pound backpacks and set off on the trail. Karin later noticed that every morning started with a steep UPHILL hike.

It is very hard to train for a mountain hike when living in Tampa, Florida. We spent the previous two months walking around flat, sea-level terrain, with backpacks full of four one-gallon jugs of water providing ballast so we could build our endurance. The main challenge we faced in Florida was sandy terrain, which definitely gave our calves a workout. It now was the middle of summer, and we were at an elevation of 3,000 to 5,000 feet, hiking rugged terrain, and drinking filtered water from the streams.

The trails often were just three feet wide, with a sheer mountain ascending to our left and a deadly cliff off to our right. We were told these were Indian trails from years gone by. We prepared ourselves for the hike by reading Bill Bryson's book *A Walk in the Woods,* in which he talked of what to do when encountering a bear. We were supposed to walk backward away from a bear—but with a sheer cliff to the left and the right of us, I could only think that we would have to back all the way down the mountain. Although we smelled the musky scent of a bear, we never actually saw one.

Each day we hiked up the trail, Karin set the pace for our group. She and I both wore brimmed hats and carried a walking stick. As I walked, I could only see her legs from the knees to her feet while she ascended the rocky terrain ahead of us. When she tired, she would plant her walking pole in the ground and bend over, catching her breath, and I would walk headlong right up into her rear end. In those days, there were young girls who would wear sweatpants with something written on the seat of their pants, such as "PINK" or "CHEER." After a few days of stumbling into Karin's stationary backside, I told her, "I need to put a stop sign on your butt!" We successfully completed our fifty-mile hike in just four days, completing seventeen miles on the final day. It was a great adventure for our family, but I distinctly remember the sensation of *following her* up the mountain.

As we go through life, we all have mountains to climb. I was following my childhood friend, Larry, up his mountain as we went through high school. Larry is a great lifelong friend of mine, born just across the street from me. He was an excellent athlete and self-confident in everything he did. He was a state champion swimmer and an acrobatic athlete, able to perform amazing feats both on the trampoline and cliff diving off the rocky ledges of Lake Travis, located west of Austin. I was happy to be in his company, but I never ascended to his feats of physicality.

When I was sixteen years old, I decided to take flying lessons and pursue my dream of becoming a pilot. Each lesson gave me more confidence as I overcame the challenges that Mother Nature threw at me. I gained self-confidence in what I was able to accomplish, both in an airplane and at the thought of pleasing my instructor, Mr. Richard Lovell. I was growing to be my own person. As I faced gusty winds or set out on a cross-country flight, navigating visually from town to town, the accomplishments I made as a seventeen-year-old started to increase my self-esteem. Aviation became my metaphorical mountain.

At age eighteen, I earned my private pilot's license in the week before setting off to college. I was no longer following Larry up his mountain but was now climbing my own. I joined the Reserve Officers Training Corps at the University of Texas and took up leadership roles during each of my four years of college. My confidence in my abilities grew by leaps and bounds, and it was only because I chose to pursue my own path and not follow somebody else up their mountain. Each of us needs to decide what is our mountain. No matter your role in life, find *your* mountain and begin the climb.

APPENDIX 3: CHANGE OF COMMAND AND RETIREMENT SPEECH

July 27, 2004

I would like to thank all of you for attending today, especially my family, my sister, Lucy, my minister, Rebekah Maul, and her husband, Derek Maul. Two years ago tomorrow, I took command of the 310th. Many of you in this room were not here that day, so I'm just going to reuse that speech.

I sincerely thank my wife, Karin, and children, Daniel and Shelby, for their patience and understanding as I put in a few long hours not only at MacDill, but for the past twenty years as well. I think my family has been proud to have been associated with the 310th, especially when the airshow VIP passes and Tampa Bay Lightning hockey tickets came out! But I don't think they will miss the cellphone calls and emails.

As for those I worked for, I thank the wing and operations group leadership for the opportunity to lead this VIP airlift squadron. Your support and trust in me have been tremendous, and I thank Col. Brian Kelly, Lt. Col. Jim Fowler, and "Uncle Mac," Steve McAllister, for their leadership, trust, and guidance during these past years.

I must also thank those at the very heart of our 310th mission—

those I have worked with day in and day out. You cannot believe the honor it has been to work with people such as Bob Giddings, Lee Icenhour, Tony Radcliffe, and all of the other proud 310th members. From the bottom of my heart, I thank those that have led this squadron—Jon Banks, Keith Kreeger, Dan Perez, the section chiefs and assistants, and Mary Shoemaker, our wonderful secretary.

I am incredibly proud of what the whole squadron has accomplished since becoming operational two years ago. For those that believe we are just the "wine and cheese squadron," let me tell you a little of the behind-the-scenes accomplishments of this unit. We, with the help of current operations and Gulfstream maintenance, are completely self-sufficient from flight planning through mission execution, with our missions tasked directly from the Pentagon, not AMC headquarters. When a problem arises, the whole squadron jumps into action to solve it. Those are the moments I have been most proud about: the way the unit tackles problems to keep our nation's military leaders on time.

Without a doubt, you have succeeded in providing a critical transportation service for our nation—from the secretary of defense, to the chairman and vice chairman of the Joint Chiefs of Staff, the seven four-star combatant commanders—and, most recently, a White House special envoy. I have swelled with pride to hear personally from three different four-star generals that they prefer to fly with MacDill's 310th crews. We could not have pulled this off without folks who are masters of their job—from each crew member, to the personnel manning our operations center, flight records, our awesome Gulfstream maintenance team, the security forces men and women, and the problem-solvers in current operations. Your work does not go unnoticed, and it is truly appreciated.

Concerning the bright future of the 310th, I will say that I have had the privilege of getting to know Lt. Col. Monty Perry and his wife, Arlis, for the past year. I am proud to say that he is a caring leader, a great aviator, and a good friend. I know he will lead the

310th to new heights, and uphold its tradition and reputation for providing five-star service for the leaders of the United States.

And now it is time to close out my twenty-year career. I can honestly say I never had a bad assignment, from B-52s, to KC-10s, to the Gulfstreams, with each aircraft newer than the last. My first aircraft was older than I was, and the last one was right off the assembly line! The Air Force has been awesome for our whole family, and I hope you enjoy your time in it, too. I will leave you with these words from the book *FISH*:

> *"As you enter this place of work, you choose to make today a great day. Your colleagues, customers, team members, and you yourself will be thankful. Find ways to play! We can be serious about our work without being serious about ourselves. Stay focused in order to be present when your customers and team members most need you. And, should you feel your energy lapsing, try this sure-fire remedy: Find someone who needs a helping hand, a word of support, or a good ear—and make their day!"*

APPENDIX 4: B-52 FACT SHEET

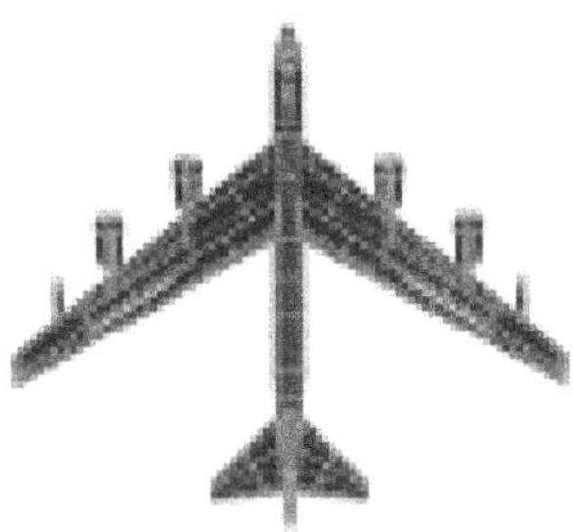

Contractor: Boeing

First B-52G Flight: February 13, 1959

Last Flight: 1994, to comply with the START II treaty

Production: 744 (Total B-52s, including 193 B-52G, the most of any variant)

Aircraft Location: Barksdale Air Force Base, Louisiana; Edwards Air Force Base, California; Minot Air Force Base, North Dakota

Active Variants: B-52H. Longer-range variant with more efficient turbofan engines

Dimensions: Span 185 feet, length 160 feet, height 40.7 feet

Weight: Max takeoff 488,000 pounds

Power Plant: Eight Pratt & Whitney J75, each 14,000 pounds thrust

Performance: Speed 634 mph, range 7,100 miles (without air refueling)

Ceiling: 46,000 feet

Armament: Nuclear: Twelve AGM-86B ALCMs externally, and eight ALCMs or gravity weapons internally. Conventional: Mk 62 sea mines, Mk 82/84 bombs, CBU-87/89 cluster bombs

Accommodation: Pilot, copilot, radar navigator, navigator, electronic warfare officer, and gunner (until 1992) on upward and downward ejection seats

Source: *Air Force Magazine,* https://www.airforcemag.com/weapons-platforms/b-52/

APPENDIX 5: KC-10 FACT SHEET

Contractors: McDonnell Douglas (now Boeing); Collins Aerospace (CNS/ATM)

First Flight: April 1980

Delivered: March 1981-April 1990

Production: Sixty

Inventory: All have retired as of September 2024

Operator: AMC, AFRC (Reserve Associate)

Aircraft Location: Travis Air Force Base, California; Joint Base McGuire-Dix-Lakehurst, New Jersey

Active Variant: KC-10A. Modified McDonnell Douglas DC-10; a multiple-role cargo-tanker

Dimensions: Span 165.4 feet, length 181.6 feet, height 58 feet

Weight: Max Takeoff 590,000 pounds

Power Plant: Three GE Aviation CF6-50C2 turbofans, each 52,500 pounds thrust

Performance: Speed 620 mph, range 11,500 miles, or 4,400 miles with max cargo

Ceiling: 42,000 feet

Fuel Capacity: 356,000 pounds, or 53,000 gallons (one gallon equals 6.7 pounds)

Fuel Offload: 1,100 gallons per minute by boom; 470 gallons per minute by hose and drogue

Accommodation: Pilot, copilot, flight engineer, boom operator

Load: 27 pallets up to 170,000 pounds, or up to seventy-five people and seventeen pallets of cargo

Source: *Air Force Magazine,* https://www.airforcemag.com/weapons-platforms/kc-10/

APPENDIX 6: C-37A FACT SHEET

Contractor: Gulfstream Aerospace

First Flight: October 1998 (C-37A)

Delivered: Oct. 14, 1998-present

IOC: Dec. 9, 1998

Production: Sixteen (planned)

Inventory: Ten (C-37A)

Operator: AMC, PACAF, USAFE

Aircraft Location: MacDill Air Force Base, Florida (until September 2019); Joint Base Andrews, Maryland; Joint Base Pearl Harbor Hickam, Hawaii; Ramstein Air Base, Germany, Chièvres Air Base, Belgium

Active Variants: C-37A and C-37B. Military version of the Gulfstream V and G-550

Dimensions: Span 93.5 feet, length 96.4 feet, height 25.8 feet

Weight: Max Takeoff 90,500 pounds

Power Plant: Two BMW/Rolls-Royce BR710A1-10 turbofans, each 14,750 pounds thrust

Performance: Speed 600 mph, range 6,300 miles

Ceiling: 51,000 feet

Accommodation: Pilot, copilot, flight engineer, communication system operator, flight attendant

Load: Up to twelve passengers

Source: *Air Force Magazine,* https://www.airforcemag.com/weapons-platforms/c-37/

ABOUT THE AUTHOR

David Dale, a native of Houston, Texas, is a fifth-generation Texan and graduated as a fourth-generation Longhorn from the University of Texas at Austin with a degree in business administration. He was commissioned in 1984 as a second lieutenant in the Air Force. His flying assignments during a twenty-year military career included navigating the B-52G, piloting both the United States KC-10 and Dutch KDC-10 air refueling tankers, and finally the Gulfstream G-III and G-V (C-20B and C-37A) for high-level dignitary missions. His aviation articles have appeared in *Plane & Pilot*, the AOPA (Aircraft Owners and Pilot Association) magazine, and on Avgeekery.com. and on Avgeekery.com. He is married to the former Karin Smith of Corpus Christi, Texas, and they have two grown children, Daniel and Shelby. David is a Boeing 737 captain for Southwest Airlines. He and Karin reside in the Texas Hill Country west of Austin.

For more about David Dale, check out his website, PilotDavidDale.com.

www.ingramcontent.com/pod-product-compliance
Lightning Source LLC
Jackson TN
JSHW071205020226
97517JS00034B/199
* 9 7 8 1 9 6 5 7 6 6 2 2 4 *